广东省哲学社会科学规划项目研究专项2020年度冷门绝学
"南海更路簿翻译研究：以苏德柳和彭正楷抄本为例"（GD20LMZZY04）成果之一

苏德柳和彭正楷『更路簿』英译本

贾绍东等 编译

中山大学出版社
·广州·

版权所有　翻印必究

图书在版编目（CIP）数据

苏德柳和彭正楷"更路簿"英译本：英文、汉文/贾绍东等编译. —广州：中山大学出版社，2024.12
ISBN 978-7-306-08307-4

Ⅰ. K296.6；H315.9

中国国家版本馆CIP数据核字第2024MS8449号

SU DELIU HE PENG ZHENGKAI "GENGLUBU" YINGYIBEN

出 版 人：	王天琪
策划编辑：	张　蕊
责任编辑：	张　蕊
封面设计：	周美玲
责任校对：	杨曼琪
责任技编：	靳晓虹
出版发行：	中山大学出版社
电　　话：	编辑部 020-84111997，84113349，84110283，84110779，84110776
	发行部 020-84111998，84111981，84111160
地　　址：	广州市新港西路135号
邮　　编：	510275　　　　传　真：020-84036565
网　　址：	http://www.zsup.com.cn　　E-mail:zdcbs@mail.sysu.edu.cn
印 刷 者：	广东虎彩云印刷有限公司
规　　格：	787mm×1092mm　1/16　14.75印张　265千字
版次印次：	2024年12月第1版　2024年12月第1次印刷
定　　价：	58.00元

如发现本书因印装质量影响阅读，请与出版社发行部联系调换

Foreword

The South China Sea Genglubu (referred to as *Genglubu*) , also known as *Shuilubu*, *Navigation Shuilubu*, *The South China Sea Shuilujing*, *The South China Sea Genglujing*, *Gengliubu for Marine Navigation*, *Shunfengdeli*, *Shuilubu for the Xisha and Nansha Islands*, *Genglubu for the East and the North Sea* etc. , is a marine navigational manual uniquely created by the fishermen of Hainan in the early Ming Dynasty (1368 – 1644). This manual was made based on the ancient compass and it is still a very valuable book that exists today because it records the activities and events as to how the fishermen of Hainan carried out their fishing and trade on the South China Sea, and as to how they explored the marine silk road, and because it also records the locations and conditions of the South China Sea islands and reefs which were given names by the fishermen of Hainan.

According to investigations and research, in the times of ancient sailing ships over the past six hundred years since the early Ming Dynasty, through the practice and explorations of many generations, the fishermen of Hainan kept recording in detail every sea route departing from Hainan Island to arrive at and land each of the islands in the Xisha and Nansha waters. And they recorded their routes to the coasts and islands of Southeast Asian countries such as Vietnam, Thailand, Cambodia, Singapore, Malaysia and Indonesia. They gave names to 136 out of 287 islands and reefs in the South China Sea in Hainan dialect. The given names of the islands and reefs, known as folk names or ancient names, gave a vivid description of their terrains and landforms, and of the hydrological characteristics, and of the distribution of fishery resources as well as their origins and legends. There is no doubt, therefore, that *Genglubu* is an art of works created by the fishermen of Hainan who had collected their sailing knowledge and experience for generations, and it is the fruit of their collective wisdom as well. For these reasons, *Genglubu* is a sufficient evidence to prove that the South China Sea has been the Chinese fishermen's ancestral waters and that all the South China Sea islands, reefs, cays, shoals and banks have been China's inherent territory.

Until now, nearly 40 versions of *Genglubu* have been discovered and studied. I think it is quite reasonable that Prof. Jia Shaodong selected Su Deliu Version of

Genglubu (referred to as Su Version) and Peng Zhengkai Version of *Genglubu* (referred to as Peng Version) as the texts for his translation studies. There are three reasons for that. Firstly, among all the versions, both Su and Peng versions are comparatively representative. Secondly, the two versions include almost all the sailing routes from Hainan Island to the islands and reefs of the South China Sea in which some routes are the same while others are different, so they can be complementary. Thirdly, Su Version, in particular, records in detail not only the routes from Hainan Island to the islands and reefs of the South China Sea, but also the routes from Hainan Island to the coast of Guangdong Province, to the coasts and islands of some Southeast Asian countries (Vietnam, Thailand, Cambodia, Singapore, Malaysia and Indonesia), as well as the return routes between coastal islands of these countries. Su Version particularly abundant and complicated, and thus translate it into English is a greater challenge for the translators, especially when translating some of the folk names or ancient names given to the islands or places of the Southeast Asian countries by the fishermen of Hainan because it is hard to determine the locations of these islands and places as well as their Chinese and English names. In addition, of course, some of the jargons in Hainan dialect are not easy to comprehend and translate.

After reading over the preface and the translated texts, I think that Prof. Jia and his team have made a bold and innovative effort to apply the theory of cultural turn, the principle of naming after the original owner and an integrated strategy to translating *Genglubu*. For instance, in terms of the translation of the South China Sea islands and reefs, by adopting the principle of naming after the original owner and that of the combination of sound and meaning, the translators employed the Hainan dialect pronunciation for the folk names and used Chinese pinyin and English common nouns for the English official names. In so doing, on the one hand, the problem of having inconsistency in the expression of the English official names of the Chinese islands and reefs can be solved; on the other hand, the negative influence of the names of the islands given by the colonialists of the West in the past can be eliminated. For another example, in dealing with the obstacles of translating the culture-loaded items such as "geng", ancient names of the places along the coasts of the Southeast Asian countries, ancient compass terminologies, Hainan dialect jargons (i. e. 打水 dashui…托 tuo) and so on, the translators managed to properly retain the original cultural elements in the translated texts so that the contents can be understood and accepted by target readers, which reflects the translators' innovation.

What's more, Prof. Jia compiled and translated the origins and legends of 90 islands, reefs, shoals and cays in the South China Sea in Su and Peng Versions on the basis of collecting, sorting and referring to a lot of literature. Moreover, he made three tables in both Chinese and English for reference: Table of the Information about the South China Sea Islands in Su Deliu and Peng Zhengkai Versions of *Genglubu*, Table of the Information about the Islands and Places of the Southeast Asian Countries in Su Deliu Version of *Genglubu*, Table of the Information about the Places along the Coast of Hainan Island to the Coast of Guangdong in Su Deliu Version of *Genglubu*.

I hereby point out, in particular, that when *Genglubu* is taken as the irrefutable evidence for defending China's sovereignty over the South China Sea islands, Prof. Jia managed to render the well-known Su and Peng Versions into English. I'm sure that the publication of the English version of *Genglubu* is bound to break a new ground for further research into it and makes it possible to become known to the outside world and have it exposed to readers in the English world, which may provide a good foundation for its promotion in the international community. Besides, its publication will surely help enhance its international influence and China's power of discourse in safeguarding its indisputable rights and interests of the South China Sea.

Zhou Weimin
Hainan University
January 24, 2024

序

《南海更路簿》（简称《更路簿》），又名《水路簿》《航海水路簿》《南海水路经》《南海更路经》《驶船更流簿》《顺风得利》《去西南沙水路簿》《东海北海更路簿》等，是明朝（1368—1644）初年中国海南渔民独创的记录南海海上交通网络的本子，也是渔民在罗盘的配合下在南海的导航手册。它记录了渔民们在南海海域开展渔业生产活动、进行海上贸易、记录和命名南海岛礁、开拓海上丝绸之路等，是流传至今的极其珍贵的民间手书。

据考证，在明朝初年以来的六百多年的风帆时代，海南渔民经过一代又一代的航海实践，详细记录了他们从海南岛出发到西沙群岛、南沙群岛，乃至东南亚各国（越南、泰国、柬埔寨、新加坡、马来西亚、印度尼西亚）的航线，他们用海南方言给南海287个岛礁中的136个命名，这些岛礁的命名被称为海南渔民俗名或古地名。这些俗名栩栩如生地描绘出了几乎所有南海被命名的岛礁的地形地貌、水文特点和渔业资源的分布，以及它们的起源与传说。《更路簿》是海南渔民世世代代航海知识与经验的积累，也是他们集体智慧的结晶。它充分证明了南海是中国渔民的"祖宗海"，南海岛礁自古以来就是中国的固有领土。

根据目前已发现和研究的近40个《更路簿》抄本，贾绍东教授选用了苏德柳和彭正楷的《更路簿》抄本（下简称苏本和彭本）作为英译文本，是合适的。主要理由有三：第一，苏本和彭本在各种版本或抄本的《更路簿》中具有较强的代表性；第二，这两个版本中都涉及海南岛往返西沙岛礁和南沙岛礁的更路，它们既具有共同的部分，又有不同的部分，彼此具有互补性；第三，尤其是苏本，除了详细记录了海南岛往返西沙岛礁和南沙岛礁的更路，还记录了从海南岛沿岸驶往广东省沿岸、东南亚各国的更路，以及往返东南亚各国之间的沿岸岛礁更路，内容特别丰富且复杂，其中对涉及的海南渔民所命名的东南亚岛礁的俗名（古地名）的地理位置和中英文标准名的确定尤为困难。当然，这当中海南渔民方言的惯用语，也给翻译工作带来了巨大的挑战。

综观译作的前言和译文，贾绍东教授在翻译《更路簿》方面做了大胆的创新性尝试，他提出了运用文化转向理论、"名从主人"原则和综合翻译策略。例如，中国南海岛礁俗名采用标准名称的翻译，渔民起的俗名采用海南方言读音，中文标准名称的英译依据"名从主人"原则，采用"音""义"结合，即汉语拼音加英语普通名词，这种译法既可解决目前南海诸岛英文名称不统一的问题，又可消除南海诸岛大量外来地名的负面影响。再如，语句的英译、"更"字的翻译、东南亚各国古地名的翻译、古代航海罗盘针术语的翻译、渔民航海习惯用语的翻译，如"打水……托"等。译文中尽可能地保留源语文化元素，又能使英文读者接受、理解，都体现了译者的创造性翻译能力。另外，他还参阅了大量的文献，收集、分类整理、编写了苏本和彭本中90个南海岛礁的起源和传说，并将它们译成英文。同时，他还制作了苏本和彭本中南海岛礁中英文信息一览表、苏本中东南亚各国岛礁中英文信息一览表，以及海南岛驶往广东省沿岸地名中英文信息一览表，供读者查阅。

这里还要特别指出，在我们将《更路簿》作为中国拥有南海诸岛主权的铁证的时候，贾绍东教授把这两版著名的《更路簿》翻译成英文，这本译作的出版将为《更路簿》研究打开新天地，使《更路簿》走向世界成为可能，让英语世界的读者们也能读到《更路簿》，为《更路簿》的国际传播提供了重要的语言基础，有利于提升《更路簿》的国际影响力和宣示南海主权的话语权，对维护我国对南海拥有无可争辩的主权大有益处。

周伟民
海南大学
2024 年 1 月 24 日

Preface

Genglubu is the historical record of Chinese fishermen's navigation and exploration of the South China Sea and beyond. It records in detail how the fishermen of Hainan gave the names of the islands, reefs, shoals, banks and cays related to the Xisha Islands and the Nansha Islands; it also records how they carried out their fishery production activities in the waters of the South China Sea by means of the ancient compass. The book demonstrates the fact that Chinese fishermen, especially the fishermen of Hainan, have been the pioneers to explore and discover the South China Sea islands. As a nation-level intangible cultural heritage, *Genglubu* is not only a precious literature for the study of China's maritime history and culture with regard to the South China Sea, but also an important folk evidence for safeguarding China's sovereignty over the South China Sea islands.

So far about 40 versions of *Genglubu* have been discovered. For the translation research in this book, we have selected two of them—Su Deliu Version and Peng Zhengkai Version as the source texts. The two versions have been used for quite a long time by the fishermen of Hainan since the early Ming Dynasty and their contents are relatively comprehensive. They recorded in detail how the fishermen of Hainan set off from Tanmen Port in Qionghai City and arrive at the Xisha Islands, the Nansha Islands and even beyond. Particularly, Su Version is different from others in that apart from the records of the navigation routes from Tanmen Port to the Xisha and Nansha waters and islands (Part Ⅰ and Part Ⅱ), it also keeps detailed records of the routes from Tanmen Port to Guangdong province as well as the routes to the coasts of the Southeast Asian countries such as Vietnam, Singapore, Indonesia, Malaysia, Thailand and Cambodia (Part Ⅲ, Part Ⅳ, Part Ⅴ, Part Ⅵ, Part Ⅶ and Part Ⅷ).

All the entries of Part Ⅰ and Part Ⅱ related with the navigational routes to the Xisha Islands and the Nansha Islands in the two source texts are numbered, and other parts (Part Ⅳ, Part Ⅴ, Part Ⅵ, Part Ⅶ and Part Ⅷ) of Su Version are also numbered so that their translated versions are in good order and can be easily read.

In view of translating *Genglubu*, the translators are faced with at least six difficulties. First, how to translate the term 更 (geng) into English? It is used for both time and distance in Chinese, but when it refers to sailing distance, how many nautical miles does "one geng" actually have? As a matter of fact, when a ship sails at sea, there are fluctuations in length affected by factors such as wind direction, wind speed, ocean currents, and navigation techniques, etc. For this reason, there exists a controversy in the academic circle about its connotation, that is, it is hard to determine how many nautical miles "one geng" should have. Similarly, how to translate the culture-loaded terms formed by the word "geng"? Second, how to render into English the folk names of the South China Sea islands given by the fishermen of Hainan and their corresponding official names? Third, how to render the ancient compass terminologies into English? When a ship sails, the needle on the ancient compass pointing towards a certain direction is composed of the Heavenly Stems and Earthly Branches, such as Zi Wu, Chou Wei, Gui Ding, Gen Kun, etc. Whether the culture-loaded items should be retained or not is hard to determine. Besides, in some entries or sentences, there are such expressions as "加/添/兼二线" "加/添/兼三线" "加/添/兼四线" which may be literally translated into "add two/three/four lines". Does it make sense? How to put them into proper English? Fourth, what is the meaning of "打水……托" in Chinese? How to translate 打水 (dashui) and 托 (tuo) into English? Fifth, how to translate into English the folk names of the places along the coasts of some Southeast Asian countries? Sixth, for the translation of the entries or sentences, what sentence pattern or patterns should be employed and how to put them into perfect nautical English? The six translation difficulties are elaborated upon one by one as follows.

1. Translation of the term "geng" into English

The term 更 (geng) is a quite important culture-loaded word in *Genglubu*. It not only refers to time, but also refers to nautical distance. When used as time, one "geng" is equivalent to 2 hours; when employed as sailing distance, it is viewed as an approximation, say, one "geng" is equivalent to 10 or 10.8 or 12.4 or 12.5 nautical miles. Li Wenhua et al. (2018) digitized the routes in *Genglubu* and used a statistical method to obtain that one "geng" is equal to 12.5 nautical miles. According to Zhang Shuoren et al. (2018), one "geng" is equal to 10.8 nautical miles. Zhou Weimin (2019), based on the experience of old fishermen and captains, believes that one "geng" is approximately equal to 10 nautical miles. Li Caixia (2019) applied Google Earth to calculating that one "geng" is equal to 12.4 nautical miles. In order to facilitate translation work, we adopt fishermen's experience that one "geng" is about 10 nautical miles.

The culture-loaded items formed by the word "geng" are very common in *Genglubu*. For example, 更半 (one and a half geng) means that the sailing time is about 3 hours, or the sailing distance is about 15 nautical miles. 九更 (nine geng) means that the sailing time is about 18 hours, or the sailing distance is approximately 90 nautical miles. In this sense, the word "geng" can be chosen as either sailing time or sailing distance when translated, but the latter is preferred to the translation. As is well-known to us, prior to the invention of steamer boats, because of the backward navigation technology or various marine or weather conditions, the sailing time might vary greatly, but the sailing distance between the places of departure and destination is basically the same or does not change a lot. On the basis of the translation theory of culture turn, in terms of the translation of "geng", the translators adopt both alienation and adaptation, that is, literal translation + transliteration + annotation (free translation). In this way, 更半 is translated into "one and a half geng" (approximately 15 nautical miles); 九更 is rendered into "nine geng" (approximately 90 nautical miles).

2. Translation of the folk names and their official names

The folk names of the islands and the reefs in the South China Sea in *Genglubu* are also known as "pet names" given by the fishermen of Hainan in the dialect of Qionghai region, so transliteration is employed to give phonetic notation to them in both Hainan dialect and Chinese Pinyin + English general words for their corresponding official names. According to the Chinese Pinyin used for *Some Official Place Names of South China Sea Islands in China* in April 1983, each of the island with its folk name is given its corresponding English official name. Here Pinyin is adopted in accordance with the documents issued, "The proper names of Chinese people and places, in principle, should be transliterated with Chinese Pinyin, and the general Chinese words such as provinces, autonomous regions, municipalities, rivers, lakes and seas, etc., can be translated into a foreign language", stipulated in Term Three of the Appendix *Regulations Concerning the Use of Chinese Pinyin as Roman Alphabet Spelling for the Proper Names of Chinese People and Places*, the attachment of the Chinese government document *Report on the Unified Standards for the Use of Chinese Pinyin as Roman Alphabet Spelling for Chinese Names and Place Names*. The document was officially issued by the State Language Commission, the Ministry of Foreign Affairs, the State Administration of Surveying and Mapping, and the China Geographical Names Commission in September, 1978. For example, 大圈 is a folk name pronounced *Ddua*¹ *Huan*¹ in the Hainan dialect while its official name is Huaguang Reef (Chinese Pinyin + an English general word), so it is translated into *Ddua*¹ *Huan*¹ (Huaguang Reef). We adopt transliteration (dialect & Pinyin) + literal translation; that is, the translation of a folk name is made up of Hainan dialect and Chinese Pinyin and an English common noun. In this way, the cultural element of the source texts can be retained in the translated texts. For more information, please see Table of the Information about the South China Sea Islands in Su Deliu and Peng Zhengkai Versions of *Genglubu*.

3. Translation of ancient compass terminology

Example 1：自牛厄去目镜，用巳亥添四线丙，九更收。对东南。

Translated Text：

At the Nansha Islands, depart from $Gu^2 Eh^7$ (Niu'e Reef) and arrive at $Mag^8 Gia^4$ (Siling Reef), the compass needle should point towards southeast between Si Hai and Ren Bing for nine geng, that is, navigate S162°E (towards southeast) for approximately 90 nautical miles.

In this entry, "巳亥添四线丙" is an important culture-loaded item on the ancient Chinese compass for navigation. After the Southern Song Dynasty, people combined the floating magnetic needle with the azimuth mark to make a compass with higher precision. The ancient compass is also known as compass needle or compass. On the compass there are eight directions formed with the 24 Chinese characters, including four out of eight trigrams (乾 Qian、坤 Kun、巽 Xun、艮 Gen), the eight heavenly stems (甲 Jia、乙 Yi、丙 Bing、丁 Ding、庚 Geng、辛 Xin、壬 Ren、癸 Gui), the twelve earthly branches (子 Zi、丑 Chou、寅 Yin、卯 Mao、辰 Chen、巳 Si、午 Wu、未 Wei、申 Shen、酉 You、戌 Xu、亥 Hai). The 子 (Zi) is at 360° due north, the 午 (Wu) is at 180° due south, the 卯 (Mao) is at 90° due east, and the 酉 (You) is at 270° due west, thus forming 子午 (Zi Wu)、壬丙 (Ren Bing)、巳亥 (Si Hai)、乾巽 (Qian Xun)、辰戌 (Chen Xu)、乙辛 (Yi Xin)、卯酉 (Mao You)、甲庚 (Jia Geng)、寅申 (Yin Shen)、艮坤 (Gen Kun)、丑未 (Chou Wei)、癸丁 (Gui Ding), which are 12 pairs altogether, representing 24 directions, each character occupies 15° in a 360° circumference; the middle of the two characters constitutes one direction, making a total of 48 directions, thus dividing the circumference into 48 equal parts, with 7.5° between every part. The above 12 pairs of individual directions are called 单针 (single needles), and between two directions are called 缝针 (sewing needles). The ancient compass needle terms belong to culture-loaded items which are often transliterated. Therefore, the expression in Example 1 "巳亥添/加/兼二/三/四线丙" can be rendered into "the compass needle should point towards southeast between Si Hai and Ren Bing; that is, navigate S162°E (towards southeast)" in which an integrated method of literal and free translation plus annotation is employed to keep the cultural elements of the original texts in the translated texts. (Figure 1)

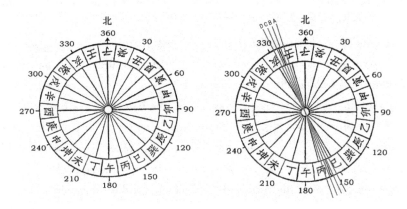

Figure 1   The ancient compass

4. Translation of "打水……托"

Example 2: 羊角离枚松极零倚即是新竹港，峙内打水十八托，外打水三十托，下边即钓壹。

Translated Text:

Navigating one geng (about 10 nautical miles) from Dua^3 $Hhui^4$ $Gang^3$ (Nuok Island, north of Hon Trau) to Mui^2 Geg^8 (Cu Lao Coni), one can arrive at Din^1 $Ddiog^7$ $Gang^3$ (Guy Nhon Port), inside which a ship can anchor in 18 tuo (roughly 16 fathoms) and outside which a ship can drop anchor in 30 tuo (approximately 27 fathoms). There fishing can be done.

打水 (dashui) is an idiomatic expression used by the fishermen of Hainan. It has two meanings: one is to anchor a ship/boat; the other is to drop anchor and place a heavy object (anchor) down onto the seabed to rub it over, so that the fishermen can know how deep the seabed is and what condition is in the area where a fishing boat anchors, and eventually the fishermen can tell what kind of seafood can be caught there. One 托 (tuo) is about 1.6 meters long, which is an approximate

5

number based on the length of the outstretching arms of an ordinary fisherman whose height is about 160 cm. Therefore, by means of free translation, 打水 is translated into "anchor" or "drop anchor"; one "tuo" is rendered into "1.6 meters", then 18 "tuo" is equal to 28.8 meters, here the word "fathom" can be utilized instead of "meter" as a unit of measuring the depth of water. One fathom is equal to 1.8 meters. So 打水十八托 can be rendered into "a ship can drop anchor/anchor in 18 tuo (roughly 16 fathoms)". 打水三十托 can be translated into "a ship can anchor/drop achor in 30 tuo (approximately 27 fathoms)."

In ancient times, Chinese fishermen employed the depth measuring weight 测深锤, also known as measurer, roped weight, and lead weight for measuring the depth of water. It involved the use of a rope with a heavy piece of lead tied to one end which would be thrown overboard and sank to the bottom to measure water depth. The unit of measurement was 托. The depth measuring weight had another function. The bottom of the weight was coated with beef tallow. When the weight hit the bottom, tallow collected sand, mud, stone or other contents of the ocean floor, allowing fishermen to determine the nature of the bottom and the water current.

5. Translation of place names of the Southeast Asian countries

There are 122 place names along the coasts of the Southeast Asian countries (Vietnam, Thailand, Cambodia, Singapore, Malaysia and Indonesia) in Su Version. For example, 大佛 ($Ddua^1 Bud^8$) and 加俑藐 ($Ge^1 Nam^2 Miao^3$) are two of them. 大佛 is also called 烟筒头 ($In^1 Ddong^2 Hao^2$), 烟头大佛 or 灵山大佛, today it refers to Cape Varella (12°53′N, 109°27′E) in the southeast of Tuy Hòa in Vietnam. 加俑藐 is also called 加滴藐 or 伽南貌 in Chinese, it refers to Hon Tre near Nha Trang in Vietnam. 浮马 ($Pu^2 Ve^3$) means a small island or reef. As for the translation of these place names, we employ Hainan dialect + English name of the island or the place in that country. For details, please see Example 2.

For more information of the place names, please see Table of the Information about the Islands and Places of the Southeast Asian Countries in Su Deliu Version of *Genglubu*.

6. Translation of the sentences (entries)

The sentences (entries) in *Genglubu* are often imperative, most of which are in such a form: depart from a certain place…arrive at/in a certain place. In the translation, we choose such words or phrases as set off from…to… (set out/set sail/start sail/leave/depart from); 收 (shou) means "arrive or end the sail". Except for the meaning of 驶往 (steer for), the characters 上 (shang) and 下 (xia) are also special directional words used by the fishermen of Hainan. Generally, 上 refers to "south and east" while 下 refers to "north and west". Special attention should be paid to the two words when translated.

Example 3: 自四江去大圈，用乾巽过头，约更半（收）。对东南。

Translated Text 1:

Set out at the Xisha Islands from $Di^4 Giang^1$ (Jinqing Island) and navigate S135°E for 15 nautical miles to $Ddua^1 Huan^1$ (Huaguang Reef); that is, the compass needle should point towards Qian Xun (towards southeast) for one and a half geng.

In the first half of the translated text, an imperative sentence and modern nautical expressions are used while in the second half, a declarative sentence and traditional nautical expressions are used, which serve as a supplement. In this way, the cultural element in the original text can be retained in the translated text as much as possible. Here, the choice of the sentence pattern and the application of the expressions is not limited, and others can also be used if possible and necessary.

Translated Text 2:

Depart at the Xisha Islands from $Di^4 Giang^1$ (Jinqing Island) and get to $Ddua^1 Huan^1$ (Huaguang Reef), the compass needle should point towards Qian Xun (towards southeast) and travel for one and a half gengs; that is, navigate S135°E for about 15 nautical miles.

Compared with Translated Text 1, Translated Text 2 is different in pattern in which traditional nautical expressions are used first so as to be faithful to the original sentence, and modern nautical expressions are followed as a supplement. Similarly, the translation theory of culture turn is applied. Strategies such as an integrated approach plus alienation, domestication, literal and free translation are employed in order to retain its cultural elements and make the translated text smooth and easy to understand.

In conclusion, there are at least six difficulties discussed above in translating Su Deliu and Peng Zhengkai Versions of *Genglubu*. What should be noted here is that, according to the research conducted by Li Wenhua (2019), in Su Version there are some deviations or omissions in view of the navigational routes which are not in accordance with the actual routes today. However, we are still faithful to the original texts without making any correction or revision in the translated texts. To properly cope with the above translation difficulties, the translators have adopted the theory of culture turn, and strategies such as alienation, adaptation, an integrated application of alienation and adaptation, annotation, compensation, etc., so that an understandable English version could be achieved.

In addition, the translators have also compiled the Chinese texts entitled "The Origins and Legends of the Folk Names of the South China Sea Islands in Su Deliu and Peng Zhengkai Versions of *Genglubu*", and then render them into English in the hope that it will help readers know more about the islands, reefs, shoals, banks and cays in the South China Sea. Besides, the translators have made three tables: Table of the Information about the South China Sea Islands in Su Deliu and Peng Zhengkai Versions of *Genglubu*, Table of the Information about the Islands and Places of the Southeast Asian Countries in Su Deliu Version of *Genglubu* as well as Table of the Information about the Places along the Coast of Hainan Island to the Coast of Guangdong in Su Deliu Version of *Genglubu*. These three tables are available for readers to acquire more information of the South China Sea islands and beyond in *Genglubu*.

This book aims to probe into translating *Genglubu* both in theory and practice. There may be mistakes and errors in the translated texts. So we're open to comments or criticism from readers.

Jia Shaodong
March 30th, 2024

前　言

　　《更路簿》是中国渔民，尤指海南渔民自古以来世世代代开发南海，在南海进行渔业生产活动与实践中形成的航海历史文献，其中详细记录了海南渔民在南海诸岛开展渔业生产活动的航海路线、古罗盘针的使用，以及给西沙群岛和南沙群岛相关的岛、礁、滩、洲命名的具体情况。更路簿作为国家级非物质文化遗产，不仅是研究我国南海航海历史和海洋文化的珍贵资料，还是中国南海维权的重要民间证据。

　　目前已发现的更路簿有近40个版本，本书主要选用苏德柳本和彭正楷本作为翻译研究文本，这两个抄本保存时间较长，内容记载比较全面。它们详细记录了海南渔民从琼海市潭门港出发前往西沙群岛和南沙群岛的更路。特别是苏德柳本，该版本的第一和第二部分记录了去西沙、南沙海域范围的内容，第三至第八部分还详细记载了从潭门港到我国广东的更路，以及到南洋，如越南、新加坡、印度尼西亚、马来西亚、泰国、柬埔寨等东南亚国家的航海更路情况。

　　苏德柳本和彭正楷本《更路簿》的原文没有数字标号，为了条目之间关系清楚，译者特意在西沙更路和南沙更路的每个条目前加上了数字编号。苏德柳本《更路簿》从第四至第八部分也加了数字编号。

　　翻译《更路簿》主要有以下六大难点：一是"更"字的翻译。"更"既表时间，又表距离。表示航行距离时，受风向、风速、洋流和航海技术等因素的影响，"一更"的实际距离会有长短的波动。因此，学术界对其内涵，即"一更"实为多少海里，存在较大争议，至今没有定论。译文应以哪个距离长度为标准？同样，对于"更"字所构成的文化负载词，如何译出？二是南海诸岛俗名（古地名或土地名）及其对应的标准名称的翻译如何处理？三是古罗盘针术语的翻译，即由天干地支构成的表示航行方位的文化负载词，如子午、丑未、癸丁、艮坤等，翻译时这些文化专有项在译文中是保留、舍弃，还是两者兼顾？还有，在某些条目中出现的"加/添/兼二线""加/添/兼三线""加/添/兼四线"等表达，如何翻译？四是"打水……托"中的"打水"和"托"分别是何意？如何翻译？五是如何翻译南洋更路中每个俗名（古地名或土地名）？六是语句（条目）的翻译，译文用什么句型？如何用地道的航海英语？在此将对上述提出的六大翻译难点逐一说明。

1. "更"字的英译

"更"字在《更路簿》中是非常重要的文化负载词,既表示时间,又表示航海距离。表示时间时,1更相当于2小时;表示航行距离时,具有明显的近似性,如1更相当于10海里,或10.8海里,或12.4海里,或12.5海里。李文化等(2018)通过将"更路"进行数字化并运用统计学方法得出1更约等于12.5海里;张朔人等(2018)对"更"数值的研究得出1更约为10.8海里;周伟民(2019)根据老船长的经验说1更约等于10海里;李彩霞(2019)运用谷歌地球(Google Earth)计算得出1更约等于12.4海里。为便于英译处理,本书采用老船长经验:1更约为10海里(approximately 10 nautical miles)。

"更"字所构成的文化负载词,在《更路簿》中几乎无所不在,如"更半"意为"1更半",就是航行时间约为3小时,或航行距离约为15海里;又如,"九更"意思是航行时间约为18小时,或航行距离约为90海里,翻译"更"字时可在航行时间和航行距离二者之间选一。在帆船时代,因航海技术落后,或因海况或天气状况不同,航行时间可能有很大的出入,但出发地与到达地之间的航行距离基本不变或者变化不大,故译文采用航行距离为佳。基于文化转向翻译理论,"更"的翻译策略采取异化与归化交互并用,即直译+音译+加注(意译),如"更半"译为 one and a half geng (approximately 15 nautical miles);"九更"译成 nine geng (approximately 90 nautical miles)。

2. 南海诸岛俗名及其标准名称的英译

《更路簿》中南海诸岛的俗名都是海南渔民用琼海潭门话给起的土地名,属于海南方言(琼文话)的范畴,故它们的英译文统一采用琼文话读音,标准名称的英译采用汉语拼音+英文普通词汇。根据1983年4月《我国南海诸岛部分标准地名》的汉语拼音,给出每个岛屿俗名相对应的标准地名的英译。依据1978年9月我国政府颁布《中国文字改革委员会、外交部、国家测绘总局、中国地名委员会关于改用汉语拼音作为我国人名地名罗马字母拼法的统一规范的报告》以及附件《关于改用汉语拼音方案拼写中国人名地名作为罗马字母拼写法的实施说明》第三条"在各外语中地名的专名部分原则上音译,用汉语拼音字母拼写,通名部分(如省、市、自治区、江、河、湖、海等)采取意译"的规定处理。例如,"大圈"是一个岛礁的俗名,海南琼文话的读音为 $Ddua^1 Huan^1$,而该岛礁的标准名称为"华光礁"(Huaguang Reef),因此译为 $Ddua^1 Huan^1$ (Huaguang Reef)。本书运用音译+直译(意译)法,即由海南琼文话读音+汉语拼音+英文普通名词构成一个俗名翻译。这样处理可以在译文中保留源语文化元素。若要了解《更路簿》中提及的南海诸岛的地理坐标信息，详见"苏德柳和彭正楷本《更路簿》南海诸岛中英文信息一览表"。

3．古罗盘术语的英译

例1：自牛厄去目镜，用巳亥添四线丙，九更收。对东南。

译文：

At the Nansha Islands, depart from $Gu^2\ Eh^7$ (Niu'e Reef) and arrive at $Mag^8\ Gia^4$ (Siling Reef), the compass needle should point towards southeast between Si Hai and Ren Bing for nine gengs, that is, navigate S162°E (towards southeast) for approximately 90 nautical miles.

本条目中，"巳亥添四线丙"是中国古代航海罗盘上的重要文化负载词。南宋以后，人们将水浮磁针与方位标志组合，形成精度更高的罗盘、经盘或罗盘指南针。罗盘由四维（八卦之四卦：乾、坤、巽、艮），八干（甲、乙、丙、丁、庚、辛、壬、癸），十二地支（子、丑、寅、卯、辰、巳、午、未、申、酉、戌、亥）24个方位构成，每个方位在360°圆周中占15°，其中，子位位于360°正北、午位位于180°正南、卯位位于90°正东、酉位位于270°正西，构成子午、壬丙、巳亥、乾巽、辰戌、乙辛、卯酉、甲庚、寅申、艮坤、丑未、癸丁 12组24个方位，每个字在360°圆周中占15°；两个方位中间又构成一个方位，共48个方位，即将圆周48等份，方位间7.5°。上述12组单独方位称单针，两方位之间称缝针。古罗盘针术语采用音译。对于"巳亥添/加/兼二/三/四线丙"等翻译，可意译为：the compass needle should point towards southeast between Si Hai and Ren Bing; that is, navigate S162°E (towards southeast)。本译文采用直译＋意译＋注释的综合法，意在保留源语文化。（见图1）

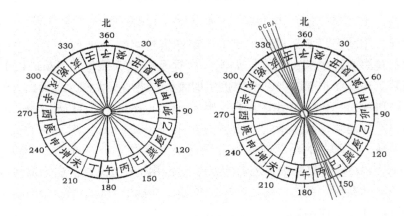

图1　古罗盘方位

4. "打水……托"句式的英译

例2：羊角离枚松极零倚即是新竹港，峙内打水十八托，外打水三十托，下边即钓壹。

译文：

Navigating one geng (about 10 nautical miles) from Dua^3 $Hhui^4$ $Gang^3$ (Nuok Island, north of Hon Trau) to Mui^2 Geg^8 (Cu Lao Coni), one can arrive at Din^1 $Ddiog^7$ $Gang^3$ (Guy Nhon Port), inside which a ship can anchor in 18 tuo (roughly 16 fathoms) and outside which a ship can anchor in 30 tuo (approximately 27 fathoms). There fishing can be done.

"打水"是海南渔民的习用语，有两层意思：一是泊船抛锚；二是通过抛锚，将重物（锚）放在海底摩擦带上泥沙，以了解渔船所在区域海底的地质情况，再根据海底地质情况，判断可以捕捞到什么样的海产品。"托"是一个长度单位，1托约等于1.6米，是依据以前普通海南渔民（平均身高约为160厘米）两臂伸直的长度所得到的概数。翻译时，可把"打水"看作动词，译为"anchor"或"drop anchor"；1托是1.6米，18托即28.8米，翻译时再换用测量水深的单位"英寻"fathom（1英寻≈1.8米），28.8米除以1.8米就约等于16英寻。采用意译法和替代法，因此，"打水十八托"译为"a ship can anchor/drop anchor in 18 tuo (roughly 16 fathoms)"；"打水三十托"译为"a ship can anchor/drop anchor in 30 tuo (approximately 27 fathoms)"。

古代海南渔民航海使用测深锤，亦称掬、背、绳驼、铅锤，沉绳水底，打量某处海水深浅，单位是托，测深锤底涂以牛油，可以粘带沙泥，以探知海底属泥底、沙底，还是石底，可以了解海底水流速度。

5. 东南亚国家（南洋）更路古地名的英译

苏德柳本《更路簿》中涉及东南亚国家（越南、泰国、柬埔寨、新加坡、马来西亚、印度尼西亚）沿岸的122个南洋古地名或土地名，它们中绝大多数名称都是海南渔民起的俗名，如例3中提及的"大佛"（$Ddua^1$ Bud^8）和"加俑藐"（Ge^1 Nam^2 $Miao^3$）。大佛也叫烟筒头，或烟头大佛，或灵山大佛，指今越南绥和（Tuy Hòa）东南的华列拉岬（Cape Varella：12°53′ N, 109°27′ E）。加俑藐，或加滴藐，或伽南貌，指越南芽庄（Nha Trang）附近的竹岛（Hon Tre）。浮马，指孤立的小岛或礁石，根据上下文关系，可译为 a small island (reef/rock)。对外洋更路中古地名的英译，采用海南渔民方言注音加涉国家的某个岛屿的标准英语名称（如上文中的竹岛，其标准英语名称为 Hon Tre）的方式处理。详见上述例2。

更多信息，详见"苏德柳本《更路簿》中东南亚（外洋）地名中英文信息一览表"。

6.《更路簿》语句（条目）的英译

《更路簿》的语句（条目）常用祈使句，绝大多数句式为：自/从/由某地……去/上/下（驶往）某地，可选用 set off from…to…（set out/set sail/start sail/leave/depart from）等英文词组或单词翻译；"收"意为到达、收帆，可译为 arrive at/in, reach 或 get to a place。条目中，"上"和"下"除有"驶往"之意外，还是海南渔民特用方位词，一般"上"为南和东，"下"为北和西，翻译时应格外注意。

例3：自四江去大圈，用乾巽过头，约更半（收）。对东南。

译文1：

Set out at the Xisha Islands from Di^4 $Giang^1$（Jinqing Island）and navigate S135°E for 15 nautical miles to $Ddua^1$ $Huan^1$（Huaguang Reef）; that is, the compass needle should point towards Qian Xun（towards southeast）for one and a half geng.

译文1的前半部分句型主要采用祈使句（现代航海表达），后半部分译文采用陈述句，遵循传统航海表达，同时，译文中尽量保留源语文化元素，海南渔民俗名在前，标准名称在后。翻译理论为文化转向，策略为归化+异化，翻译方法为意译+直译。对于句型和词汇的选择与选用，不限于以上提到的，也可用其他的句型和词汇。

译文2：

Depart at the Xisha Islands from Di^4 $Giang^1$（Jinqing Island）and get to $Ddua^1$ $Huan^1$（Huaguang Reef）, the compass needle should point towards Qian Xun（towards southeast）and travel for one and a half geng, that is, navigate S135°E for about 15 nautical miles.

译文2与译文1的不同点是，前半部分忠实于原文表述，后半部分用现代航海表达作为补充；翻译理论为文化转向，先用异化以便保留源语文化，再用归化，采用直译+意译，可使译文流畅易懂。

总之，翻译《更路簿》至少有以上六大难点。除此之外，根据李文化（2019）的研究，苏德柳本中个别条目的更路描述与实际更路存在偏差，或存在漏字现象，但翻译时仍忠实于源语文本，不做偏差校正和补漏。解决以上翻译难点，译者主要采用文化转向翻译理论，翻译策略包括异化与归化及其融合使用、夹注、补偿等，以便获得地道的译文。

本项目除了提供苏德柳和彭正楷本《更路簿》原文的英译文，译者还提供了上述两版抄本中有关南海诸岛俗名（土地名）的起源和传说的中英文稿，以帮助读者了解更多中国南海诸岛。此外，译者还制作了"苏德柳和彭正楷本《更路簿》南海诸岛中英文信息一览表""苏德柳本《更路簿》中东南亚（外洋）地名中英文信息一览表"，以及"苏德柳本《更路簿》海南岛沿岸至广东省沿岸地名中英文信息一览表"，这三个表格将有助于读者获得更多《更路簿》中涉及南海诸岛信息、东南亚国家岛屿名称信息和海南岛沿岸至广东省沿岸地名信息。

本书是对"更路簿"英译的大胆探索，译文中或有错误或不妥之处，欢迎广大读者批评指正。

贾绍东
2024 年 3 月 30 日

Contents

1 English Version of Su Deliu *Genglubu* ·· 1
  1.1 Navigational Routes towards $Ddang^1 Hhai^3$ (the Xisha Islands) ······ 1
  1.2 Navigational Routes towards $Bag^7 Hhai^3$ (the Nansha Islands) ········ 7
  1.3 Other Navigational Routes ··· 28

2 English Version of Peng Zhengkai *Genglubu* ································ 53
  2.1 Navigational Routes towards *Donghai* (the Xisha Islands) ············ 53
  2.2 Navigational Routes towards *Beihai* (the Nansha Islands) ············ 57

3 The Origins and Legends of the Folk Names of the South China Sea Islands in Su Deliu Version and Peng Zhengkai Version of *Genglubu* ··· 93
  3.1 Navigational Routes towards $Ddang^1 Hhai^3$ (the Xisha Islands) ······ 93
  3.2 Navigational Routes towards $Bag^7 Hhai^3$ (the Nansha Islands) ······ 98

4 Tables ·· 111
  4.1 Table of the Information about the South China Sea Islands in Su Deliu and Peng Zhengkai Versions of *Genglubu* ···················· 111
  4.2 Table of the Information about the Islands and Places of the Southeast Asian Countries in Su Deliu Version of *Genglubu* ········ 130
  4.3 Table of the Information about the Places along the Coast of Hainan Island to the Coast of Guangdong in Su Deliu Version of *Genglubu* ··· 144

Postscript ·· 147

目　　录

1 苏德柳本《更路簿》原文及释义 …………………………… 150
　1.1　立东海更路（西沙更路） ………………………………… 150
　1.2　立北海更路（南沙更路） ………………………………… 154
　1.3　其他更路（南洋更路） …………………………………… 165

2 彭正楷本《更路簿》原文及释义 …………………………… 173
　2.1　立东海更路（西沙更路） ………………………………… 173
　2.2　立北海更路（南沙更路） ………………………………… 176

3 苏德柳本和彭正楷本《更路簿》南海诸岛俗名起源与传说 …… 194
　3.1　立东海更路（西沙更路） ………………………………… 194
　3.2　立北海更路（南沙更路） ………………………………… 197

参考文献 …………………………………………………………… 204

后　　记 …………………………………………………………… 207

1 English Version of Su Deliu *Genglubu*

1.1 Navigational Routes towards *Ddang¹ Hhai^β* (the Xisha Islands) ①

Entry 1

Set out from *Dua¹ Ham²* (Tanmen Port), Qionghai and sail towards *Ddang¹ Hhai³* (the Xisha Islands). First, you should travel 120 nautical miles bearing S135°E. In traditional measurements, travel for about twelve geng; the needle on the compass should point towards Qian Xun (towards southeast). This will bring you to the halfway point of the journey, at which point you should set course at S142.5°E for 150 nautical miles. In other words, the compass needle should point between Qian Xun and Si Hai (towards southeast) for fifteen geng.

Entry 2

Set out from the Xisha Islands, leave *Da¹ Di⁶* (Nandao Island) bearing 255°W with a southerly wind or 285°W with a northerly wind, and sail towards *Gan¹ Ddao¹* (Beijiao Reef). You should navigate for about 30 nautical miles. Using traditional directions, the needle on the compass should point towards Jia Geng for three geng when the wind blows south, but if the wind blows north, the compass needle should point towards Yi Xin.

Entry 3

At the Xisha Islands, leave *Da¹ Di⁶* (Nandao Island), navigate S247.5°W for approximately 30 nautical miles to arrive at *Zio⁵ Ddo²* (the Yongle Islands). The

---

① **Notes**: For more information about the folk names given by the Chinese fishermen, please refer to The Origins and Legends of the Folk Names of the South China Sea Islands in Su Deliu and Peng Zhengkai Versions of *Genglubu* and Table of the Information about the South China Sea Islands in Su Deliu and Peng Zhengkai Versions of *Genglubu*.

compass needle should point between Gen Kun and Yin Shen (towards southwest) for three geng.

Entry 4

Set off at the Xisha Islands from $Da^1 Di^6$ (Nandao Island) and sail towards $Yi^1 Huan^1$ (Yuzhuo Reef) at S202.5°W for 35 nautical miles; the compass needle should point between Gui Ding and Chou Wei (towards southwest) for three and a half geng.

Entry 5

Depart from the Xisha Islands, leave $Da^1 Di^6$ (Nandao Island) and sail S157.5°E for approximately 40 nautical miles to reach $Da^1 Huan^1$ (Langhua Reef); the compass needle should point between Ren Bin and Si Hai (towards southeast) for four geng.

Entry 6

At the Xisha Islands, leave $Va^1 Du^4$ (Yongxing Island) and sail N292.5°W for roughly 45 nautical miles to arrive at $Gan^1 Ddao^1$ (Beijiao Reef); the compass needle should point between Yi Xin and Chen Xu (towards northwest) for four and a half geng if the wind blows north.

Entry 7

At the Xisha Islands, leave $Va^1 Du^4$ (Yongxing Island) and sail S232.5°W for approximately 40 nautical miles to arrive at $E^5 Di^6$ (the Yongle Islands); that is, the compass needle should point between Gen Kun and Yin Shen (towards southwest) for four geng.

Entry 8

At the Xisha Islands, leave $Va^1 Du^4$ (Yongxing Island) and navigate south bearing 202.5°S for roughly 35 nautical miles. That is, the compass needle should point between Gui Ding and Chou Wei (towards south) for three and a half geng. You should then arrive at $Yi^1 Huan^1$ (Yuzhuo Reef).

Entry 9

Leaving $Yi^1 Huan^1$ (Yuzhuo Reef) at the Xisha Islands to sail N300°W for about 10 nautical miles, one will arrive at $E^5\ Di^6$ (the Yongle Islands). During this voyage, the compass needle should point towards Chen Xu (towards northwest) for one geng.

Entry 10

At the Xisha Islands, leave $Zio^5\ Ddo^2$ (the Yongle Islands) and sail S112.5°E for approximately 20 nautical miles and you will arrive at $Yi^1\ Huan^1$ (Yuzhuo Reef). The compass needle should point towards southeast, between Yi Xin and Chen Xu for two geng.

Entry 11

From the Xisha Islands, depart from $Di^4\ Giang^1\ Mui^2$ (Jinqing Pass) at $Zio^5\ Ddo^2$ (the Yongle Islands) and navigate 75°E for roughly 60 nautical miles to arrive at $Va^1\ Du^4$ (Yongxing Island). During this trip, the compass needle should point towards Jia Geng (towards east) for six geng.

Entry 12

Set out at the Xisha Islands from $Di^4\ Giang^1$ (Jinqing Island) and navigate S135°E for 15 nautical miles to $Ddua^1\ Huan^1$ (Huaguang Reef); that is, the compass needle should point towards Qian Xun (towards southeast) for one and a half geng.

Entry 13

Set off at the Xisha Islands from $Ngin^2\ Di^6$ (Yinyu Bank) and navigate 345°N for approximately 35 nautical miles to $Gan^1\ Ddao^1$ (Beijiao Reef). The needle on the compass should point towards Ren Bing (towards north) for three and a half geng.

Entry 14

From the Xisha Islands, leave $Va^1\ Hheng^1$ (Dongdao Island) and sail roughly 35 nautical miles at 202.5°S to arrive at $Da^1\ Huan^1$ (Langhua Reef). The compass needle should point between Gui Ding and Chou Wei (towards south) for three and a half geng.

Entry 15

From the Xisha Islands, depart from *Va¹ Du⁴* (Yongxing Island) and navigate 165°S for roughly 40 nautical miles to arrive at *Da¹ Huan¹* (Langhua Reef). The compass needle should point towards Ren Bing (towards south) for four geng.

Entry 16

At the Xisha Islands, depart from *Ddua¹ Huan¹* (Huaguang Reef), travel for approximately 30 nautical miles bearing 216°S to arrive at *Bua⁴ Lou¹* (Zhongjian Island). The compass needle should point south between Gen Kun and Chou Wei for three geng.

Entry 17

At the Xisha Islands, leave *Yi¹ Huan¹* (Yuzhuo Reef), bearing N315°W for approximately 45 nautical miles to arrive at *Gan¹ Ddao¹* (Beijiao Reef). The compass needle should point towards Qian Xun, sailing northwest for four and a half geng.

Entry 18

At the Xisha Islands, depart from *Vue³ Di⁶* (Jinyin Island) and sail 35 nautical miles bearing S195°W to reach *Bua⁴ Lou¹* (Zhongjian Island). The needle on the compass should point towards Gui Ding, navigating southwest for three and a half geng.

Entry 19

At the Xisha Islands, depart from *Da¹ Huan¹* (Langhua Reef) and sail S255°W for roughly 65 nautical miles to arrive at *Bua⁴ Lou¹* (Zhongjian Island). During this voyage of six and a half geng, the needle on the compass should point towards Jia Geng (towards southwest).

Entry 20

At the Xisha Islands, depart from *Yi¹ Huan¹* (Yuzhuo Reef) and sail for about 15 nautical miles bearing 210°S to arrive at *Be⁵ Di⁶ Gia³* (Panshi Island). The compass needle should point towards Chou Wei while one sails south for one and a half geng.

Entry 21

At the Xisha Islands, set off from *Ddua¹ Huan¹* (Huaguang Reef) and navigate 180°S for about 10 nautical miles to arrive at *Be⁵ Di⁶ Gia³* (Panshi Island); that is, the compass needle should point south towards Zi Wu for one geng.

Entry 22

At the Xisha Islands, set out from *Ang² Sao³ Mui²* (Hongcao Pass), navigating S135° E for roughly 20 nautical miles to reach *Diang¹ Pan²* (the Gaojian Rocks). During this voyage, the compass needle should point towards Qian Xun (towards southeast) for two geng.

Entry 23

At the Xisha Islands, depart from *Ang² Sao³ Mui²* (Hongcao Pass) bearing S105°E and sail approximately 20 nautical miles to reach *Va¹ Hheng¹* (Dongdao Island); that is, the compass needle should point towards Yi Xin (towards southeast) for two geng.

Entry 24

At the Xisha Islands, leave *Be⁵ Di⁶ Gia³* (Panshi Island) and sail roughly 30 nautical miles bearing S240° W to arrive at *Bua⁴ Lou¹* (Zhongjian Island). The needle on the compass should point towards Yin Shen (towards southwest) for three geng.

Entry 25

From the Xisha Islands, leave *Bua⁴ Lou¹* (Zhongjian Island) and sail bearing S247.5°W for approximately 150 nautical miles to arrive at *Hhua¹ Lo²* (Dao Ly Son) which is not far from the central coast of Vietnam. The needle on the compass should point southwest between Jia Geng and Yin Shen for fifteen geng.

Entry 26

At the Xisha Islands, depart from *Yi¹ Huan¹* (Yuzhuo Reef) and set sail at 240°W for about 10 nautical miles to reach *Ddua¹ Huan¹* (Huaguang Reef). The compass needle should point towards Yin Shen (towards west) for one geng.

Entry 27

At the Xisha Islands, departing from $Da^1\ Huan^1$ (Langhua Reef), set course at 262.5°W and sail roughly 50 nautical miles to arrive at $Be^5\ Di^6\ Gia^3$ (Panshi Island). During this voyage, the needle on the compass should point west between Jia Geng and Mao You for five geng.

Entry 28

At the Xisha Islands, depart from $Be^5\ Di^6\ Gia^3$ (Panshi Island) and sail 90°E for approximately 50 nautical miles to arrive at $Da^1\ Huan^1$ (Langhua Reef). The needle on the compass should point towards Mao You (towards east) for five geng.

Entry 29

Set out from the Xisha Islands, leaving $Dun^2\ Ngam^2\ Vue^3$ (Xisha Sand Bank), bearing 277.5°W and sail roughly 40 nautical miles to reach $Gan^1\ Ddao^1$ (Beijiao Reef). The needle on the compass should point west between Yi Xin and Mao You for four geng.

1.2 Navigational Routes towards *Bag⁷ Hhai⁸* (the Nansha Islands) ①

Entry 1

From the Xisha Islands, leave $Da^1\ Huang^4$ (Langhua Reef), sail S135°E for approximately 130 nautical miles. At the half-way point where semidiurnal tide occurs, re-orient the compass to S150°E and sail an additional 130 nautical miles to arrive at $Diang^1\ Di^6$ (the Shuangzi Islands) on the Nansha Islands. To restate using traditional terms, when leaving $Da^1\ Huang^4$ (Langhua Reef), the compass needle should point towards Qian Xun for 13 geng. After having sailed nearly half the total distance and reaching the aera of semidiurnal tide, adjust the direction and navigate with the compass needle pointing towards Si Hai for another 13 geng to arrive at $Diang^1\ Di^6$ (the Shuangzi Islands) on the Nansha Islands.

Entry 2

From the Xisha Islands, leave $Be^5\ Di^6\ Gia^3$ (Panshi Island), bearing S135°E and sail for approximately 380 nautical miles to arrive at $Diang^1\ Di^6$ (the Shuangzi Islands). During this voyage, the needle on the compass should point towards Qian Xun (towards east) for 38 geng.

Entry 3

Navigate 105°E from the Nansha Islands, leave $Diang^1\ Di^6$ (the Shuangzi Islands), sail for 20 nautical miles to arrive at $Hhong^2\ Sao^3\ Dua^4\ Bai^2$ (Lesi Shoal). The needle on the compass should point towards Yi Xin (towards east) for two geng.

Entry 4

At the Nansha Islands, depart from $Diang^1\ Di^6$ (the Shuangzi Islands),

---

① **Notes**: For more information about the folk names given by the Chinese fishermen, please refer to The Origins and Legends of the Folk Names of the South China Sea Islands in Su Deliu and Peng Zhengkai Versions of *Genglubu* and Table of the Information about the South China Sea Islands in Su Deliu and Peng Zhengkai Versions of *Genglubu*.

navigate 150°S and sail about 30 nautical miles to arrive at Hih^7 Di^6 (Zhongye Island). The needle on the compass should point towards Si Hai (towards south) for three geng.

Entry 5

Leave $Hhong^2$ Sao^3 (Xiyue Island) and navigate N300°W from the Nansha Islands for 20 nautical miles to arrive at Dua^4 Bai^2 (Changtan Bank). During this trip, the needle on the compass should point towards Chen Xu (towards northwest) for two geng.

Entry 6

From the Nansha Islands, leave $Hhong^2$ Sao^3 (Xiyue Island) and navigate S225°W for roughly 30 nautical miles to arrive at $Ddoi^1$ Da^1 Di^6 (Nanyue Island). The compass needle should point towards Gen Kun (towards southwest) for three geng.

Entry 7

From the Nansha Islands, depart from $Hhong^2$ Sao^3 (Xiyue Island) and set course at 90°E for approximately 50 nautical miles to arrive at Lo^2 $Hong^2$ (Mahuan Island). During this voyage, the needle on the compass should point east towards Mao You for five geng.

Entry 8

From the Nansha Islands, leave $Hhong^2$ Sao^3 (Xiyue Island), setting course at S195°W for about 20 nautical miles to arrive at $Hhue^3$ Ai^1 (Huo'ai Reef); that is, the compass needle should point southwest towards Gui Ding for two geng.

Entry 9

Navigate S255°W from the Nansha Islands, leave $Hhong^2$ Sao^3 Dua^4 Bai^2 (Changtan Bank) and sail for roughly 20 nautical miles to arrive at Hih^7 Di^6 (Zhongye Island), that is, the compass needle should point southwest towards Jia Geng for two geng.

1 English Version of Su Deliu *Genglubu*

Entry 10

From the Nansha Islands, leave *Hhong² Sao³ Dua⁴ Bai²* (Changtan Shoal), navigate S127.5°E for about 20 nautical miles, arrive at *Hhue³ Ai¹* (Huo'ai Reef). Using Chinese traditional terms of direction and distance, the compass needle should point southeast between Qian Xun and Chen Xu for two geng.

Entry 11

Navigate 277.5°W from the Nansha Islands, sail about 20 nautical miles from *Hhue³ Ai¹* (Huo'ai Reef) to arrive at *Hou⁴ Gui* (Kugui Reef). That is, the compass needle should point west between Yi Xin and Mao You for two geng.

Entry 12

Sail S135°E from the Nansha Islands, leave *Hhue³ Ai¹* (Huo'ai Reef) to travel 30 nautical miles. This will bring you to *Da¹ Gag⁷* (Sanjiao Reef). During this trip, the compass needle should point towards Qian Xun (towards southeast) for three geng.

Entry 13

Depart from *Da¹ Gag⁷* (Sanjiao Reef) at the Nansha Islands and sail for about 20 nautical miles bearing S120°E. Thus, one can arrive at *Diang¹ Mui²* (Meiji Reef); that is, the compass needle should point towards Chen Xu (towards southeast) for two geng.

Entry 14

Leave *Hhong² Sao³* (Xiyue Island), navigate S120°E for approximately 40 nautical miles. This will take you to *Ngou⁵ Hhuang¹* (Wufang Reef). The compass needle should point southeast towards Chen Xu (towards southeast) for four geng.

Entry 15

Leave the Nansha Islands from *Diang¹ Mui²* (Meiji Reef), navigate 97.5°E for about 20 nautical miles to arrive at *Ddui⁵ Dad⁷* (Ren'ai Reef). That is, the compass needle should point east between Yi Xin and Mao You for two geng.

Entry 16

From the Nansha Islands, leave $Diang^1$ Mui^2 (Meiji Reef) and navigate 165°S for about 20 nautical miles to arrive at $Ziao$ $Shua$ (Xian'e Reef). That is, the compass needle should point towards Ren Bing (towards south) for two geng.

Entry 17

At the Nansha Islands, navigate S135°E from $Diang^1$ Mui^2 (Meiji Reef) and sail for approximately 40 nautical miles to arrive at $Diang^1$ $Hiao^1$ (Xinyi Reef). During this voyage, the compass needle should point towards Qian Xun (towards southeast) for four geng.

Entry 18

From the Nansha Islands, leave $Ddui^5$ Dad^7 (Ren'ai Reef) and navigate S157.5°E for about 20 nautical miles to arrive at $Diang^1$ $Hiao^1$ (Xinyi Reef). That is, the compass needle should point between Ren Bing and Si Hai (towards southeast) for two geng.

Entry 19

At Nansha, leave $Ddui^5$ Dad^7 (Ren'ai Reef) and navigate S112.5°E for roughly 20 nautical miles to arrive at Gu^2 Sia^1 Eng^1 (Niuchelun Reef). The compass needle should point southeast between Yi Xin and Chen Xu for two geng.

Entry 20

At Nansha, leave $Ddui^5$ Dad^7 (Ren'ai Reef), sail N15°E for approximately 50 nautical miles to arrive at $Ngou^5$ $Hhuang^1$ (Wufang Reef). The compass needle should point towards Gui Ding (towards northeast) for five geng.

Entry 21

At Nansha, leave Gu^2 Sia^1 Eng^1 (Niuchelun Reef) and sail for roughly 30 nautical miles bearing S135°E to arrive at Ha^1 $Buad^7$ (Haikou Reef). In other words, the compass needle should point towards Qian Xun (towards southeast) for three geng.

1   English Version of Su Deliu *Genglubu*

Entry 22

At Nansha, leave $Gu^2\ Sia^1\ Eng^1$ (Niuchelun Reef) navigating N315°W for about 20 nautical miles to arrive at $Ddui^5\ Dad^7$ (Ren'ai Reef). During this trip, the compass needle should point towards Qian Xun (towards northwest) for two geng.

Entry 23

At Nansha, leave $Ha^1\ Buad^7$ (Haikou Reef) bearing 90°E and sail for roughly 20 nautical miles to arrive at $Zio^5\ Liang^2$ (Jianzhang Reef). That is, the compass needle should point towards Mao You (towards east) for two geng.

Entry 24

At Nansha, leave $Zio^5\ Liang^2$ (Jianzhang Reef), navigate 360°N and sail for approximately 40 nautical miles to arrive at $Hhu^2\ Lin^2$ (Xianbin Reef). That is, the needle on the compass should point towards Zi Wu (towards north) for four geng.

Entry 25

At Nansha, leave $Ha^1\ Buad^7$ (Haikou Reef) and bear N337.5°W, sail for roughly 30 nautical miles to arrive at $Gu^2\ Sia^1\ Eng^1$ (Niuchelun Reef). That is, the compass needle should point northwest between Ren Bing and Si Hai for three geng.

Entry 26

At Nansha, leave $Zio^5\ Liang^2$ (Jianzhang Reef) and navigate N292.5°W, sail about 20 nautical miles to arrive at $Ha^1\ Buad^7$ (Haikou Reef). In Chinese traditional terms, the compass needle should point northwest between Yi Xin and Chen Xu for two geng.

Entry 27

At Nansha, depart from $Hhu^2\ Lin^2$ (Xianbin Reef) and sail about 30 nautical miles bearing 99°E to arrive at $Ddang^1\ Hao^2\ Id^7\ Din^1$ (Pengbo Shoal). That is, the compass needle should point east between Yi Xin and Mao You for three geng.

Entry 28

From Nansha, leave Hhu^2 Lin^2 (Xianbin Reef), navigate 352.5° N for approximately 50 nautical miles to arrive at Hho^1 $Ddin^2$ (Houteng Reef). The compass needle should point north between Zi Wu and Ren Bing for five geng.

Entry 29

At Nansha, leave Hhu^2 Lin^2 (Xianbin Reef), navigate 270° W for about 20 nautical miles to arrive $Ddui^5$ Dad^7 (Ren'ai Reef). In traditional terms, the compass needle should point towards Mao You (towards west) for two geng.

Entry 30

At Nansha, leave $Diang^1$ $Hiao^1$ (Xinyi Reef), bear S129°E and sail roughly 30 nautical miles to arrive at $Hhai^3$ $Gong^1$ (Banyue Reef). The compass needle should point southeast between Qian Xun and Chen Xu for three geng.

Entry 31

Navigate 276° W for approximately 20 nautical miles, leave $Diang^1$ $Hiao^1$ (Xinyi Reef), you will arrive at $Ziao$ $Shua$ (Xian'e Reef); that is, the compass needle should point west between Yi Xin and Mao You for two geng.

Entry 32

Sail N345°W for approximately 50 nautical miles, leave $Ziao$ $Shua$ (Xian'e Reef), you will arrive at $Ngin^2$ Bia^3 (Anda Reef); the compass needle should point towards Ren Bing (towards northwest) for five geng.

Entry 33

At the Nansha Islands, sail 90°E for approximately 20 nautical miles, leave Lo^2 $Hong^2$ (Mahuan Island) to arrive at Hho^1 $Ddin^2$ (Houteng Reef); the needle on the compass should point towards Mao You (towards east) for two geng.

Entry 34

At the Nansha Islands, navigate 165°S for approximately 15 nautical miles, leave Lo^2 $Hong^2$ (Mahuan Island) to arrive at $Ngou^5$ $Hhuang^1$ (Wufang Reef); the needle on the compass should point between Ren Bing and Zi Wu (towards south) for one and a half geng.

Entry 35

Sail 165°S from the Nansha Islands for approximately 40 nautical miles, leave *Ngou⁵ Hhuang¹* (Wufang Reef), you should arrive at *Ddui⁵ Dad⁷* (Ren'ai Reef); that is, the compass needle should point towards Ren Bing (towards south) and navigate for four geng.

Entry 36

Sail S120°E from the Nansha Islands for approximately 40 nautical miles, leave *Ngou⁵ Hhuang¹* (Wufang Reef), you should arrive at *Hhu² Lin²* (Xianbin Reef); that is, the compass needle should point towards Chen Xu (towards southeast) for four geng. However, there is a dark sand belt half-way to *Hhu² Lin²* which was named *Bua⁴ Lou¹ Dua⁴* (Banlu Reef).

Entry 37

Sail S135°E from the Nansha Islands for approximately 20 nautical miles, leave *Ngou⁵ Hhuang¹ Hao* (Wufangtou Reef), you should arrive at *Bua⁴ Lou¹ Dua⁴* (Banlu Reef); that is, the compass needle should point towards Qian Xun (towards southeast) for two geng.

Entry 38

Navigate S120°E at the Nansha Islands and sail for approximately 20 nautical miles, leave *Hih⁷ Di⁶* (Zhongye Island), you should arrive at *Hou⁴ Gui* (Kugui Reef); the needle on the compass should point towards Chen Xu (towards southeast) for two geng.

Entry 39

Navigate S135°E for roughly 20 nautical miles, leave *Hih⁷ Di⁶* (Zhongye Island), you should arrive at *Ddang² Gim¹* (Yangxin Cay); that is, the needle on the compass should point towards Qian Xun (towards southeast) for two geng.

Entry 40

Navigate S225°W for about 20 nautical miles. Depart from *Hih⁷ Di⁶* (Zhongye Island) to arrive at *Siu³ Vi¹* (Zhubi Reef); that is, the needle on the compass should point towards Gen Kun (towards southwest) for two geng.

Entry 41

Navigate S210°W for approximately 20 nautical miles, leave $Hih^7 Di^6 Dua^4 Gia^3$ (Tiezhi Reef) to arrive at $Siu^3 Vi^1$ (Zhubi Reef); that is, the needle on the compass should point towards Chou Wei (towards southwest) for two geng.

Entry 42

Navigate S165°E at the Nansha Islands for approximately 20 nautical miles; leave $Hih^7 Di^6$ (Zhongye Island), then you should arrive at $Diang^1 Uang^2$ (Shuanghuang Cay); that is, the needle on the compass should point towards Ren Bing (towards southeast) for two geng.

Entry 43

Navigate S135°E from the Nansha Islands for approximately 25 nautical miles; depart from $Hih^7 Di^6$ (Tiexian Reef), you should arrive at $Hou^4 Gui$ (Kugui Reef); that is, the needle on the compass should point towards Qian Xun (towards southeast) for two and a half geng.

Entry 44

At the Nansha Islands, navigate S120°E for roughly 20 nautical miles; leave $Siu^3 Vi^1$ (Zhubi Reef), then you should arrive at $Diang^1 Uang^2$ (Shuanghuang Cay); that is, the needle on the compass should point towards Chen Xu (towards southeast) for two geng.

Entry 45

At the Nansha Islands, navigate S135°E for approximately 30 nautical miles; depart from $Siu^3 Vi^1$ (Zhubi Reef), then you will arrive at $Ui^2 Dua^1 Ve^3$ (Taiping Island); that is, the needle on the compass should point towards Qian Xun (towards southeast) for three geng.

Entry 46

At the Nansha Islands, navigate S150°E for about 20 nautical miles; depart from $Hih^7 Di^6$ (Zhongye Island), you should arrive at $Ddoi^1 Da^1$ (Nanyue Island); that is, the needle on the compass should point towards Si Hai (towards southeast)

1 English Version of Su Deliu *Genglubu*

for two geng.

Entry 47

At the Nansha Islands, navigate 172.5°S for approximately 20 nautical miles, leave *Ddoi¹ Da¹* (Nanyue Island), then you should arrive at *Ui² Dua¹ Ve³* (Taiping Island); that is, the needle on the compass should point south towards the middle line between Zi Wu and Ren Bing for two geng.

Entry 48

At the Nansha Islands, navigate S135°E for roughly 30 nautical miles; leave *Ddoi¹ Da¹* (Nanyue Island), then you will arrive at *Ngin² Bia³* (Anda Reef); that is, the needle on the compass should point towards Qian Xun (towards southeast) for three geng.

Entry 49

From the Nansha Islands, sail S120°E for approximately 50 miles. Set off from *Hou⁴ Gui* (Kugui Reef), the trip will bring you to *Da¹ Gag⁷* (Sanjiao Reef). During this trip, the compass needle should point towards Chen Xu (towards southeast) for five geng.

Entry 50

At the Nansha Islands, navigate S150°E for approximately 20 nautical miles. Depart from *Ddang² Gim¹* (Yangxin Cay), the trip will bring you to *Ngin² Bia³* (Anda Reef); that is, the needle on the compass should point towards Si Hai (towards southeast) for two geng.

Entry 51

At the Nansha Islands, navigate S255°W for about 20 nautical miles. Leave *Ddang² Gim¹* (Yangxin Cay), you will arrive at *Ddoi¹ Da¹* (Nanyue Island); that is, the needle on the compass should point towards Jia Geng (towards southwest) for two geng.

Entry 52

At the Nansha Islands, sail S120°E for approximately 50 nautical miles; leave *Ngin² Bia³* (Anda Reef) and you should arrive at *Ziao Shua* (Xian'e Reef); that is, the compass needle should point towards Chen Xu (towards southeast) for five geng.

Entry 53

At the Nansha Islands, sail 270°W for 20 nautical miles; leave $Ngin^2\ Bia^3$ (Anda Reef), you will arrive at $Ui^2\ Dua^1\ Ve^3$ (Taiping Island). that is, the compass needle should point towards Mao You (towards west), sailing for two geng.

Entry 54

At the Nansha Islands, sail S195°W for about 20 nautical miles; leave $Ngin^2\ Bia^3$ (Anda Reef), the trip will bring you to $Gu^2\ Eg^7$ (Niu'e Reef); that is, the compass needle should point towards Gui Ding (towards southwest) for two geng.

Entry 55

At the Nansha Islands, navigate N337.5°W for approximately 30 nautical miles; depart from $Ui^2\ Dua^1\ Ve^3$ (Taiping Island), you should then arrive at $Siu^3\ Vi^1$ (Zhubi Reef); that is, the needle on the compass should point towards the middle line between Ren Bing and Si Hai (towards northwest) for three geng.

Entry 56

At the Nansha Islands, navigate S135°E for approximately 30 nautical miles; set off from $Ui^2\ Dua^1\ Ve^3$ (Taiping Island), then you will arrive at $Gu^2\ Eg^7$ (Niu'e Reef); that is, the needle on the compass should point towards Qian Xun (towards southeast) for three geng.

Entry 57

At the Nansha Islands, navigate S240°W for about 30 nautical miles; depart from $Ui^2\ Dua^1\ Ve^3$ (Taiping Island), you will arrive at $Lao^2\ Gu^2\ Lao^2$ (Daxian Reef); that is, the needle on the compass should point towards Yin Shen (towards southwest) for three geng.

Entry 58

From the Nansha Islands, navigate S165°E for 10 nautical miles. Leave $Ui^2\ Dua^1\ Ve^3$ (Taiping Island), you should then arrive at $Nam^2\ Id^7\ Di^6$ (Hongxiu Island); that is, the needle on the compass should point towards Ren Bing (towards southeast) for one geng.

Entry 59

At the Nansha Islands, navigate 180°S for approximately 20 nautical miles; set off from $Nam^2\ Id^7\ Di^6$ (Hongxiu Island), then you will arrive at $Sin^4\ Gao^1$ (Jinghong Island); that is, the needle on the compass should point towards Zi Wu (towards south) for two geng.

Entry 60

At the Nansha Islands, navigate S165°E; set off from $Nam^2\ Id^7\ Di^6$ (Hongxiu Island) and sail for roughly 20 nautical miles, you should then arrive at $Sin^4\ Gao^1\ Dua^4$ (Huajiao Reef); that is, the needle on the compass should point towards Ren Bing (towards southeast) for two geng.

Entry 61

At the Nansha Islands, sail S162°E for approximately 90 nautical miles. Leave $Gu^2\ Eg^7$ (Niu'e Reef) will bring you to $Mag^8\ Gia^4$ (Siling Reef); that is, the compass needle should point southeast between Si Hai and Ren Bing for nine geng.

Entry 62

At the Nansha Islands, navigate S240°W for roughly 20 nautical miles. Leave $Mag^8\ Gia^4$ (Siling Reef), you should arrive at $Sim^1\ Huang^1$ (Yuya Shoal); that is, the compass needle should point towards Yin Shen (towards southwest) for two geng.

Entry 63

At the Nansha Islands, navigate N315°W. Leave $Mag^8\ Gia^4$ (Siling Reef) and sail for approximately 30 nautical miles, you will arrive at $Vo^2\ Mi^6\ Dua^4$ (Wumie Reef); that is, the compass needle should point towards Qian Xun (towards northwest) for three geng.

Entry 64

At the Nansha Islands, sail S172.5°E; depart from *Nise Zio* (Ranqingdong Reef) and sail for approximately 50 nautical miles, you will arrive at $Vo^2\ Mi^6\ Dua^4$ (Wumie Reef); that is, the compass needle should point towards the middle line between Zi Wu and Ren Bing (towards southeast) for five geng.

Entry 65

Set sail from the Nansha Islands at Vo^2 Mi^6 Dua^4 (Wumie Reef) and navigate S165°E for about 20 nautical miles, the trip will bring you to Sim^1 $Huang^1$ (Yuya Shoal); that is, the compass needle should point towards Ren Bing (towards southeast) for two geng.

Entry 66

Set sail from the Nansha Islands at Sim^1 $Huang^1$ (Yuya Shoal) and navigate S247.5°W for approximately 20 nautical miles, the trip will bring you to Po^1 Gi^1 (Boji Reef); that is, the compass needle should point towards the middle line between Jia Gen and Yin Shen (towards southwest) for two geng.

Entry 67

Set sail from the Nansha Islands at Po^1 Gi^1 (Boji Reef) and navigate S240°W for about 10 nautical miles, the trip will bring you to $Ddang^2$ $Ziang^1$ (Nanhai Reef); that is, the compass needle should point towards Yin Shen (towards southwest) for one geng.

Entry 68

Set sail from the Nansha Islands at $Ddang^2$ $Ziang^1$ (Nanhai Reef) and navigate N315°W for approximately 30 nautical miles, you can arrive at $Hhai^3$ Hao^3 Dua^4 (Baijiao Reef); the compass needle should point towards the middle line between Qian Xun and Chen Xu (towards northwest) for three geng.

Entry 69

Set sail from the Nansha Islands at $Ddang^2$ $Ziang^1$ (Nanhai Reef) and navigate S157.5°E for approximately 25 nautical miles, you can arrive at $Guang^1$ Se^1 Gia^3 (Guangxingzai Reef); that is, the compass needle should point southeast towards the middle line between Ren Bing and Si Hai for two and a half geng.

Entry 70

Set sail from the Nansha Islands at $Guang^1 Se^1 Gia^3$ (Guangxingzai Reef) and navigate 270°W for about 10 nautical miles, you should arrive at $Ddua^1 Guang^1 Se^1$ (Guangxing Reef); namely, the compass needle should point towards Mao You (towards west) for one geng.

Entry 71

Set sail from the Nansha Islands at $Guang^1 Se^1 Gia^3$ (Guangxingzai Reef) and navigate N352.5°W for approximately 40 nautical miles, you can arrive at $Hhai^3 Hao^3 Dua^4$ (Baijiao Reef); namely, the compass needle should point northwest towards the middle line between Ren Bing and Zi Wu for four geng.

Entry 72

Set sail from the Nansha Islands at $Guang^1 Se^1 Gia^3$ (Guangxingzai Reef) and navigate S135°E for about 20 nautical miles, you should arrive at $Zio^5 Gong^1 Li^3$ (Danwan Reef); namely, the compass needle should point towards Qian Xun (towards southeast) for two geng.

Entry 73

Set sail from the Nansha Islands at $Zio^5 Gong^1 Li^3$ (Danwan Reef) and navigate S202.5°W for approximately 25 nautical miles, and you will arrive at $Ngou^5 Be^6 Yi^1$ (Huanglu Reef); that is, the compass needle should point southwest towards the middle line between Gui Ding and Chou Wei for two and a half geng.

Entry 74

Set sail from the Nansha Islands at $Ngou^5 Be^6 Yi^1$ (Huanglu Reef) and navigate S202.5°W for approximately 30 nautical miles, you can arrive at $Ddan^1 Dad^7$ (Nantong Reef); that is, the compass needle should point southwest towards the middle line between Chou Wei and Gui Ding for three geng.

Entry 75

Set sail from the Nansha Islands at $Ddan^1 Dad^7$ (Nantong Reef) and navigate S217.5°W for approximately 60 nautical miles, you should arrive at $Vag^8 Gue^1 Dua^4$

(Nanping Reef); that is, the compass needle should point southwest towards the middle line between Gen Kun and Chou Wei for six geng.

Entry 76

Set sail from the Nansha Islands at Sin^4 Gao^1 (Jinghong Island) and navigate S186°W for approximately 50 nautical miles. This should take you to Hho^2 Leg^7 Mui^2 (Nanhua Reef); that is, the compass needle should point southwest towards the two separate lines between Zi Wu and Gui Ding for five geng.

Entry 77

Set sail from the Nansha Islands at Sin^4 Gao^1 (Jinghong Island) and navigate S195°W for approximately 50 nautical miles, you will arrive at Lag^8 Mui^2 (Liumen Reef); that is, the compass needle should point towards Gui Ding (towards southwest) for five geng.

Entry 78

Set sail from the Nansha Islands at Hho^2 Leg^7 Mui^2 (Nanhua Reef) and navigate S165°E for approximately 40 nautical miles, you can arrive at Po^1 Gi^1 (Boji Reef); namely, the compass needle should point towards Ren Bing (towards southeast) for four geng.

Entry 79

Set sail from the Nansha Islands at Lag^8 Mui^2 (Liumen Reef) and navigate S150°E for approximately 40 nautical miles; that is, the compass needle should point towards Si Hai (towards southeast) for four geng. Then you can arrive at Po^1 Gi^1 (Boji Reef).

Entry 80

Set sail from the Nansha Islands at Hho^2 Leg^7 Mui^2 (Nanhua Reef) and navigate 180°S for approximately 40 nautical miles; namely, the compass needle should point towards Zi Wu (towards south) for four geng. Then you will arrive at $Ddang^2$ $Ziang^1$ (Nanhai Reef).

Entry 81

Set sail from the Nansha Islands at $Hho^2 \ Leg^7 \ Mui^2$ (Nanhua Reef) and navigate S120°E for approximately 40 nautical miles; that is, the needle on the compass should point towards Chen Xu (towards southeast) for four geng. Thus, you can arrive at $Sim^1 \ Huang^1$ (Yuya Shoal).

Entry 82

Set sail from the Nansha Islands at $Lag^8 \ Mui^2$ (Liumen Reef) and navigate S165°E for approximately 40 nautical miles; namely, the compass needle should point towards Ren Bing (towards southeast) for four geng. Thus, you will arrive at $Ddang^2 \ Ziang^1$ (Nanhai Reef).

Entry 83

Set sail from the Nansha Islands at $Lag^8 \ Mui^2$ (Liumen Reef) and navigate N300°W for roughly 20 nautical miles; namely, the compass needle should point towards Chen Xu (towards northwest) for two geng. This route will bring you to $Zio^5 \ Bua^2$ (Bisheng Reef).

Entry 84

At the Nansha Islands, depart from $Lao^2 \ Gu^2 \ Lao^2$ (Daxian Reef) and arrive at $Lag^8 \ Mui^2$ (Liumen Reef), one should navigate S165°E for approximately 50 nautical miles; that is, the needle on the compass should point southeast towards Ren Bing for five geng.

Entry 85

From the Nansha Islands, embark from $Lao^2 \ Gu^2 \ Lao^2$ (Daxian Reef) and head for $Hho^2 \ Leg^7 \ Mui^2$ (Nanhua Reef), you should navigate S150°E for approximately 50 nautical miles; that is, the needle on the compass should point towards Si Hai (towards southeast) for five geng.

Entry 86

From the Nansha Islands, navigate S195°W, namely, the needle on the compass should point towards Gui Ding (towards southwest). By leaving $Lao^2 \ Gu^2 \ Lao^2$ (Daxian Reef) and sailing for five geng (approximately 50 nautical miles), you can arrive at $Zio^5 Bua^2$ (Bisheng Reef).

Entry 87

From the Nansha Islands, embark at $Lao^2 Gu^2 Lao^2$ (Daxian Reef) and head for $Sin^4 Gao^1$ (Jinghong Island), navigate S120°E for approximately 30 nautical miles; namely, the needle on the compass should point towards Chen Xu (towards southeast) for three geng.

Entry 88

Set sail from the Nansha Islands at $Hho^2 Leg^7 Mui^2$ (Nanhua Reef) and navigate N300°W for about 10 nautical miles, you can thus arrive at $Lag^8 Mui^2$ (Liumen Reef); namely, the compass needle should point towards Chen Xu (towards northwest) for one geng.

Entry 89

From the Nansha Islands, depart from $Lao^2 Gu^2 Lao^2$ (Daxian Reef) and arrive at $Zio^1 Vu^5$ (Yongshu Reef), one should navigate S240°W for approximately 40 nautical miles; namely, the needle on the compass should point towards Yin Shen (towards southwest) for four geng.

Entry 90

Set sail from the Nansha Islands at $Hhai^3 Hao^3 Dua^4$ (Baijiao Reef) and navigate N330°W for approximately 50 nautical miles, you should then arrive at $Ddang^2 Song^4$ (Dongjiao Reef); namely, the compass needle should point towards Si Hai (towards northwest) for five geng.

Entry 91

Set sail from the Nansha Islands at $Ddang^2 Song^4$ (Dongjiao Reef) and navigate N285°W for 20 nautical miles, you will then arrive at $Long^6 Pi^1$ (Xijiao Reef). That is, the compass needle should point towards Yi Xin (towards northwest) for two geng.

1 English Version of Su Deliu *Genglubu*

Entry 92

Set sail from the Nansha Islands at *Long⁶ Pi¹* (Xijiao Reef) and navigate S240°W for approximately 20 nautical miles. Namely, the compass needle should point towards Yin Shen (towards southwest) for two geng. Thus, you can arrive at *Ziao³ Gia³ Di⁶* (Nanwei Island).

Entry 93

Set sail from the Nansha Islands at *Ziao³ Gia³ Di⁶* (Nanwei Island) and navigate N285°W for approximately 20 nautical miles. That is, the compass needle should point towards Yi Xin (towards northwest) for two geng. You should then arrive at *Dai¹ Hao² Id⁷ Din¹* (Riji Reef).

Entry 94

Set sail from the Nansha Islands at *Dai¹ Hao² Id⁷ Din¹* (Riji Reef) and navigate N330°W for approximately 200 nautical miles. That is, the compass needle should point towards Si Hai (towards northwest) for more than twenty geng. You can arrive at *Annamite* (in Vietnam).

Entry 95

Set sail from the Nansha Islands at *Dai¹ Hao² Id⁷ Din¹* (Riji Reef) and navigate N315°W for approximately 220 nautical miles, then you can arrive at *Lo² Uan¹ Hao²* (Cape of Padaran) in Vietnam; that is, the compass needle should point towards Qian Xun (towards northwest) for twenty-two geng.

Entry 96

At the Nansha Islands, setting off from *Nam² Id⁷* (Hongxiu Island), navigate N285°W for about 10 nautical miles; that is, the needle on the compass should point towards Yi Xin (towards northwest) for one geng. You can then arrive at *Nam² Id⁷ Dua⁴ Gia³* (Nanxun Reef).

Entry 97

At the Nansha Islands, setting off from *Nam² Id⁷ Dua⁴ Gia³* (Nanxun Reef), navigate 262.5°W for roughly 25 nautical miles. That is, sail for two and a half geng with the needle on the compass pointing towards the middle line between Jia Geng and Mao You (towards west). You should then arrive at *Lao² Gu² Lao²* (Daxian Reef).

Entry 98

At the Nansha Islands, leaving *Ddang² Gim¹* (Yangxin Cay), navigate S210°W for about 20 nautical miles. That is, the compass needle should point towards Chou Wei (towards southwest) for two geng. You can then arrive at *Ui² Dua¹ Ve³* (Taiping Island).

Entry 99

At the Nansha Islands, leave *Ddang² Gim¹* (Yangxin Cay) and navigate S210°W for approximately 20 nautical miles. That is, the compass needle should point towards between Yi Xin and Mao You (towards east) while sailing for five geng. Thus, you will arrive at *Da¹ Gag⁷* (Sanjiao Reef).

Entry 100

At the Nansha Islands, leave *Ddui⁵ Dad⁷* (Ren'ai Reef) and navigate N322.5°W for approximately 20 nautical miles. That is, the compass needle should point towards the middle line between Qian Xun and Si Hai (towards northwest). Sail for two geng to arrive at *Diang¹ Mui²* (Meiji Reef).

Entry 101

At the Nansha Islands, leave *Diang¹ Mui²* (Meiji Reef) and sail N337.5°W for about 20 nautical miles. That is, the compass needle should point towards the middle line between Ren Bing and Si Hai (towards northwest). One should navigate two geng to arrive at *Da¹ Gag⁷* (Sanjiao Reef).

Entry 102

Set sail from the Nansha Islands at *Hhai³ Hao³ Dua⁴* (Baijiao Reef) and navigate N22.5°E for approximately 30 nautical miles; that is, the compass needle should point towards the middle line between Gui Ding and Chou Wei (towards northeast) for three geng, then you will arrive at *Lag⁸ Mui²* (Liumen Reef).

1 English Version of Su Deliu *Genglubu*

Entry 103

At the Nansha Islands, leaving *Diang*[1] *Mui*[2] (Meiji Reef), sail N352.5°W for approximately 20 nautical miles. That is, navigate for two geng with the compass needle pointing towards the middle line between Zi Wu and Ren Bing (towards northwest). You can thus arrive at *Id*[7] *Dua*[4] (Lusha Reef).

Entry 104

At the Nansha Islands, sail S294°W for approximately 35 nautical miles, leaving *Da*[1] *Gag*[7] (Sanjiao Reef) to arrive at *Ngin*[2] *Bia*[3] (Anda Reef). That is, the compass needle should point between Yi Xin and Chen Xu (towards southwest) while navigating for three and a half geng.

Entry 105

Set sail from the Nansha Islands at *Ddan*[1] *Dad*[7] (Nantong Reef) and navigate 15°N for about 100 nautical miles to arrive at *Hhai*[3] *Hao*[3] *Dua*[4] (Baijiao Reef). That is, the compass needle should point towards Gui Ding (towards north) for ten geng with the north wind.

Entry 106

Set sail from the Nansha Islands at *Vag*[8] *Gue*[1] *Dua*[4] (Nanping Reef) and navigate S231°W for approximately 250 nautical miles, and you will arrive at *Natuna Besar*. During this voyage, the compass needle should point towards between Yin Shen and Gen Shen (towards southwest) for twenty-five geng.

Entry 107

Set sail from the Nansha Islands at *Vag*[8] *Gue*[1] *Dua*[4] (Nanping Reef) and navigate S255°W for approximately 250 nautical miles to arrive at *Hhong*[2] *Ngou*[5] *Luan*[2] (Ranai). The compass needle should point towards Jia Geng (towards southwest) for twenty-five geng.

Entry 108

Set sail from the Nansha Islands and navigate 262.5°W for approximately 250 nautical miles to arrive at *Subi*. That is, the compass needle should point between Jia Geng and Mao You (towards west) for this trip of twenty-five geng.

Entry 109

Navigate S202.5°W from the Nansha Islands for approximately 20 nautical miles, leaving *Hhong² Sao³ Dua⁴ Bai²* (Changtan Bank) to arrive at *Hou⁴ Gui* (Kugui Reef). That is, the compass needle should point between Gui Ding and Chou Wei (towards southwest) for two geng.

Entry 110

Setting sail from the Nansha Islands at *Ddan¹ Dad⁷* (Nantong Reef) and navigating S243°W for approximately 320 nautical miles, you can arrive at *Natuna Besar*. That is, the compass needle should point between Jia Geng and Yin Shen (towards southwest) for this trip of thirty-two geng.

Entry 111

Setting sail from the Nansha Islands at *Guang¹ Se¹ Gia³* (Guangxingzai Reef) and navigating S174°E for approximately 15 nautical miles, you can arrive at *Zio⁵ Gong¹ Li³* (Danwan Reef). During your voyage, the compass needle should point between Zi Wu and Ren Bing (towards southeast) for one and a half geng.

Entry 112

From the Nansha Islands, leave *Zio⁵ Bua²* (Bisheng Reef) and navigate N315°W for approximately 40 nautical miles. You should thus arrive at *Zio¹ Vu⁵* (Yongshu Reef). The needle on the compass should point between Qian Xun and Si Hai (towards northwest) while sailing for four geng.

Entry 113

Set sail from the Nansha Islands at *Lag⁸ Mui²* (Liumen Reef) and navigate S225°W for approximately 30 or 35 nautical miles. Thus, you can arrive at *Hhai³ Hao³ Dua⁴* (Baijiao Reef). During this trip, the compass needle should point towards Gen Kun (towards southwest) for three geng, or for three and a half geng.

Entry 114

Setting sail from the Nansha Islands at *Ngou⁵ Be⁶ Yi¹* (Huanglu Reef) and navigating 7.5°N for approximately 70 nautical miles, you should arrive at *Hhai³ Hao³*

Dua^4 (Baijiao Reef). If the wind blows north, you will travel for seven geng with the compass needle pointing between Zi Wu and Gui Ding (towards north).

Entry 115

At the Nansha Islands, leave Ui^2 Dua^1 Ve^3 $Ddang^1$ (Dunqian Cay), navigate S150°E, and sail for 20 nautical miles. You will arrive at Gao^3 $Ziang^1$ (the Jiuzhang Banks and Reefs). The needle on the compass should point towards Si Hai (towards southeast) for two geng.

Entry 116

Set sail from the Nansha Islands at $Ddang^2$ $Song^4$ Gia^1 (Huayang Reef) and navigate 262.5° W for about 20 nautical miles to arrive at $Ddua^1$ $Ddang^2$ $Song^4$ (Dongjiao Reef). The compass needle should point between Jia Geng and Mao You (towards west) for two geng.

1.3　Other Navigational Routes[1]

1.3.1　Routine Navigational Routes

Navigate south along $Hhua^1 Lo^2 Dua^1$ (Dao Ly Son), the eastern central coast of Vietnam, but do not sail too far east. Continue observing the sea current and the wind direction for three days. Sail west, but not too far west. It is the right route when the water is clear and there is rotten wood flowing. The water will be getting shallow and peach-colored, and there will be seagulls flying overhead. Along $Hhua^1 Lo^2$ (Dao Ly Son), the central coast of Vietnam, sail south for seven geng (approximately 70 nautical miles), you will arrive at $Siang^2 Sa^1$ (the Nansha Islands), which is far away from $Zio^5 Ddo^2$ (the Yongle Islands), the circular reef. In its north are $Suan^2 Pu^4 Di^6$ (Quanfu Island), $Lao^5 Sou^1 Di^6$ (Shanhu Island), $Di^4 Giang^1 Di^6$ (Jingqin Island), $Da^1 Ha^1 Di^6$ (Chenhang Island) and $Vue^3 Di^6$ (Jinyin Island). If you see $Sid^7 Ziu^1 Io^2$ (the Qizhou Islands) to the east, sail back at once by navigating N75°E or 90°E or somewhere between. That is, the compass needle should point towards Jia Geng (N75°E) or Mao You (90°E), or between these two points.

If you see $Hhua^1 Lo^2 Dua^1$ (Dao Ly Son) near the central coast of Vietnam and try to sail towards $Tang^2 Dua^1$ (坐山) from $In^1 Ddong^2 Hao^2$ (Cape Varella) to $Ziam^1 Bi^7 Lo^2$ (Champa Island), it is quite all right, and your boat should be about one geng (10 nautical miles) distance away from $Tang^2 Dua^1$. When getting close to $Tang^2 Dua^1$, you would better navigate 255°W. When approaching $Sid^7 Ziu^1 Io^2$ (the Qizhou Islands), which is situated in the northeast of Hainan Island, you may see treacherous currents, then you will arrive at $Nam^2 Heng^2 Mui^2$ (Dawanshan Island) which lies near the southeast coast of Zhuhai City, Guangdong province, the mouth of the Pearl River. When sailing towards $Ziam^1 Bi^7 Lo^2$ (Champ

---

[1] **Notes:** 1. For more detailed information of the places or islands along the coast of Hainan Island to the coast of Guangdong province in this *Genglubu*, please refer to Information Table of the Places along the Coast of Hainan Island to the Coast of Guangdong in Su Deliu Version of *Genglubu*.

2. For more detailed information about the islands concerning the Southeast Asian countries in this *Genglubu*, please refer to Table of the Information about the Islands and Places of the Southeast Asian Countries in Su Deliu Version of *Genglubu*.

3. The English version of Sections 1 – 12 of Part IV are also numbered based on the original texts for a clear-cut structure between entries.

Island) from *Sid*^{7} *Ziu*^{1} *Io*^{2} (the Qizhou Islands), navigate S127°E, that is, the needle on the compass should point towards the middle line between Qian Xun and Chen Xu (towards southeast). Sail for three geng (approximately 30 nautical miles) to pass by *Hhua*^{1} *Lo*^{2} (Dao Ly Son). Then sail 172.5°S, with the compass needle pointing towards the middle line between Ren Bing and Zi Wu so as to arrive at *In*^{1} *Ddong*^{2} *Hao*^{2} (Cape Varella). Navigate S187.5°W for eight geng (approximately 80 nautical miles); that is, the needle on the compass should point towards the middle line between Gui Ding and Zi Wu (towards southeast), then you will get to *Lo*^{2} *Uan*^{1} *Hao*^{2} (Padaran).

1.3.2 Navigational Routes from *Dua*^{1} *Ham*^{2} (Tanmen Port) to the Coast of Hainan Island, to the Coast of Guangdong Province, to the Xisha Islands, to China – Indochina Peninsula, to Malay Archipelago and to the Coast of Indonesia.

1.3.2.1

1. Navigate N30°E, that is, the needle on the compass points northeast (Chou Wei), departing from *Dua*^{1} *Ham*^{2} (Tanmen Port) and sail for approximately 150 nautical miles (fifteen geng), you will arrive in the coast of Guangdong.

2. Departing from *Dua*^{1} *Ham*^{2} (Tanmen Port) and arriving at *Ddan*^{1} *Nang*^{2} *Di*^{6} (单人峙), sail for about 10 nautical miles (one geng).

3. Navigate 75°E – 90°E, that is, the compass needle points towards west (between Jia Geng and Mao You) for 40 nautical miles (four geng), leaving from *Ddang*^{2} *Zi*^{2} (Mount Tonggu) and arriving at *Dua*^{1} *Ham*^{2} (Tanmen Port).

4. Departing from *Zio*^{1} *Di*^{6} (the Xuande Islands) and arriving at *E*^{5} *Di*^{6} (the Yongle Islands), sail for 160 nautical miles (sixteen geng) by navigating N30°E – S210°W, with the compass needle pointing towards Chou Wei (towards either northeast or southwest).

5. Navigate 82.5°E, that is, the needle on the compass points towards due east between Jia Geng and Mao You for approximately 30 nautical miles (three geng), departing from *Ddang*^{2} *Zi*^{2} (Mount Tonggu) and arriving at *Nam*^{2} *Hhang*^{2} *Liao*^{3} (南行了).

6. Navigate 180°S, that is, the compass needle points towards due south (Zi Wu) for approximately 100 nautical miles (ten geng), departing from *Ddang*^{2} *Zi*^{2} (Mount Tonggu) and arriving at *Bag*^{7} *Di*^{6} (Beishi Island).

7. Set off *Bag*^{7} *Di*^{6} (Beishi Island) and travel for about 10 nautical miles (one geng), and then sail past *Ddang*^{2} *Zi*^{2} (Mount Tonggu) for approximately 30 nauti-

cal miles (three geng). That is, sail 165°S – 180°S, the compass needle points towards due south (Zi Wu and Ren Bing), one can arrive at $Ddang^2$ Gou^3 (Mount Tonggu) near which there are some small islands. To the north there is a bay known as Dua^1 Ao^4 Mui^2 (Da'ao Fishing Village).

8. Sail S215°W – S210°W, that is, the needle on the compass points towards southwest (Gen Kun and Chou Wei) and travel for about 30 nautical miles (three geng) departing from Bag^7 Di^6 (Beishi Island) and arriving at $Ddang^2$ Gou^3 (Mount Tonggu).

9. Navigate 180°S/360°N, that is, the needle on the compass points towards due south/north (Zi Wu) for approximately 130 nautical miles (thirteen geng), leaving from Bag^7 Di^6 (Beishi Island) and arriving at $Ddang^2$ Zi^2 (Mount Tonggu).

10. Departing from Bag^7 Di^6 (Beishi Island), navigate S135°E – S150°E, that is, the compass needle points towards southwest between Qian Xun and Si Hai, and travel for approximately 140 nautical miles (fourteen geng), you will arrive at Gan^1 $Ddao^1$ (Beijiao Reef), one of the Xisha Islands.

11. Navigate S195°W – S210°W; that is, the compass needle points towards southwest between Gui Ding and Chou Wei if your ship departs from Bag^7 Di^6 (Beishi Island) and arrives at Dua^1 Ham^2 (Tanmen Port), travel for approximately 160 nautical miles (sixteen geng).

12. Set off $Ddang^2$ Gou^3 (Mount Tonggu) and sail for approximately 10 nautical miles (one geng), and then navigate S190.5°W, with the compass needle pointing towards southwest between Gui Ding and Chou Wei. Travel for approximately 50 nautical miles (five geng), then you will arrive at Dua^1 Ziu^1 (Yanwo Island). Sailing past Dua^1 Ziu^1 (Yanwo Island), navigate S202.5°W, with the compass needle pointing towards southwest between Gui Ding and Chou Wei, you will get to $Siah^7$ Hho^3 (Gia^3) inside which there are some small islands. To the south there is a bay where a ship can anchor.

13. Leaving $Ddang^2$ Gou^3 (Mount Tonggu), navigate S127.5°E, with the compass needle pointing towards southeast between Qian Xun and Chen Xu. Sail for approximately 100 nautical miles (ten geng), you will arrive at Gan^1 $Ddao^1$ (Beijiao Reef) at the Xisha Islands.

14. Navigate S195°W – S210°W, that is, the compass needle points towards southwest between Gui Ding and Chou Wei, departing from $Ddang^2$ Gou^3 (Mount Tonggu) and traveling for approximately 160 nautical miles (sixteen geng), you will arrive at Dua^1 Ham^2 (Tanmen Port).

1 English Version of Su Deliu *Genglubu*

15. Navigate N37.5°E, with the compass needle pointing towards northeast between Gen Kun and Chou Wei. Departing from *Log*[8] *An*[1] (Padaran) and travelling for approximately 250 nautical miles (twenty-five geng), you will arrive at *Ddang*[2] *Gou*[3] (Mount Tonggu).

16. Navigate 97.5°S – 120°E, with the needle on the compass pointing towards southeast between Yi Xin and Chen Xu. Departing from *Dua*[1] *Ziu*[1] (Yanwo Island) and sailing for approximately 120 nautical miles (twelve geng), you will arrive at *Gan*[1] *Ddao*[1] (Beijiao Reef).

17. Sail S157.5°E, with the compass needle pointing towards southeast between Ren Bing and Si Hai. Navigate for approximately 150 nautical miles (fifteen geng), departing from *Dua*[1] *Ziu*[1] (Yanwo Island), you will arrive at *Zio*[5] *Ddo*[2] (the Yongle Islands).

18. Departing from *Dua*[1] *Ziu*[1] (Yanwo Island), navigate S210°W – S215°W, that is, the compass needle points towards southwest between Gen Kun and Chou Wei. Sail approximately 180 nautical miles (eighteen geng), you will arrive at *Ziam*[1] *Bi*[7] *Lo*[2] (Champa Island).

19. Setting off *Dua*[1] *Ziu*[1] (Yanwo Island), navigate S210°W, that is, the compass needle points towards southwest (Chou Wei). Travel for approximately 180 nautical miles (eighteen geng), you will arrive at *Ddan*[1] *Di*[6] (Hon Ong) in Vietnam.

20. Leaving *Dua*[1] *Ziu*[1] (Yanwo Island), sail S202.5°W, with the needle on the compass pointing towards southwest between Chou Wei and Gui Ding. Travel for approximately 200 nautical miles (twenty geng), you can arrive at *Hhua*[1] *Lo*[2] (Dao Ly Son).

21. Departing from *Dua*[1] *Ziu*[1] (Yanwo Island), sail 187.5°S, that is, the compass needle points towards south between Zi Wu and Gui Ding. Sail for approximately 280 nautical miles (twenty-eight geng), you will arrive at *Din*[1] *Ddiog*[7] (Quy Nhon, Vietnam).

22. Departing from *Dua*[1] *Ziu*[1] (Yanwo Island) and arriving at *Ddua*[1] *Bud*[8] (Cape Varella) in Vietnam. Navigate 180°S, with the compass needle pointing due south (Zi Wu). Travel for approximately 360 nautical miles (thirty-six geng).

23. Departing from *Leng*[2] *Dui*[3] (Lingshui Jiao), navigate S210°W, with the compass needle pointing towards southwest (Chou Wei). Sail for approximately 160 nautical miles (sixteen geng), one can arrive at *Ziam*[1] *Bi*[7] *Lo*[2] (Champa Island) in Vietnam.

24. Departing from *Leng² Dui³* (Lingshui Jiao) and arriving at *Hhua¹ Lo²* (Dao Ly Son), navigate 180°S – 187.5°S, that is, the needle on the compass points towards south between Zi Wu and Gui Ding. Sail for approximately 170 nautical miles (seventeen geng).

25. Navigate 180°S, with the compass needle pointing due south (Zi Wu), and travel for approximately 140 nautical miles (fourteen geng), departing from *Yi² Lim²* (Yulin Port) and arriving at *Hhua¹ Lo²* (Dao Ly Son) in Vietnam.

26. Departing from *Yi² Lim²* (Yulin Port), navigate 180°S – 187.5°S; that is, the compass needle points due south (Zi Wu) and (Gui Ding). Sail for approximately 140 nautical miles (fourteen geng), you will arrive at *Ziam¹ Bi⁷ Lo²* (Champa Island) in Vietnam.

1.3.2.2

1. Depart from *Hhua¹ Lo²* (Dao Ly Son) and arrive at *Ddua¹ Bud⁸* (Cape Varella), the compass needle points due south (Zi Wu) and travel for twelve geng; that is, sail 180°S for approximately 120 nautical miles.

2. Departing from *Hhua¹ Lo²* (Dao Ly Son) and arriving at the Nansha Islands (It needs further exploring), the compass needle points due east between Mao You and Jia Geng and travel for fourteen geng; that is, sail 75°E – 90°E for approximately 140 nautical miles.

3. Departing from *Hhua¹ Lo²* (Dao Ly Son) and arriving at *Sao³ Di⁶* (Con Co), the needle on the compass points towards northwest (Qian Xun) and travel for twelve geng; that is, sail N315°W for approximately 120 nautical miles.

4. Departing from *Hhua¹ Lo²* (Dao Ly Son) and arriving at *Dua¹ Pi³ Gag⁷* (Ba Lang An Mui), Thanh pho Quang Ngai in Vietnam, the needle on the compass points towards southwest between Gen Kun and Yin Shen and sail for one geng; that is, navigate S232.5°W – S240°W for approximately 10 nautical miles.

5. Departing from *Hhua¹ Lo²* (Dao Ly Son) and arriving at *Mui² Geg⁸* (Cu Lao Coni, Vietnam), the compass needle points towards south between Gui Ding and Chou Wei and sail for ten geng; that is, navigate S187.5°W – S210°W for approximately 100 nautical miles.

6. Leaving *Hhua¹ Lo²* (Dao Ly Son) and arriving at *O¹ Hao²* (Dung Quat, Thanh Thuy, Thanh pho Quang Ngai, Vietnam), the compass needle points due west (Mao You) and sail for one and a half geng; that is, navigate 270°W for approximately 15 nautical miles.

7. Leaving *Hhua¹ Lo²* (Dao Ly Son) and arriving at *Nge⁵ Li³* (the east of

Thanh pho Quang Ngai, Vietnam), the needle on the compass points towards west (Jia Geng) and sail for one geng; that is, navigate 255°W for about 10 nautical miles.

8. Departing from $Hhua^1 Lo^2$ (Dao Ly Son) and arriving at $Dua^3 Hhui^4 Gang^3$ (Nuok Island, north of Quy Nhon, Vietnam), the needle on the compass points due south between Zi Wu and Gui Ding (navigate 180°S – 187.5°S).

9. Depart from $Hhua^1 Lo^2$ (Dao Ly Son) and arrive at $Ziu^1 A^6$ (Phu Quy, Vietnam), the compass needle points due south (Zi Wu) and (Ren Bing); that is, navigate 172.5°S – 180°S.

10. Departing from $Hhua^1 Lo^2$ (Dao Ly Son) and arriving at $Ziam^1 Bi^7 Lo^2$ (Champa Island, Vietnam), the compass needle points towards southeast (between Qian Xun and Chen Xu) and sail for three geng; that is, navigate N300°W – N315°W for approximately 30 nautical miles.

11. Departing from $Hhua^1 Lo^2$ (Dao Ly Son) and arriving at $Du^1 O^1 Hao^2$ (Dung Quat, east of Thanh Thuy, Thanh pho Quang Ngai, Vietnam), the compass needle points due west (Mao You) and sail for one geng; that is, navigate 270°W for 10 nautical miles, and then sail due south (180°S). The pass is accessible to vessels.

12. Departing from $Hhua^1 Lo^2$ (Dao Ly Son), the compass needle points northeast (Yin Shen) and travel for six geng; that is, sail N60°E for approximately 60 nautical miles, you should arrive at $Gan^1 Ddao^1$ (Beijiao Reef).

13. Departing from $Hhua^1 Lo^2$ (Dao Ly Son), the compass needle should point due south (between Zi Wu and Gui Ding); that is, sail 180°S – 187.5°S, you should arrive at $Ddiog^7 Go^1 Di^6$ (Nuok Island, north of Quy Nhon, Vietnam).

14. Setting off $Hhua^1 Lo^2$ (Dao Ly Son) and getting to the west of Zhongjian Island at the Xisha Islands, the compass needle points due east between Yi Xin and Mao You, that is, sail 90°E – 97.5°E. Navigate for seven geng (approximately 70 nautical miles).

1.3.2.3

1. Departing from $Ve^3 Lou^1 Seng^1$ (Pulau Gambir, Vietnam) and arriving at $Ddua^1 Bud^8$ (Cape Varella), the needle of the compass points due south between Zi Wu and Ren Bing, and sail for four geng; that is, navigate S172.5 – 180°E for approximately 40 nautical miles.

2. Leaving $Io^2 Gag^7 Di^6$ (Nuok Island, Hon Trau, Vietnam) for $Din^1 Ddiog^7 Gang^3$ (Guy Nhon Port, Vietnam), the compass needle points due south (between

Zi Wu and Ren Bing) and sail for one geng; that is, navigate 175°S – 180°S for approximately 10 nautical miles, one can arrive at Guy Nhon Port.

3. Setting out from $Io^2 \ Gag^7 \ Di^6$ (Nuok Island, Hon Trau, Vietnam) and arriving at $Be^5 \ Ddao^1 \ Seng^1$ (Pulau Gambir, Vietnam), the compass needle points south between Zi Wu and Ren Bing and voyage for two geng; that is to say, sail 175°S – 180°S and travel for approximately 20 nautical miles.

4. Navigating one geng (about 10 nautical miles) from $Io^2 \ Gag^7 \ Di^6$ (Nuok Island, Hon Trau, Vietnam) to $Mui^2 \ Dong^2 \ Geg^8$ (Cu Lao Coni, Vietnam), one can arrive at $Din^1 \ Ddiog^7 \ Gang^3$ (Guy Nhon Port), inside which a ship can anchor in 15 fathoms and outside which a ship can anchor in 25 fathoms. There fishing can be done.

5. Departing from $Io^2 \ Gag^7 \ Di^6$ (Nuok Island, Hon Trau) to arriving at $Din^1 \ Ddiog^7$ (Guy Nhon Port), the compass needle points due south between Zi Wu and Ren Bing and sail for one geng; that is, navigate 180°S – 172.5°S for about 10 nautical miles.

1.3.2.4

1. Leaving $Din^1 \ Ziu^1$ (Quy Nhon) for $Ddua^1 \ Bud^8$ (Cape Varella), there is about one geng (approximately 10 nautical miles) away from where a ship sets off. But for $Ddua^1 \ Bud^8$ (Cape Varella), the compass needle should point south (Ren Bing) and sail for four geng; that is, navigate 165°S for 40 nautical miles.

2. Leaving $Io^2 \ Gag^7 \ Di^6$ (Nuok Island, Hon Trau) for $Be^5 Ddao^1 Seng^1$ (Pulau Gambir), the compass needle points south between Zi Wu and Ren Bing; that is, sail 180°S – 172.5°S. To the south of $Be^5 \ Ddao^1 \ Seng^1$ (Pulau Gambir) there is a bay where fishing ships can anchor when the wind blows northeast. Inside there is also a bay where ships can anchor when the wind blows northeast and southwest.

3. Depart from $Ddua^1 \ Bud^8$ (Cape Varella) to get to $Yun^2 \ Hiu^2$ (Nha Trang Port), the needle on the compass points south (Gui Ding), and sail for three geng, that is, navigates S195°W for approximately 30 nautical miles, one should arrive at $Yun^2 \ Hiu^2$ (Nha Trang Port).

4. Departing from $Ddua^1 \ Bud^8$ (Cape Varella) to arrive at $Yun^2 \ Dud^8 \ Zio^1 \ Mui^2$ (the northern entrance of Nha Trang Port), near which there are a few small islands, the compass needle points southwest between Gen Kun and Yin Shen and sail for less than one geng, that is, navigate S232.5°W – S240°W for less than 10 nautical miles, on the way to the entrance there is a sign to show how one can get into $Yun^2 \ Hiu^2$ (Nha Trang Port).

5. Departing from *Ddua*^{1} *Bud*^{8} (Cape Varella) to *Ziu*^{1} *A*^{6} (the south of Phu Guy), the compass needle points due south (Zi Wu and Ren Bing), that is, sail 180°S.

6. If you depart from *In*^{1} *Ddong*^{2} *Hao*^{2} (Cape Varella) and arrive at *Ziu*^{1} *A*^{6} (Phu Guy Island, Vietnam), the compass needle should point towards south between Zi Wu and Gui Ding and voyage for twelve geng; that is, navigate south bearing 180°S – 187.5°S for approximately 120 nautical miles.

7. Departing from *In*^{1} *Ddong*^{2} *Hao*^{2} (Cape Varella) to get to *Dua*^{1} *Sa*^{1} (Zhongnan Shoal), the compass needle points towards east between Jia Geng and Yin Shen as well as between Mao You, that is, navigate 67.5°E – 90°E.

8. Depart from *Ddua*^{1} *Bud*^{8} (Cape Varella) where a ship can anchor in 53 fathoms, the compass needle points towards south between Zi Wu and Gui Ding, and travel for three geng, that is, sail 180°S – 187.5°S for about 30 nautical miles, then one can arrive at *Ge*^{1} *Nam*^{2} *Miao*^{3} (Ben Hoi/Hon Tre, Vietnam). In Hainan Dialect, *Ddua*^{1} *Bud*^{8} is also known as *In*^{1} *Ddong*^{2} *Hao*^{2} (Cape Varella) near which there are a few small islands where ships can anchor when wind blows northeast.

9. Leaving from *Yun*^{2} *Hiu*^{2} (Nha Trang) to *Lo*^{2} *Uan*^{1} *Hao*^{2} (Padaran), the compass needle points south between Zi Wu and Gui Ding; that is, sail 180°S – 187.5°S. Outside *Yun*^{2} *Hiu*^{2} (Nha Trang) there is a quay/jetty. Sail for five geng (approximately 50 nautical miles), one should arrive at several small islands or rocks close to *Lo*^{2} *Uan*^{1} *Hao*^{2} (Padaran).

10. Departing from the quay outside *Yun*^{2} *Hiu*^{2} (Nha Trang) and arriving at *Ziu*^{1} *A*^{6} (Phu Quy Island), the needle on the compass points towards south between Zi Wu and Ren Bing; that is, navigate 172.5°S – 180°S. Sail for eight geng (approximately 80 nautical miles), one can arrive at a small island close to *Ziu*^{1} *A*^{6} (Phu Quy Island). To the south of the island, the water is shallow, which is a stretch of about two geng (approximately 20 nautical miles).

11. Setting off *Lo*^{2} *Uan*^{1} *Hao*^{2} (Padaran) and getting to *Hun*^{1} *Lun*^{2} (Con Dao), the needle on the compass points towards southwest between Gen Kun and Chou Wei; that is, navigate S210°W – S217.5°W. Sail for seventeen geng (approximately 170 nautical miles), you can arrive at *Hun*^{1} *Lun*^{2} (Con Dao).

12. Leaving *Lo*^{2} *Uan*^{1} *Hao*^{2} (Padaran) for *Siah*^{7} *Ai*^{1} *Hao*^{2} (Ke Ga), the compass needle points towards southwest between Jia Geng and Yin Shen; that is, navigate S240° – 247.5°W and sail for three geng (approximately 30 nautical miles).

13. Leaving *Lo*^{2} *Uan*^{1} *Hao*^{2} (Padaran) for *Dai*^{1} (the southeastern coast of Tuy

Phong), the compass needle points towards southwest between Jia Geng and Yin Shen, that is, navigate S240°W – S247.5°W. Sail for one and a half geng (approximately 15 nautical miles), one can arrive at Dai^1 (the southeastern coast of Tuy Phong).

14. Departing from $Siah^7 Ham^4$ (Ke Ga) and arriving at $Ziu^1 A^6$ (Phu Guy Island), the needle on the compass points towards southeast (Qian Xun), that is, sail S135°E.

1.3.2.5

This section is related with the navigational routes from $Lo^2 Uan^1 Hao^2$ (Padaran) to $Hun^1 Lun^2$ (Con Dao).

1. If a ship departs from $Lo^2 Uan^1 Hao^2$ (Padaran) and arrives at $Hun^1 Lun^2$ (Con Dao), the compass needle points towards southwest between Gen Kun and Chou Wei, that is, sail S210°W – S215°W. Travel for seventeen geng (approximately 170 nautical miles), you will arrive at $Hun^1 Lun^2$ (Con Dao).

2. Outside $Lo^2 Uan^1 Hao^2$ (Padaran) a ship can anchor in 17 – 18 tuo (approximatly 14 – 15 fathoms) if it voyages straight to $Hun^1 Lun^2$ (Con Dao) and pass by. How many geng are taken depends on the direction and distance. To get to $Hun^1 Lun^2$ (Con Dao), the compass needle points towards southwest between Gen Kun and Chou Wei, that is, navigate S215°W. On the route, the depth of waters can be tested by dropping anchor, some waters are about twenty tuo (approximately 17 fathoms) deep while some waters are 30 tuo (roughly 25 fathoms) deep or about 40 tuo (approximately 33 fathoms) deep. Then the compass needle points towards west and northwest between Xin and You and Xu; that is to say, sail 270°W – S300°W. Ships must not anchor around $Hun^1 Lun^2$ (Con Dao) where there are some rocks sticking out.

3. Sail from $Fog^7 Ddia^3$ (the northeast of Nui Son Linh) to $Hhag^8 Ddeng^3$ (Nui Son Linh), the compass needle points towards southwest (Jia Geng), that is, navigate S255°W. Travel for one geng (10 nautical miles).

4. Leaving from $Hhag^8 Ddeng^3$ (Nui Son Linh) to $Hhua^1 Yim^5$ (the mouth of Mekong River), the compass needle points towards southwest and west between Jia Geng and Mao You; that is to say, sail northwest between S255°W and due west (270°W). Make a voyage for one and half geng (about 15 nautical miles).

5. $Hun^1 Lun^2 Gia^3$ (Moi Ba Non) is opposite $Hun^1 Lun^2$ (Con Dao). The compass needle points due west (Mao You), that is, sail 270°W. There may be two geng (about 20 nautical miles) between them. Departing from $Hun^1 Lun^2$ (Con

Dao) and arriving at $Hun^1 Lun^2 Gia^3$ (Moi Ba Non), the compass needle points east between Jia Geng and Mao You; that is, navigate 82.5° E. Sail for three geng (about 30 nautical miles), then you can get to $Hun^1 Lun^2 Gia^3$ (Moi Ba Non).

1.3.2.6

1. Departing from $Hun^1 Lun^2$ (Con Dao) to $Dden^1 Ge^1 Ngi^2$ (Trengganu, Malaysia), the compass needle points southwest between Gen Kun and Yin Shen, that is, sail S225°W – S240°W. Travel for thirty geng (approximately 300 nautical miles), one can arrive at $Dden^1 Ge^1 Ngi^2$ (Trengganu).

2. Departing from $Hun^1 Lun^2$ (Con Dao) to arriving at $Gid^7 Lin^2 Ziu^1$ (Kelantan/Kota Bharu, Malaysia) the compass needle points southwest between Jia Geng and Yin Shen, that is, navigate S240°W – S255°W. Make a voyage for thirty geng (approximately 300 nautical miles).

3. Leaving from $Hun^1 Lun^2$ (Con Dao) to $Ddou^3 Se^3$ (Pulau Tenggul, Malaysia), the compass needle points southwest (Chou Wei), that is, navigate S210°W. Make a voyage for twenty-nine geng (approximately 290 nautical miles).

4. Leaving $Hun^1 Lun^2$ (Con Dao) for $Sao^3 Se^3$ (Pulau Perhentian, Malaysia), the compass needle points southwest between Gen Kun and Yin Shen, that is, navigate S225°W – S240°W. Make a voyage for thirty geng (approximately 300 nautical miles).

5. Departing from $Hun^1 Lun^2$ (Con Dao) to arrive at $Dai^2 Sin^2$ (Jemaja Island, Malaysia), the needle on the compass points south between Zi Wu and Ren Bing, that is, navigate 180°S – 165°S. Travel for thirty-eight geng (approximately 380 nautical miles).

6. Leaving $Hun^1 Lun^2$ (Con Dao) for $Ddang^1 Ddiog^7$ (Pulau Aur, Malaysia), the compass needle points south between Zi Wu and Gui Ding, that is, navigate 180°S – 195°S. Sail for thirty-eight geng (approximately 380 nautical miles).

7. Set out at the south of $Hun^1 Lun^2$ (Con Dao) and sail for one geng (about 10 nautical miles), and then in order to get to $Zin^1 Se^3$ (Khoai, Vietnam), the needle on the compass points due west (Mao You), that is, sail 270°W. Set out at the north of $Hun^1 Lun^2$ (Con Dao) and sail for one geng (about 10 nautical miles) and get to $Zin^1 Se^3$ (Khoai), the compass needle points due west (Mao You) and west by south (Jia Geng), that is, navigate 270°W and between 270°W and S255°W, one can arrive at $Zin^1 Se^3$ (Khoai). One geng (about 10 nautical miles) away from outside $Hun^1 Lun^2$ (Con Dao) to the north, the compass needle points northwest (Gen Kun), that is, navigate N45°W and voyage for eight geng (approxi-

mately 80 nautical miles), one can arrive at $Ddai^6 Mao^6$ (Wallace, Vietnam).

8. Depart from $Ddai^6 Mao^6$ (Wallace) and get to $Hhag^8 Ddeng^3 Dua^1$ (Nui Son Linh), the compass needle points northwest (Chou Wei), that is, navigate N30°W. Sail for five geng (approximately 50 nautical miles) and one can arrive at $Hhag^8 Ddeng^3 Dua^1$ (Nui Son Linh). Then depart from $Hun^1 Lun^2$ (Con Dao) and arrive at $Ddang^1 Dai^1 Ddong^5$ (Sapate Island, Vietnam), the compass needle points northwest (Yin Shen), that is, navigate N60°W. Travel for fifteen geng (about 150 nautical miles). Outside $Ddang^1 Dai^1 Ddong^5$ (Sapate Island) there are several cap-like rocks.

9. When a ship leaves $Hun^1 Lun^2$ (Con Dao) and sail for one geng (about 10 nautical miles) and then sets off for $Lu^5 Dang^4$ (吕宋), the compass needle points southwest between Gui Ding and Chou Wei, that is, navigate S195°W – S210°W. Make a voyage for fourteen geng (approximately 140 nautical miles). Be cautious of the shallow waters on the way.

10. When a ship leaves $Hun^1 Lun^2$ (Con Dao) and sails for one geng (about 10 nautical) and then sets out for $Zin^1 Se^3 Lim^2$ (east Phan Thiet, Vietnam), the compass needle points northeast (Chou Wei), that is, sail N30° E. Travel for seventeen geng (approximately 170 nautical miles), you will arrive at $Zin^1 Se^3 Lim^2$ (east Phan Thiet), near which there are shallow waters.

11. When a ship passes through $Hun^1 Lun^2$ (Con Dao) and sets out for Sin^3 (Royal Bisho), the compass needle points northwest between Gen Kun and Yin Shen, that is, navigate N45°W. Make a voyage for twelve geng (approximately 120 nautical miles), then one can arrive at an unknown island close to Sin^3 (Royal Bisho).

12. Depart from $Hun^1 Lun^2$ (Con Dao) and arrive at $Dang^4 Lu^5$ (宋吕), the compass needle points northwest (Gen Kun), that is, navigate N45°W. Sail for fourteen geng (approximately 140 nautical miles), one can get to $Dang^4 Lu^5$ (宋吕).

13. Passing through $Hun^1 Lun^2$ (Con Dao), the compass needle points northeast between Gen Kun and Yin Shen, that is, navigate N45°E – N60°E. Make a voyage for sixteen geng (approximately 160 nautical miles), one can arrive at $Ddai^6 Mao^6$ (Phu Guy Island).

14. Leaving $Ddai^6 Mao^6$ (Phu Guy Island) for $Hun^1 Lun^2$ (Con Dao), the compass needle points southwest between Chou and Gen and Gui; that is, sail S225°W – S210°W – S195°W respectively, and you can arrive at $Hun^1 Lun^2$ (Con Dao). But you will come to an unknown hill if the needle on the compass points

1 English Version of Su Deliu Genglubu

southwest (Yin Shen), that is, navigate S240°W.

15. Depart from $Hun^1 Lun^2$ (Con Dao) and get to $Ddi^5 Bua^2$ (Tioman, Malaysia), when you voyage half way where your ship can anchor in 20 tuo or in 40 tuo (around 17 or 33 fathoms), that is $Zia^4 Lou^1 Ni^2 Ddi^5$ (Tioman).

16. Depart from $Hun^1 Lun^2$ (Con Dao) and arrive at $Ddi^5 Bua^2 Gia^3$ (Pulau Seri Buat, Malaysia), the compass needle points southwest (Chou Wei), that is, navigate S210°W. Make a voyage for forty geng (approximately 400 nautical miles). Also, the compass needle points southwest between Gui Ding and Chou Wei, that is, sail S202.5°W. Travel for thirty-eight geng (approximately 380 nautical miles), one can arrive at $Ddi^5 Bua^2 Gia^3$ (Pulau Seri Buat).

17. If a ship departs from $Hun^1 Lun^2$ (Con Dao) and sails west a little far where it can anchor in 40 tuo (around 33 fathoms), there is an island known as $Siah^7 Ziao^1$ (Hon Tre Lon, Vietnam) in sight.

18. Leaving $Hun^1 Lun^2$ (Con Dao) for $Zin^1 Se^3$ (Khoai, Vietnam), the compass needle points west (Jia Geng), that is, navigate 255°W. Travel for eight geng (approximately 80 nautical miles), one can arrive at $Zin^1 Se^3$ (Khoai). On the route there are two small islands sitting face to face.

19. Set out at $Hun^1 Lun^2$ (Con Dao) and arrive at $Niao^7 Hun^1 Lun^2$ (Moi Ba Non), the compass needle points west (Mao You), that is, sail 270°W. $Hun^1 Lun^2$ (Con Dao) lies to the east of $Niao^7 Hun^1 Lun^2$ (Moi Ba Non).

20. Depart from $Hun^1 Lun^2$ (Con Dao) and arrive at $Zin^1 Se^3$ (Khoai), the compass needle points west (Jia Geng), that is, navigate 255°W. Travel for eight geng (approximately 80 nautical miles), one can arrive at $Zin^1 Se^3$ (Khoai). But if your ship sets out from the northwest end of $Hun^1 Lun^2$ (Con Dao) and arrives at $Ddi^5 Bua^2$ (Tioman), the compass needle points southwest between Gui Ding and Chou Wei, that is, sail S202.5°W. Make a voyage for thirty-eight geng (approximately 380 nautical miles).

21. Or if your ship departs from the northwest of $Hun^1 Lun^2$ (Con Dao), sail for one geng (around 10 nautical miles) and get to $Siah^7 Ham^4$ (Ke Ga, Vietnam), the compass needle points northeast between Chou Wei and Gui Ding, that is, navigate N15°E – N30°E. Sail for fifteen geng (approximately 150 nautical miles), one can arrive at $Siah^7 Ham^4$ (Ke Ga). Set out for $Zin^1 Se^3$ (Khoai), the compass needle points towards the opposite direction, that is, navigate southwest.

1.3.2.7

1. Departing from $Zin^1 Se^3$ (Khoai) and arriving at $Gid^7 Lin^2 Ziu^1$ (Kelantan/

Kota Bharu, Malaysia), the needle on the compass points northeast/southwest (Chou Wei), that is, navigate N30°E/S210°W. Travel for ten geng (about 100 nautical miles).

2. Departing from Zin^1 Se^3 (Khoai) and arriving at Sou^1 Bue^4 (Koh Samui/Kra Island, Thailand), the compass needle points due east/west (Mao You), that is, sail 90°E/270°W. Make a voyage of eighteen geng (approximately 180 nautical miles).

3. Leaving Zin^1 Se^3 (Khoai) for Ham^4 $Hhao^5$ Gag^7 (Mui Ca Mau, Vietnam), the compass needle points southeast/northwest between Ren Bing and Si Hai, that is, sail S150 – 165°E/ N345°W – N330°W for one geng (about 10 nautical miles).

4. If a ship sets out from Zin^1 Se^3 (Khoai) and arrives at $Ddua^1$ $Hhue^2$ (Pulau Panjang), the compass needle points southeast/northwest (Qian Xun), that is, navigate S135° E/N315°W. Travel for eight geng (approximately 80 nautical miles), one can get to $Ddua^1$ $Hhue^2$ (Pulau Panjang).

5. Departing from Zin^1 Se^3 (Khoai) and arriving at Bid^7 Ge^4 (Koh Khram Yai, Thailand), the compass needle points southeast/northwest between Qian Xun and Si Hai, that is, navigate S135°E – S150°E/N315°W – N330°W.

6. Leaving $Ddua^1$ $Hhue^2$ (Pulau Panjang) for $Niao^7$ $Hhue^2$ (Ko Wai), the needle on the compass points southeast/northwest (Chen Xu), that is, sail S120°E/N300°W for five geng (approximately 50 nautical miles).

7. Sail from Ge^3 Se^3 (Fausse Obi, Vietnam) to $Ddua^1$ $Hhue^2$ (Pulau Panjang), the compass needle points southeast/northwest between Qian Xun and Chen Xu, that is, navigate S120°E – S135°E/N300°W – N315°W.

8. Set off at $Niao^7$ $Hhue^2$ (Ko Wai) and get to Bid^7 Ge^4 (Koh Khram Yai), the compass needle points southeast/northwest between Qian Xun and Chen Xu, that is, sail S120°E – S135°E/N300°W – N315°W. Travel for twenty-three geng (approximately 230 nautical miles), one can arrive at Bid^7 Ge^4 (Koh Khram Yai). For return, the compass needle points southeast (Qian Xun), that is, navigate S135°E.

9. Sail from Bid^7 Ge^4 Hao^2 (Khao Sam Roi Yod) to Di^4 $Siang^3$ Mui^2 (east of Khao Sam Roi Yod), the compass needle points east/west (Mao You), that is, navigate 90°E/ 270°W.

10. Sailing from $Ddan^2$ $Gong^1$ Di^6 (Ko Khi Nok) to $Ddiog^7$ Di^6 (Samut Sakhon) in Thailand, the compass needle points south/north between Gui Ding and Zi

1 English Version of Su Deliu Genglubu

Wu, that is, navigate 180°S – 195°S/360°N – 15°N.

11. Sailing from Gin^4 Bud^8 Dou^1 (Chonburi) to Pi^3 (the east of Phetcha Buri), the needle on the compass points east/west (Jia Geng), that is, navigate 75°E/255°W.

12. Sailing from $Ddan^2$ $Gong^1$ Di^6 (Ko Lan) to $Dang^1$ Di^4 $Siang^3$ Mui^2 (east of Ko Lan), the compass needle points east/west (Mao You), that is, navigate 90°E/ 270°W.

13. Sailing from $Ddiog^7$ Di^6 (Samut Sakhon) to $Ziao^3$ Hao^2 $Siang^3$ (Nong Thale, Krabi Town, Thailand), the needle on the compass points south/north (Gui Ding), that is, navigate 195°S/15°N.

14. Departing from Zin^1 Se^3 (Khoai) to Dde^2 Bua^2 (Koh Kut, Malaysia), the needle on the compass points southeast/northwest between Ren Bing and Si Hai, that is, navigate S150°E – S165°E/N330°W – N345°W. Sail for sixteen geng (approximately 160 nautical miles), one can arrive at Dde^2 Bua^2 (Koh Kut).

1.3.2.8

This section is related with the navigational routes from Zin^1 Se^3 (Khoai) to Din^1 Ziu^1 $Gang^3$ (Port of Singapore).

1. Depart from the west of Zin^1 Se^3 (Khoai), the needle of the compass points south between Ren Bing and Zi Wu, that is, navigate 165°S – 180°S. Travel for thirty-eight geng (approximately 380 nautical miles), sailing by its east, one can arrive at Ddi^5 Bua^2 (Tioman). To the southeast end of Ddi^5 Bua^2 (Tioman), there are three tall rocks sticking out like dragon horns.

2. Depart from Zin^1 Se^3 (Khoai), the compass needle points south between Ren Bing and Zi Wu, that is, navigate 165°S – 180°S. Travel for three and a half geng (approximately 35 nautical miles), one can get through the middle pass of $Ddang^1$ Dai^1 $Ddiog^7$ (Pulau Aur, east of Johor, Malaysia).

3. Depart from Zin^1 Se^3 (Khoai), the compass needle points south (Ren Bing), that is, navigate 165°S. Travel for three geng (approximately 30 nautical miles), one can arrive at $Jiang^1$ Gun^1 Mao^4 (Pulau Tinggi) stretching long from east to west. Passing through $Jiang^1$ Gun^1 Mao^4 (Pulau Tinggi), the compass needle points south (Gui Ding), that is, sail 195°S, one can arrive at the outside of Lo^2 $Hhan^4$ Di^6 (Lima Island). To its southeast end, there is a small white rock on which stands a pharos.

4. If your ship enters the middle of Lo^2 $Hhan^4$ Di^6 (Petra Branca) and sets off for $Siah^7$? (east Singapore), the compass needle first points east between Jia Geng

and Mao You bearing 75°E – 90°E and traveling for one and a half geng (about 15 nautical miles); then the compass needle points east (Mao You) bearing 90°E. Travel for two and a half geng (about 25 nautical miles), you can arrive at *Pou*⁴ (Port of Singapore) and drop anchor there.

1.3.2.9

This section is related with the navigational routes from *Zin*¹ *Se*³ (Khoai) to *Dden*¹ *Ge*¹ *Ngi*² (Trengganu).

1. Depart from the outside of *Zin*¹ *Se*³ (Khoai) and travel for one geng (about 10 nautical miles), then the compass needle points south (Gui Ding), with navigating S195°W. Sail for twenty geng (approximately 200 nautical miles), you can arrive at *Sao*³ *Di*⁶ (Pulau Redang), and there *Min*² *Hhue*¹ *Di*⁶ (Pulau Kapas) is in sight. *Sao*³ *Di*⁶ (Pulau Redang) is a small island around which a ship can anchor when there is northeast wind.

2. Not far from *Zin*¹ *Se*³ (Khoai), there are three or four islets, among which a ship can enter and drop anchor in 14 or 15 tuo (12 – 13 fathoms). Here there is sand or mud bottom. Passing by *Zin*¹ *Se*³ (Khoai), the compass needle points northwest between Yi Xin and Chen Xu, with navigating N285°W – N300°W. Make a voyage for eight geng (approximately 80 nautical miles), you can arrive at *Ddua*¹ *Hhue*² (Pulau Panjang).

3. Departing from *Zin*¹ *Se*³ (Khoai) and arriving at *Ge*³ *Se*³ (Fausse Obi), the compass needle points southeast/northwest (Si Hai), bearing S150°E/N330°W. The distance between the two places is three geng (about 30 nautical miles) and a ship can anchor in 15 fathoms there.

4. Inside *Ddua*¹ *Hhue*² (Pulau Panjang), a ship can anchor in 16 tuo (around 13 fathoms) while outside it a ship can anchor in 25 tuo (around 20 fathoms). At the bottom there is sand or mud. Departing from *Ddua*¹ *Hhue*² (Pulau Panjang) and arriving at *Niao*⁷ *Hhue*² (Ko Wai), the compass needle points northwest between Yi Xin and Chen Xu, with navigating N285°W – N300°W.

5. At the southern side of *Niao*⁷ *Hhue*² (Ko Wai), a ship can anchor in 24 tuo (about 20 fathoms). In distance, there appears to be three or four islets, tall in the west and low in the east. Between each of them there are treacherous currents.

6. Departing from *Niao*⁷ *Hhue*² (Ko Wai), the compass needle points northwest (Qian Xun), with navigating N315°W. Travel for ten geng (approximately 100 nautical miles), and then the compass needle points towards northwest between Qian Xun and Chen Xu, that is, navigate N315°W – N300°W. Sail for fifteen geng

(approximately 150 nautical miles), you can arrive at $Bid^7\ Ge^4$ (Koh Khram Yai) which is also known as $Bid^7\ Ge^4\ Hao^2$ (Khao Sam Roi Yod), near which a ship can anchor in 20 tuo (around 17 fathoms). $Bid^7\ Ge^4$ (Koh Khram Yai) looks like a penholder and so the name was given Bijiashan (笔架山), on the top of which is full of sharp points and plants.

7. Departing from $Bid^7\ Ge^4$ (Koh Khram Yai), the compass needle points northwest (Ren Bing), with navigating N345°W, you will arrive at $Ddan^2\ Gong^1\ Di^6$ (Ko Khi Nok). There one side of $Li^2\ Hao^2\ Dua^1$ (Mount Limu) of Hainan Island is in sight.

8. Departing from $Ddan^2\ Gong^1\ Di^6$ (Ko Khi Nok), the needle on the compass points northwest between Ren Bing and Zi Wu, that is, navigate N345°W – N360°N. Travel for five geng (approximately 50 nautical miles), you can arrive at $U^1\ Hao^2\ Sin^3$ (Nong Thale). Pass through the east side, your ship can drop anchor in 20 tuo (around 17 fathoms). Set off at $U^1\ Hao^2\ Sin^3$ (Nong Thale), the compass needle points northeast (Gui Ding), with navigating N15°E. Sail for three geng (about 30 nautical miles), and one can arrive at $Ddiog^7\ Di^6$ (the outside of Samut Sakhon Port); departing from Samut Sakhon, the compass needle points northwest or due north between Ren Bing and Zi Wu, that is, navigate N345°W – 360°N and travel for another three geng (30 nautical miles), one can arrive at $Ddiog^7\ Di^6$ (Samu Sakhon Port).

1.3.2.10

1. In order to get to $Siam^2\ Lo^2\ Gang^3$ (Port of Siam or Siam Container Terminal) in the right direction and avoid sailing to $Pe^2\ Heng^1\ Gang^3$ (Port of Samut Sakhon), the compass needle should point due north or northwest (Zi Wu and Gui Ding), that is, navigate N360° – N15°W.

2. Departing from $Ddua^1\ Hhue^2$ (Pulau Panjang) and arriving at $Siah^7\ Gia^3\ Gang^3\ Hao^3$ (Koh Phangan), the compass needle should point northwest (Yi Xin), with navigating S105°E – N285°W and sailing for thirty geng (approximately 300 nautical miles).

3. Depart from $Ddua^1\ Hhue^2$ (Pulau Panjang) and arrive at $Dou^1\ Vue^2$ (Ko Sa Mui), the compass needle should point due west (Mao You) and northwest (Yi Xin); that is, navigate 90°E – 270°W and 105°E – N285°W respectively. Travel for thirty-five geng (approximately 350 nautical miles).

4. Depart from $Ddua^1\ Hhue^2$ (south of Pulau Panjang) and sail for half a geng (about 5 nautical miles), then the compass needle should point southwest (Jia Geng

and Yin Shen), with navigating between S240°W and S255°W. Travel for thirty-one geng (approximately 310 nautical miles), one can arrive at $Va^1 Siu^3$ (the two islands outside Songkhla Port).

5. Sail from $Ddua^1 Hhue^2$ (Pulau Panjang) to $Vo^2 Lai^2 U^5 Ao^4$ (Port of Ban Pak Phanang), the compass needle points southwest (Gen Kun), with navigating S225°W.

6. Sail from $Ddua^1 Hhue^2$ (Pulau Panjang) to $Siah^7 Gia^3 Gang^3 Hao^3$ (Port of Phangan), the compass needle should point northwest (Yi Xin) and due west (Mao You); that is, sail N285°W – N270°W and travel for twenty-five geng (approximately 250 nautical miles), one can arrive at $Siah^7 Gia^3 Gang^3 Hao^3$ (Port of Phangan).

7. Sail from $Niao^7 Hhue^2$ (Ko Wai) to $Dou^1 Vue^2$ (Ko Sa Mui), the compass needle should point due east or due west (Mao You), with navigating 90°E – 270°W and traveling for twenty geng (approximately 200 nautical miles).

8. Sail from $Niao^7 Hhue^2$ (Ko Wai) to $Vo^2 Lai^2 U^5 Ao^4$ (Port of Ban Pak Phanang), the compass needle points southwest (Chou Wei) bearing N30°E – S210°W.

9. Sail from $Zin^1 Du^2$ (Khoai) to $Ddang^1 Ddiog^7$ (Pulau Aur, Malaysia), the compass needle should point southeast/northwest between Ren Bing and Si Hai; that is, navigate S150°E – S165°E/N330°W – N345°W respectively and travel for ten geng (roughly 100 nautical miles).

10. Leaving $Zin^1 Di^6$ (Khoai) and arriving at $Diag^7 Di^6$ (Natuna Islands), the compass needle should point southeast/northwest between Ren Bing and Si Hai; that is, navigate S165°E – S150°E/N345°W – N330°W respectively. Travel for thirty geng (roughly 300 nautical miles).

11. Depart from $Zin^1 Du^2$ (south of Khoai) and sail for half a geng (about 5 nautical miles), then the compass needle points southeast/northwest (Qian Xun), that is, navigate S135°E/N315°W and sail for seven geng (about 70 nautical miles), one will arrive at $Ddua^1 Hhue^2$ (Pulau Panjang).

12. Sail from $Zin^1 Du^2$ (Khoai) to $Hang^4 Gia^3 Ddo^2$ (Port of Sihanoukville), the compass needle should point southeast/northwest (Ren Bing), with navigating S165°E/ N345°W and traveling for seventeen geng (approximately 170 nautical miles).

13. Sail from $Zin^1 Du^2$ (Khoai) to $Da^1 Gag^7$ (Perhentian Islands), the compass needle should point southwest (Gui Ding and Chou Wei), that is, navigate

S195°W – S210°W/ N15°E – N30°E. Travel for two geng (approximately 20 nautical miles).

14. Depart from west of $Zin^1 Du^2$ (Khoai) and sail for half a geng (about 5 nautical miles), then the compass needle should point southwest/northwest (Gui Ding), that is, navigate S195°W/ N15°E. Travel for twenty-five geng (approximately 250 nautical miles), one can arrive at $Ddou^3 Yi^3$ (Pulau Tenggul).

15. Sail from $Ge^3 Se^3$ (Fausse Obi) to $Ddua^1 Hhue^2$ (Pulau Panjang), the compass needle should point southeast/northwest between Yi Xin and Chen Xu, that is, navigate S105°E – S120°E/N285°W – N300°W for four geng (approximately 40 nautical miles).

16. Depart from $Ge^3 Se^3$ (Fausse Obi) and arrive at $Zin^1 Du^2$ (Khoai), the compass needle points due south (Zi Wu) and southeast (Ren Bing), with navigating 180°S – 360°N/S165°E – N345°W.

17. Sail out at $Li^2 Hhai^3 Dua^1$ (Mount Limu), the compass needle points southeast/northwest between Qian Xun and Si Hai, that is, navigate S150°E – S120°E/ N330°W – N315°W, one can arrive at $Bo^3 Di^6$ (Bech Long Vi).

18. Navigate from $Li^2 Hhai^3 Dua^1$ (Mount Limu) to $Hhua^1 Lo^2$ (Dao Ly Son), the compass needle points southeast (Ren Bing), with sailing S165°E/N345°W.

19. Sailing south from $Hhua^1 Lo^2$ (Dao Ly Son) to $Ddi^5 Bua^2$ (Tioman), first the compass needle should point southwest between Gui Ding and Chou Wei, with navigating S195°W – S210°W and sail for eighteen geng (approximately 180 nautical miles); and then sail north from $Ddi^5 Bua^2$ (Tioman) to $Hun^1 Lun^2$ (Con Dao), the compass needle points northwest (Gui Ding), that is, navigate N15°W and travel for twenty geng (approximately 200 nautical miles).

1.3.2.11

1. Set off $Ddang^1 Ddiog^7$ (Hon Tre, southwest of Vietnam) and get to $Ddo^2 Io^1$ (Bintan Island), the compass needle should point southeast between Ren Bing and Si Hai, that is, navigate S157.5°E. Travel for eight geng (approximately 80 nautical miles) and one can arrive at $Ddo^2 Io^1$ (Bintan Island), around which there are treacherous rocks and reefs inaccessible.

2. Being away from $Ddo^2 Io^1$ (Bintan Island, Singapore) for half a geng (about 5 nautical miles) and getting to $Ddu^1 Vo^3 Hao^2$ (east of Lingga Island, Indonesia), the compass needle points south between Ren Bing and Zi Wu, that is, navigate 175°S. Sail for eight geng (approximately 80 nautical miles), one can ar-

rive at Ddu^1 Vo^3 Hao^2 (east of Lingga Island) where ships are inaccessible and should be cautious because there are many rocks and reefs inside the bay.

3. If a ship leaves Ddu^1 Vo^3 Hao^2 (east of Lingga Island) and arrives at Man^6 Hao^2 Di^6 (Saya, east Sumatra Island, Indonesia), the compass needle points south (Gui Ding), with navigating 195°S and sailing for three geng (about 30 nautical miles).

4. Departing from Man^6 Hao^2 Di^6 (Saya, east of Sumatra Island), the compass needle first points southeast between Ren Bing and Si Hai, that is, navigate S157.5°E. Travel for seven geng (approximately 70 nautical miles), one can arrive at Nam^2 $Mang^1$ (north Palembang); then the compass needle points towards due south (Zi Wu), with navigating 180°S and sailing for three geng (approximately 30 nautical miles), one can arrive at I^1 $Ddeng^1$ (eastern entrance of Palembang).

5. Vun^2 $Ddou^3$ Wan^1 (Selat Bangka) where ships can anchor lies to Beg^7 $Ddeng^1$ (mouth of Palembang). Set out at Ddu^1 Vo^3 Hao^2 (east of Lingga Island), the compass needle points south (Ren Bing), with navigating south bearing S165°E and traveling for four geng (approximately 40 nautical miles), one can arrive at Sid^7 Se^1 (Seven Island/Tudju Island). Then the compass needle points south between Ren Bing and Zi Wu, that is, navigate 172.5°S, and sail for four geng (approximately 40 nautical miles), one can arrive at Nam^2 $Mang^1$ (north of Palembang). After that, the compass needle points due south (Zi Wu), that is, navigate 180°S. Sail for three geng (approximately 30 nautical miles), one can arrive at I^1 $Ddeng^1$ (the eastern entrance of Palembang). To the west of I^1 $Ddeng^1$ (Palembang) stands a huge unknown rock. Away from the rock for half a geng (about 5 nautical miles), there are treacherous currents.

1.3.2.12

This section is related to the navigational routes from Ddu^1 Vo^3 Hao^2 (Pulau Sibu/Baobi, Malaysia) to Gu^1 $Gang^3$ (Palembang, Indonesia).

1. Set out at Ddu^1 Vo^3 Hao^2 (Pulau Sibu/Baobi) and arrive at $Mang^1$ Hao^2 Di^6 (Saya, east of Sumatra Island), the compass needle points south (Gui Ding), with navigating 195°S and sailing for three geng (approximately 30 nautical miles). Leaving Ddu^1 Vo^3 Hao^2 (Pulau Sibu/Baobi) and arriving at the south of Ko Wai where ships can anchor in 24 tuo (around 20 fathoms). Looking ahead, $Niao^7$ $Hhue^2$ (Ko Wai) appears to be three separate sticking-out rocks.

2. Leaving Ddu^1 Vo^3 Hao^2 (Pulau Sibu/Baobi) for Palembang, first sail for one geng (about 10 nautical miles), with the compass needle pointing south between

1 English Version of Su Deliu *Genglubu*

Gui Ding and Zi Wu and Ren Bing; that is, navigate 195°S – 180°S – 172.5°S respectively. Travel for eleven geng (roughly 110 nautical miles), one can arrive at *Gu¹ Gang³* (Palembang).

3. Departing from *Gu¹ Gang³* (Palembang) to arrive at *Vun² Ddou³* (Selat Bangka), the compass needle points southwest between Jia Geng and Yin Shen, navigate S255°W – S240°W

4. Departing from *Ddu¹ Vo³ Hao²* (Pulau Sibu/Baobi, Malaysia), first sail south for one geng (about 10 nautical miles), then the compass needle points south (Gui Ding), navigate south bearing 195°S and sailing for eight geng (approximately 80 nautical miles), one can arrive at *Ddo² Io¹* (east of Bintan Island).

5. Departing from *Ddo² Io¹* (Pulau Sibu/Baobi) and first sailing north for one geng (about 10 nautical miles), then the compass needle points north between Ren Bing and Zi Wu, that is, navigate 352.5°N. Travel for seven geng (approximately 70 nautical miles), one can arrive at *Ddang¹ Ddiog⁷* (Pulau Aur, Vietnam).

6. Set off at *Din¹ Ziu¹ Gang³* (Port of Singapore) and arrive at *Lo² Hhan⁴ Di⁶* (Lima Island, Singapore), the compass needle points due east (Mao You), navigate 90°E and travel for five geng (approximately 50 nautical miles). To the southeast of *Lo² Hhan⁴ Di⁶* (Lima Island) stand eleven tall white rocks, around which it is dangerous to pass through and sail across into the high sea.

7. Departing from *Ddang¹ Ddiog⁷* (Pulau Aur, Vietnam) and arriving at *Ddo² Io¹* (Pulau Sibu/Baobi), the compass needle points due south/north (Zi Wu), with navigating 180°S/360°N and traveling for nine geng (approximately 90 nautical miles).

1.3.3

1. Departing from *Hun¹ Lun²* (Con Dao) and arriving at *Zin¹ Se⁶* (Khoai), the compass needle points west between Jia Geng and Mao You, with navigating 255°W – 270°W and sailing for nine geng (approximately 90 nautical miles).

2. Departing from *Zin¹ Se⁶* (Khoai) and arriving at *Ddua¹ Hhue²* (Pulau Panjang), the compass needle points northwest (Qian Xun), that is, navigate N315°W and sail for six geng (approximately 60 nautical miles).

3. Departing from *Ddua¹ Hhue²* (Pulau Panjang) and arriving at *Niao⁷ Hhue²* (Ko Wai), the compass needle points Chen Xu (towards northwest), with navigating N300°W.

4. Departing from *Ddua¹ Hhue²* (Pulau Panjang) and arriving at *Hhun² Mao⁵* (Koh Tang, Cambodia), the compass needle points northwest between Qian Xun

and Si Hai, that is, navigate N315°W – N330°W and sail for six geng (approximately 60 nautical miles).

5. Leaving $Niao^7\ Hhue^2$ (Ko Wai) for $Hhun^2\ Mao^5$ (Koh Tang), the compass needle points northwest (between Yi Xin and Chou Wei), navigate N285°W and sail for two geng (approximately 20 nautical miles).

6. Set off at $Hhun^2\ Mao^5$ (Koh Tang) and get to $Gog^7\ Hhui^5$ (Ko Tao), the compass needle points due west (Mao You); that is, navigate 270°W and sail for eighteen geng (approximately 180 nautical miles). To arrive at $Hhun^2\ Mao^5\ Gia^3$ (Depond Reef/Kas Prins), sail for three geng (about 30 nautical miles).

1.3.4

1. Departing from $Se^1\ Ziu^1$ (Port of Singapore), the compass needle points due west (Mao You) bearing 270° W, one can arrive at $Be^5\ Zio^5\ Bua^2\ Hhab^8$ (Pedra Branca or Pulau Batu Puteh, Singapore).

2. Departing from $Be^5\ Zio^5\ Bua^2\ Hhab^8$ (Pedra Branca or Pulau Batu Puteh), the needle on the compass points northwest between Ren Bing and Si Hai, that is, navigate N345°W. Travel for seven geng (approximately 70 nautical miles), one can arrive at $Ddo^2\ Io^1$ (Pulau Sibu).

3. Leave $Ddo^2\ Io^1$ (Pulau Sibu) for Pulau Baobi, the compass needle points at Ren Bing (towards northwest), with navigating N345°W. Travel for less than one geng (less than 10 nautical miles).

4. Leave $Ddu^1\ Vo^3\ Hao^2$ (Pulau Baobi) for $Ddi^5\ Bua^2\ Gia^3$ (Pulau Seri Buat), the compass needle points towards Ren Bing (towards northwest), that is, navigate N345°W. Sail for two geng (about 20 nautical miles).

5. Leave $Ddi^5\ Bua^2\ Gia^3$ (Pulau Seri Buat) for $Hih^7\ Liam^2\ Di^6$ (Berhala, Malaysia), the compass needle points northwest between Ren Bing and Si Hai, with sailing N337.5°W and traveling for three geng (about 30 nautical miles).

6. Departing from the inside of $Hih^7\ Liam^2\ Di^6$ (Berhala), the needle on the compass points north between Zi Wu and Ren Bing, that is, navigate 352.5°N. Sail for eight geng (approximately 80 nautical miles), you will arrive at $Ddou^3\ Di^6$ (Kuala Pahang).

7. Depart from $Ddou^3\ Di^6$ (Kuala Pahang) and arrive at $Gam^1\ Ve^3\ Se^6$ (Kemasik), the needle on the compass points towards Gen Kun (towards southwest/northeast), that is, navigate S215°W/N45°E. The former is half a geng (about 5 nautical miles) away from the latter.

1 English Version of Su Deliu *Genglubu*

1.3.5 This part is related to the navigational routes from $Se^1 \, Ziu^1$ (Singapore) to $Ba^5 \, Li^8$ (Bali Island, Indonesia).

1. Leave $Liao^2 \, Mui^2 \, Ddeng^1$ (Rhio Strait) for $Se^1 \, Di^6 \, Gia^3$ (a small unknown island of south Rhio Strait), the compass needle points towards Qian Xun (towards southeast), with navigating S135° E. Travel for four geng (about 40 nautical miles).

2. Set out at $Se^1 \, Di^6 \, Gia^3$ (a small unknown island of south Rhio Strait) and arrive at $Ddu^1 \, Vo^3 \, Hao^2$ (east Lingga Island), the compass needle points south (Ren Bing), that is, navigate 165°S. Travel for seven geng (about 70 nautical miles).

3. Depart from $Ddu^1 \, Vo^3 \, Hao^2$ (east Lingga Island) to get to $Man^6 \, Hao^2 \, Di^6$ (Saya, east Sumatra Island), the compass needle points towards Gui Ding (towards south by west), that is, navigate 195°S. Travel for three geng (about 30 nautical miles). Your ship should pass by $Man^6 \, Hao^2 \, Di$ (Saya) to the east.

4. Set off at $Man^6 \, Hao^2 \, Di^6$ (Saya, east Sumatra Island) and arrive at $Sin^4 \, Se^1$ (Seven Island/Tudju Island), the compass needle points towards Qian Xun (towards southeast), that is, navigate S135°E. Travel for three geng (about 30 nautical miles). Your ship should pass by Seven Island to the west.

5. Leave $Sin^4 \, Se^1$ (Seven Island/Tudju Island) for $Bud^8 \, Ddou^3 \, Ddeng^1$ (northeast of Palembang), the compass needle points towards Gui Ding (towards south by west), that is, navigate S195°W. Travel for three geng (about 30 nautical miles). Passing by west, you can arrive at $Him^2 \, Dda^3 \, Ddeng^1$ (north of Palembang).

6. Leave $Him^2 \, Dda^3 \, Ddeng^1$ (north of Palembang) for $Id^7 \, Din^1 \, Ddeng^1$ (the protruding part of Palembang along east coast), the compass needle points towards Yi Xin (towards east by south), that is, navigate S195°E. Travel for two geng (about 20 nautical miles).

7. Depart from $Id^7 \, Din^1 \, Ddeng^1$ (the protruding part of Palembang along east coast) and arrive at $Mui^2 \, Zio^1 \, Ddeng^1$ (southwest Toboali Port), the compass needle points towards Si Hai, that is, navigate southeast by bearing S150°E. Travel for seven geng (about 70 nautical miles).

8. Depart from $Mui^2 \, Zio^1 \, Ddeng^1$ (southwest of Toboali Port) and arrive at $Da^1 \, Lib^8$ (三立洋), the compass needle points towards Ren Bing (towards south by east), that is, navigate S165°E. Travel for two geng (about 20 nautical miles).

9. Depart from $Da^1 \, Lib^8$ (三立洋) and arrive at $Gid^7 \, Li^3 \, Vun^2$ (Karimun

Jawa), the compass needle points southeast between Qian Xun and Chen Xu, with navigating S135°E – S120°E. Travel for twenty-nine geng (about 290 nautical miles).

10. Depart from *Gid*[7] *Li*[3] *Vun*[5] (Karimun Jawa) and arrive at *Yio*[1] *Liang*[2] *Hou*[2] (north of Surabaya), the compass needle points southeast between Yi Xin and Chen Xu, that is, navigate S105°E – S120°E. Sail for nineteen geng (about 190 nautical miles). Leaving *Yio*[1] *Liang*[2] *Hou*[2] (north of Surabaya), sail east, you will arrive at *Gag*[7] *Ban*[5] *Di*[6] (Iyan Island). Passing by Iyan Island and continuing to sail east, one can arrive at *Da*[1] *Mui*[2] *Ddeng*[1] (Sumenep).

11. Depart from *Da*[1] *Mui*[2] *Ddeng*[1] (Sumenep) to arrive at *Ziao*[3] *Gu*[1] *Bai*[2] *Ddeng*[1] (克桑比兰帕), the compass needle points towards Ren Bing (towards south by east), that is, navigate S165°E. Travel for three and a half geng (about 35 nautical miles).

12. Departing from the east of *Ziao*[3] *Gu*[1] *Bai*[2] *Ddeng*[1] (克桑比兰帕) and arriving at *Dai*[1] *Dim*[1] *Dua*[4] *Ddeng*[1] (Pulau Menjangan), the compass needle points towards Zi Wu (towards due south), with navigating 180°S and traveling for two and a half geng (about 25 nautical miles).

13. Departing from *Dai*[1] *Dim*[1] *Dua*[4] *Ddeng*[1] (Pulau Menjangan) and arriving at *Hhua*[1] *Nam*[2] *Hhang*[2] *Mui*[2] (Banyu Wangi), along both places there are pharos at either side of the entrances, the compass needle points towards Gui Ding and Chou Wei (towards south by west), that is, navigate between S195°W – S210°W, one can arrive at *Gia*[1] *Lo*[2] *Ve*[3] (Sobo Banyu Wangi).

14. Set out from *Gia*[1] *Lo*[2] *Ve*[3] (Sobo Banyu Wangi), the compass needle points southeast between Qian Xun and Chen Xu, with navigating S135°E – S120°E. Sail for five geng (approximately 50 nautical miles), one can arrive at *Se*[1] *Hhu*[2] *Hao*[2] (South of Kota Denpasar).

1.3.6

1. Departing from *Dua*[1] *Ziu*[1] (Yanwo Island) to get to *Ziam*[1] *Bi*[7] *Lo*[2] (Champa Island), the needle on the compass points northeast between Chou Wei and Gen Kun, that is, navigate northeast/southwest by bearing N30°E – N210°W/N45°E – S215°W and sail for eighteen geng (approximately 180 nautical miles), one can arrive at *Ziam*[1] *Bi*[7] *Lo*[2] (Champa Island).

2. Depart from *Dua*[1] *Ziu*[1] (Yanwo Island) to get to *Hhua*[1] *Lo*[2] (Dao Ly Son), the needle on the compass points towards Gui Ding and Chou Wei, that is, navigate south by west and due south by bearing S195°W – 180°S, and travel for twenty-one

geng (210 nautical miles), you will arrive at $Hhua^1\ Lo^2$ (Dao Ly Son).

3. Setting out at $Hhua^1\ Lo^2$ (Dao Ly Son) to arrive at $Be^5\ Ddao^1\ Seng^1$ (Pulau Gambir), the needle on the compass points due south (Zi Wu) and south by east (Ren Bing), with navigating 180°S – 165°S. Travel for eleven geng (110 nautical miles), one can arrive at $Be^5\ Ddao^1\ Seng^1$ (Pulau Gambir).

4. Depart from $Be^5\ Ddao^1\ Seng^1$ (Pulau Gambir), the compass needle points due south (Zi Wu) or south by east (Ren Bing), that is, navigate 180°S – 165°S. Travel for four geng (about 40 nautical miles), one can arrive at $Ddua^1\ Bud^8$ (Cape Varella).

5. Set off at $Ddua^1\ Bud^8$ (Cape Varella), the compass needle points due south (Zi Wu) or south by west (Gui Ding), with navigating 180°S – 195°S. Travel for four geng (about 40 nautical miles), you will arrive at $Yun^2\ Hiu^2$ (Port of Nha Trang).

6. Leave $Ddua^1\ Bud^8$ (Cape Varella) for $Ziu^1\ A^6$ (Phu Quy Island), the needle on the compass points due south (Zi Wu) and south by east (Ren Bing), that is, navigate 180°S – 165°S.

7. Leave $Yun^2\ Hiu^2$ (Port of Nha Trang), the needle on the compass points due south (Zi Wu) and south by west (Gui Ding), with navigating 180°S – 195°S. Sail for five geng (approximately 50 nautical miles), one can arrive at $Log^8\ An^1$ (Cape of Padaran).

8. Depart from $Log^8\ An^1$ (Cape of Padaran), the compass needle points south by west between Gen Kun and Chou Wei, that is, navigate S225°W – S210°W. Sail for nineteen geng (approximately 190 nautical miles), you will arrive at $Hun^1\ Lun^2$ (Con Dao).

9. Start sailing at $Log^8\ An^1$ (Cape of Padaran), the compass needle points due south (Zi Wu), that is, navigate 180°S. Sail for three geng (approximately 30 nautical miles), you will get to $Ziu^1\ A^6$ (Phu Quy Island).

10. Set out at $Hun^1\ Lun^2$ (Con Dao), the needle on the compass points south by west (Ding), that is, navigate 195°S. Sail for thirty-six geng (approximately 360 nautical miles), one can arrive at $Ddi^5\ Bua^2$ (Tioman Island, Malaysia).

11. Set off at $Hun^1\ Lun^2$ (Con Dao), the compass needle points towards Si Hai (towards southeast), with navigating S150°E. Sail for twenty-four geng (approximately 240 nautical miles), you will arrive at $Pu^2\ Lo^2\ Li^5\ Ud^7$ (Subi).

12. Depart from $Pu^2\ Lo^2\ Li^5\ Ud^7$ (Subi) to arrive at $Hhong^2\ Ngou^5\ Luan^2$ (Ranai, the capital city of Natuna Islands), the needle on the compass points

northwest between Qian Xun and Si Hai, with sailing northwest by bearing N315°W – N330°W.

13. Depart from *Ddi⁵ Bua²* (Tioman Island), the needle on the compass points south by east (Ren Bing), with navigating 165° S. Sail for three geng (approximately 30 nautical miles), one can arrive at *Ddang¹ Ddiog⁷* (Pulau Aur, Malysia).

14. Set out at *Ddang¹ Ddiog⁷* (Pulau Aur), the compass needle points due south (Zi Wu) and south by west (Gui Ding), that is, navigate 180°S – 195°S. Sail for six geng (approximately 60 nautical miles), one will arrive at *Be⁵ Zio⁵ Bua² Hhab⁸* (Pedra Branca).

2 English Version of Peng Zhengkai *Genglubu*

2.1 Navigational Routes towards *Donghai* (the Xisha Islands) ①

Entry 1

If you set off at the Xisha Islands from $Vue^3 Di^6$ (Jinyin Island) and sail to $Bua^4 Lou^1$ (Zhongjian Island), navigate S187.5° and travel for about two geng (approximately 20 nautical miles); that is, the needle on the compass should point towards the middle line between Gui Ding and Zi Wu (towards south).

Entry 2

If you set off at the Xisha Islands from $Da^1 Huan^1$ (Langhua Reef) and sail to $Bua^4 Lou^1$ (Zhongjian Island), navigate S247.5°W and travel for about six geng (approximately 60 nautical miles); that is, the needle on the compass should point towards the middle line between Jia Geng and Yin Shen (towards southwest).

Entry 3

If you set off at the Xisha Islands from $Bua^4 Lou^1$ (Zhongjian Island) and sail to $Gan^1 Ddao^1$ (Beijiao Reef), navigate N15°E to travel for about five and a half geng (approximately 55 nautical miles); that is, the compass needle should point towards Gui Ding (towards northeast).

Entry 4

If you set off at the Xisha Islands from the northeast part of $Ddua^1 Huan^1$ (Hua-

---

① **Notes**: For more information about the folk names given by the Chinese fishermen, please refer to The Origins and Legends of the Folk Names of the South China Sea Islands in Su Deliu and Peng Zhengkai Versions of *Genglubu*, and Table of the Information about the South China Sea Islands in Su Deliu and Peng Zhengkai Versions of *Genglubu*.

guang Reef) and sail to $Da^1 Huan^1$ (Langhua Reef), navigate S120°E to travel for about three geng (approximately 30 nautical miles) if wind blows south, that is, the compass needle should point towards Chen Xu (towards southeast).

Entry 5

If you set off at the Xisha Islands from $Lao^5 Sou^1 Ddua^1 Mui^2$ (Laocu Reef) and sail to $Di^4 Giang^1 Mui^2$ (Jinqing Pass), navigate S135°E and travel for two geng (approximately 20 nautical miles); that is, the compass needle should point towards the middle line between Qian Xun and Chen Xu (towards southeast).

Entry 6

If you set off at the Xisha Islands from $Da^1 Ha^1$ (Chenhang Island) and make a round trip to $Ngin^2 Di^6$ (Yinyu Island), navigate N352.5°; that is, the compass needle should point towards the middle line between Zi Wu and Ren Bing (towards north).

Entry 7

If you set off at the Xisha Islands from $Va^1 Du^4$ (Yongxing Island) and sail to $Gan^1 Ddao^1$ (Beijiao Reef), navigate N292.5°W and travel for three geng (approximately 30 nautical mile); that is, the compass needle should point towards the middle line between Chen Xu and Yi Xin (towards northwest).

Entry 8

If you set off at the Xisha Islands from $Da^1 Di^6$ (Nandao Island) and sail to $Va^1 Du^4$ (Yongxing Island), navigate S180°; that is, the compass needle should point towards Zi Wu (towards south).

Entry 9

If you set off at the Xisha Islands from $Ang^2 Sao^3 Mui^2$ (Hongcao Pass) and sail to $Va^1 Hheng^1$ (Dongdao Island), navigate S105°E and travel for one and a half geng (approximately 15 nautical miles); that is, the compass needle should point towards Yi Xin (towards southeast).

Entry 10

If you set off at the Xisha Islands from $Di^4 Giang^1$ (Jinqing Island) and sail to

Va^1 $Hheng^1$ (Dongdao Island), navigate S255°W to travel for about four and a half geng (approximately 45 nautical miles); that is, the compass needle should point towards Jia Geng (towards southwest).

Entry 11

If you set off at the Xisha Islands from Zio^5 Ddo^2 (the Yongle Islands) and sail to $Ddua^1$ $Huan^1$ (Huaguang Reef), navigate S135°E and travel for about one geng (approximately 10 nautical miles); that is, the compass needle should point towards Qian Xun (towards southeast).

Entry 12

If you set off at the Xisha Islands from Gan^1 $Ddao^1$ (Beijiao Reef) and sail to Zio^5 Ddo^2 (the Yongle Islands), navigate S150°E to travel for about two geng (approximately 20 nautical miles); that is, the compass needle should point towards Si Hai (southeast).

Entry 13

If you set off at the Xisha Islands from Va^1 Du^4 (Yongxing Island) and sail to Yi^1 $Huan^1$ (Yuzhuo Reef), navigate S202.5°W and travel for about two and a half geng (approximately 25 nautical miles); that is, the compass needle should point towards the middle line between Gui Ding and Chou Wei (towards southwest).

Entry 14

If you set off at the Xisha Islands from Dun^2 Ham^4 Vue^3 (Xisha Sand Bank) and sail to Gan^1 $Ddao^1$ (Beijiao Reef), navigate W277.5° to travel for about three geng (approximately 30 nautical miles); that is, the compass needle should point towards the middle line between Yi Xin and Mao You (towards west).

Entry 15

If you set off at the Xisha Islands from Ang^2 Sao^3 (Nansha Sand) and sail to Zio^5 Ddo^2 (the Yongle Islands), you must travel for about three geng (approximately 30 nautical miles) and navigate S240°W; that is, the compass needle should point towards Yin Shen (towards southeast).

Entry 16

At the Xisha Islands, set off from *Yi^1 Huan^1* (Yuzhuo Reef) and sail to *Zio^5 Ddo^2* (the Yongle Islands), navigate S315°W to travel for about one and a half geng (approximately 15 miles); that is, the compass needle should point towards Qian Xun (southwest).

Entry 17

If you set off at the Xisha Islands from *Yi^1 Huan^1* (Yuzhuo Reef) and sail to *Ddua^1 Huan^1* (Huaguang Reef), navigate S240°W and travel for about one geng (approximately 10 nautical miles); that is, the compass needle should point towards Yin Shen (southwest).

Entry 18

At the Xisha Islands, set off from *Da^1 Huan^1* (Langhua Reef) and sail to *Nai^6 Lo^2* (the Shuangzi Islands), navigate S150°E to travel for thirty geng (approximately 300 nautical miles) with the compass needle pointing towards Si Hai (southeast), and then continue to sail S165°E with the compass needle pointing towards Ren Bing (southeast) and travel for another thirty geng.

2.2 Navigational Routes towards *Beihai* (the Nansha Islands) [①]

Entry 1

At the Xisha Islands, depart from $Be^5\ Siu^1\ Gia^3$ (Panshi Island) and arrive at $Diang^1\ Di^6$ (the Shuangzi Islands) at the Nansha Islands, navigate S142.5°E and travel for about twenty-eight geng (approximately 280 nautical miles); that is, the compass needle should point towards the middle line between Qian Xun and Si Hai (towards southeast).

Entry 2

At the Xisha Islands, leave $Da^1\ Huan^1$ (Langhua Reef) and arrive at $Lo^2 Hong^2$ (Mahuan Island) at the Nansha Islands, navigate S142.5°E to travel for about twenty-eight geng (approximately 280 nautical miles); that is, the compass needle should point towards Qian Xun (towards southeast).

Entry 3

Set out from the Nansha Islands, leave $Diang^1\ Di^6$ (the Shuangzi Islands) and arrive at $Hih^7\ Di^6$ (Zhongye Island), navigate S187.5° to travel for about two geng (approximately 20 nautical miles); that is, the compass needle should point towards the middle line between Zi Wu and Gui Ding (towards south).

Entry 4

At the Nansha Islands, leave $E^5\ Di^6\ Dua^1\ Gia^3$ (Nailuo Reef) to arrive at $Hih^7\ Ddao^2\ Dua^4\ Bai^2$ (Tiezhi Reef), navigate S165°E and travel for two geng (approximately 20 nautical miles); that is, the compass needle should point towards the middle line between Ren Bing and Si Hai (towards southeast).

[①] **Notes**: For more information about the folk names given by the Chinese fishermen, please refer to The Origins and Legends of the Folk Names of the South China Sea Islands in Su Deliu and Peng Zhengkai Versions of *Genglubu*, and Table of the Information about the South China Sea Islands in Su Deliu and Peng Zhengkai Versions of *Genglubu*.

Entry 5

Set out from the Nansha Islands, leave *Hih*[7] *Di*[6] (Zhongye Island) to arrive at *Hou*[4] *Gui* (Kugui Reef), navigate S112.5°E to travel for about two geng (approximately 20 nautical miles); that is, the compass needle should point towards the middle line between Yi Xin and Chen Xu (towards southeast).

Entry 6

At the Nansha Islands, depart from *Hou*[4] *Gui* (Kugui Reef) to arrive at *Da*[1] *Gag*[7] (Sanjiao Reef), navigate S112.5°E and travel for five geng (approximately 50 nautical miles); that is, the compass needle should point towards the middle line between Yi Xin and Chen Xu (towards southeast).

Entry 7

At the Nansha Islands, leave *Da*[1] *Gag*[7] (Sanjiao Reef) to travel for about two geng (approximately 20 nautical miles) and navigating S135°E will bring you to *Diang*[1] *Mui*[2] (Meiji Reef); that is, the compass needle should point towards Qian Xun (southeast). For a return voyage, navigate N345°W; that is, the compass needle should point towards Ren Bing (towards northwest).

Entry 8

At the Nansha Islands, leave *Diang*[1] *Mui*[2] (Meiji Reef) to arrive at *Ddui*[5] *Dad*[7] (Ren'ai Reef), navigate E97.5° and travel for about two geng (approximately 20 nautical miles); that is, the compass needle should point towards the middle line between Yi Xin and Mao You (towards east). For a return voyage, navigate N307.5°W, that is, the compass needle should adjust to the middle line between Qian Xun and Chen Xu (towards northwest).

Entry 9

At the Nansha Islands, departing from *Ddui*[5] *Dad*[7] (Ren'ai Reef) to travel for about two geng (approximately 20 nautical miles) and navigating S105°E will bring you to *Gu*[2] *Sia*[1] *Eng*[1] (Niuchelun Reef), that is, the compass needle should point towards to Yi Xin (southeast). For a return voyage, navigate N307.5°W, that is, the compass needle should point towards the middle line between Qian Xun and Chen Xu (towards northwest).

Entry 10

At the Nansha Islands, leaving $Gu^2 Sia^1 Eng^1$ (Niuchelun Reef) to arrive at $Ha^1 Buad^7$ (Haikou Reef), you should navigate S135°E and travel for about three geng (approximately 30 nautical miles); that is, the compass needle should point towards Qian Xun (southeast). For a return voyage, navigate N345°W; that is, the compass needle points towards Ren Bing (towards northwest).

Entry 11

At the Nansha Islands, setting out from $Ha^1 Buad^7$ (Haikou Reef) to arrive at $Zio^5 Liang^2$ (Jianzhang Reef), you should navigate E97.5° to travel for about two geng (approximately 20 nautical miles); that is, the compass needle should point towards the middle line between Yi Xin and Mao You (towards east).

Entry 12

At the Nansha Islands, leaving $Zio^5 Liang^2$ (Jianzhang Reef) and navigating N15°E to travel for about four geng (approximately 40 nautical miles) will bring you to $Hhu^2 Lin^2$ (Xianbin Reef); that is, the compass needle should point towards Gui Ding (towards northeast).

Entry 13

At the Nansha Islands, depart from $Hhu^2 Lin^2$ (Xianbin Reef) and navigate N330°W to travel for about four geng (approximately 40 nautical miles), you will arrive at $Ngou^5 Hhuang^1$ (Wufang Reef); that is, the compass needle should point towards Si Hai (towards northwest).

Entry 14

At the Nansha Islands, leaving $Gong^4 Se^5 Dua^1$ (Gongshi Reef) to arrive at $Ang^2 Sao^3 Dua^4 Bai^2$ (Changtan Bank), you should navigate S112.5°E to voyage for three geng (approximately 30 nautical miles); that is, the compass needle should point towards the middle line between Yi Xin and Chen Xu (towards southeast).

Entry 15

At the Nansha Islands, set out from ($Ang^2 Sao^3$) $Dua^4 Bai^2$ (Changtan Bank) and navigate S135°E to travel for about two geng (approximately 20 nautical miles), you will arrive at *Hhue³ Ai¹* (Huo'ai Reef); that is, the compass needle should point towards Qian Xun (towards southeast).

Entry 16

At the Nansha Islands, departing from *Hhue³ Ai¹* (Huo'ai Reef) to arrive at *Da¹ Gag⁷* (Sanjiao Reef), you should navigate S135°E and voyage for four geng (approximately 40 nautical miles); that is, the compass needle should point towards Qian Xun (towards southeast).

Entry 17

At the Nansha Islands, leaving *Ang² Sao³ Dua⁴ Bai²* (Changtan Bank) to arrive at *Hhong² Sao³* (Xiyue Island), you should navigate N285°W and travel for two geng (approximately 20 nautical miles); that is, the compass needle should point towards Yi Xin (towards northwest).

Entry 18

At the Nansha Islands, set sail at *Hhong² Sao³* (Xiyue Island), navigate 97°E, travel for five geng (approximately 50 nautical miles), you can arrive at *Lo² Hong²* (Mahuan Island); that is, the compass needle should point towards the middle line between Yi Xin and Mao You (towards east).

Entry 19

At the Nansha Islands, leaving *Lo² Hong²* (Mahuan Island) to arrive at *Hhao¹ Ddin²* (Houteng Reef), navigate 97°E and voyage for about two geng (approximately 20 miles); that is, the compass needle should point towards the middle line between Yi Xin and Mao You (towards east).

Entry 20

At the Nansha Islands, leaving *Hhong² Sao³* (Xiyue Island), navigating S112.5°E and traveling for about four geng (approximately 40 nautical miles) will bring you to *Ngou⁵ Hhuang¹* (Wufang Reef); that is, the compass needle should point towards the middle line between Yi Xin and Chen Xu (towards southeast).

Entry 21

At the Nansha Islands, set sail at *Ngou^5 Hhuang^1* (Wufang Reef) and navigate S165°E to travel for about four geng (approximately 40 nautical miles), you can arrive at *Ddui^5 Dad^7* (Ren'ai Reef); that is, the compass needle should point towards Ren Bing (towards southeast).

Entry 22

At the Nansha Islands, leaving *Ddui^5 Dad^7* (Ren'ai Reef) to arrive at *Diang^1 Dda^1* (Xinyi Reef), navigate S150°E and sail for about two geng (approximately 20 nautical miles); that is, the compass needle should point towards Si Hai (towards southeast).

Entry 23

At the Nansha Islands, departing from *Diang^1 Dda^1* (Xinyi Reef) to arrive at *Hhai^3 Gong^1* (Banyue Reef), navigate S127°E and make a voyage for three geng (approximately 30 nautical miles); that is, the compass needle should point towards the middle line between Qian Xun and Chen Xu (towards southeast).

Entry 24

At the Nansha Islands, departing from *Hhai^3 Gong^1* (Banyue Reef), navigate N345°W and travel for about three geng (approximately 30 nautical miles), you can arrive at *Diang^1 Dda^1* (Xinyi Reef); that is, the compass needle should point towards Ren Bing (towards northwest).

Entry 25

At the Nansha Islands, leaving *Diang^1 Dda^1* (Xinyi Reef) to arrive at *Ziao Shua* (Xian'e Reef), you should navigate N285°W and travel for two geng (approximately 20 nautical miles); that is, the compass needle should point towards Yi Xin (towards northwest).

Entry 26

At the Nansha Islands, setting sail at *Ziao Shua* (Xian'e Reef) and arriving at *Ngin^2 Bia^3* (Anda Reef), navigate N337.5°W and make a voyage for five geng (approximately 50 nautical miles); that is, the compass needle should point towards the middle line between Ren Bing and Si Hai (towards northwest).

Entry 27

At the Nansha Islands, leaving Hih^7 $Ddao^2$ (Zhongye Island) to arrive at $Ddang^2$ Gim^1 (Yangxin Cay), navigate S120°E and travel for two geng (approximately 20 nautical miles); that is, the compass needle should point towards Chen Xu (towards southeast).

Entry 28

At the Nansha Islands, departing from $Ddang^2$ Gim^1 (Yangxin Cay) to arrive at $Ngin^2$ Bia^3 (Anda Reef), you should navigate S135°E to travel for about two geng (approximately 20 nautical miles); that is, the compass needle should point towards Qian Xun (towards southeast).

Entry 29

At the Nansha Islands, departing from $Ngin^2$ Bia^3 (Anda Reef) to arrive at Ui^2 Dua^1 Ve^3 (Taiping Island), navigate 270°W and travel for three geng (approximately 30 nautical miles); that is, the compass needle should point towards Mao You (towards west).

Entry 30

At the Nansha Islands, departing from Ui^2 Dua^1 Ve^3 (Taiping Island) to arrive at Gu^2 Eh^7 (Niu'e Reef), navigate S135°E and travel for two geng (approximately 20 nautical miles); that is, the compass needle should point towards Qian Xun (towards southeast).

Entry 31

At the Nansha Islands, depart from Ui^2 Dua^1 Ve^3 (Taiping Island), navigate S165°E to travel for one geng (approximately 10 nautical miles), you can arrive at Nam^2 Mid^8 (Hongxiu Island); that is, the compass needle should point towards Ren Bing (towards southeast).

Entry 32

At the Nansha Islands, leaving Gu^2 Eh^7 (Niu'e Reef) to arrive at Mag^8 Gia^4

(Siling Reef), you should navigate S165°E and travel for nine geng (approximately 90 nautical miles); that is, the compass needle should point towards the middle line between Ren Bing and Si Hai (towards southeast).

Entry 33

At the Nansha Islands, set sail at $Mag^8\ Gia^4$ (Siling Reef) to arrive at $Vo^2\ Mi^6\ Dua^4$ (Wumie Reef), navigate N307.5°W and travel for three geng (approximately 30 nautical miles); that is, the compass needle should point towards the middle line between Qian Xun and Chen Xu (towards northwest).

Entry 34

At the Nansha Islands, leave $Vo^2\ Mi^6\ Dua^4$ (Wumie Reef), navigate S165°E to travel for three geng (approximately 30 nautical miles), you can arrive at $Sim^1\ Huan^1$ (Yuya Shoal); that is, the compass needle should point towards Ren Bing (towards southeast).

Entry 35

At the Nansha Islands, depart from $Vo^2\ Mi^6\ Dua^4$ (Wumie Reef) to arrive at $Og^7\ Log^7\ Mui^2$ (Nanhua Reef), navigate S240°W to voyage for three geng (approximately 30 nautical miles); that is, the compass needle should point towards Yin Shen (towards southwest).

Entry 36

At the Nansha Island, setting out from $Sim^1\ Huan^1$ (Yuya Shoal), navigating S247.5°W to travel for two geng (approximately 20 nautical miles) will bring you to $Bua^4\ Gi^1$ (Boji Reef); that is, the compass needle should point towards the middle line between Jia Geng and Yin Shen (towards southwest).

Entry 37

At the Nansha Islands, leaving $Bua^4\ Gi^1$ (Boji Reef), navigate S247.5°W and travel for one geng (approximately 10 nautical miles), one can arrive at $Ddang^2\ Ziang^1$ (Nanhai Reef); that is, the compass needle should point towards the middle line between Yin Shen and Jia Geng (towards southwest).

Entry 38

At the Nansha Islands, depart from *Ddang² Ziang¹* (Nanhai Reef) to arrive at *Guang¹ Se¹ Gia³* (Guangxingzai Reef) and navigate S165°E and travel for two geng (approximately 20 nautical miles); that is, the compass needle should point towards Ren Bing (towards southeast).

Entry 39

At the Nansha Islands, set out from *Guang¹ Se¹ Gia³* (Guangxingzai Reef) and arrive at *Zio⁵ Gong¹ Li²* (Danwan Reef), navigate S180° and travel for one and a half geng (approximately 15 nautical miles); that is, the compass needle should point towards Zi Wu (towards due south).

Entry 40

At the Nansha Islands, leaving *Zio⁵ Gong¹ Li²* (Danwan Reef) to arrive at *Ngou⁵ Be⁶ Yi¹* (Huanglu Reef), navigate S195°W and travel for three geng (approximately 30 nautical miles) with the compass needle pointing towards Gui Ding (towards southwest).

Entry 41

At the Nansha Islands, departing from *Ngou⁵ Be⁶ Yi¹* (Huanglu Reef) to arrive at *Ddan¹ Dad⁷* (Nantong Reef), navigate S202.5°W and travel for three geng (approximately 30 nautical miles); that is, the compass needle should point towards the middle line between Gui Ding and Chou Wei (towards southwest).

Entry 42

At the Nansha Islands, set sail from *Ddang² Ziang¹* (Nanhai Reef) and arrive at *Hhai³ Hao³ Dua⁴* (Baijiao Reef), you should navigate N303.5°W to travel for three geng (approximately 30 nautical miles). The compass needle should point towards the middle line between Chen Xu and Qian Xun (towards northwest).

Entry 43

Set out from the Nansha Islands, departing from *Hhai³ Hao³ Dua⁴* (Baijiao Reef) and navigating N315°W to travel for five geng (approximately 50 nautical miles), with the compass needle pointing towards Qian Xun (towards northwest), then you can arrive at $Ddua^1$ $Ddang^2$ $Song^4$ (Dongjiao Reef).

Entry 44

Set out from the Nansha Islands, leaving $Ddang^2$ $Song^4$ Gia^3 (Huayang Reef) to arrive at $Ddua^1$ $Ddang^2$ $Song^4$ (Dongjiao Reef), travel for one geng (approximately 10 nautical miles) by navigating S255°W, and the compass needle should point towards Jia Geng (towards southwest).

Entry 45

Set out from the Nansha Islands, leaving $Ddang^2$ $Song^4$ (Dongjiao Reef) to arrive at $Long^6$ Pi^1 (Xijiao Reef), you should travel for two geng (approximately 20 nautical miles) by navigating N285°W, the compass needle should point towards Yi Xin (towards northwest).

Entry 46

At the Nansha Islands, leaving $Long^6$ Pi^1 (Xijiao Reef) to arrive at $Ziao^3$ Gia^3 Di^6 (Nanwei Island), you should travel for two geng (approximately 20 nautical miles) by navigate S236.5°W; that is, the compass needle should point towards the middle line between Yin Shen and Gen Kun (towards southwest).

Entry 47

At the Nansha Islands, set out from Ui^2 Dua^1 Ve^3 (Taiping Island) and navigate S165°E to voyage for one geng (approximately 10 nautical miles) with the compass needle pointing towards Ren Bing (towards southeast), you can arrive at Nam^2 Id^7 (Hongxiu Island).

Entry 48

At the Nansha Islands, leaving Nam^2 Id^7 (Hongxiu Island) to arrive at Sin^4 Gao^1 (Jinghong Island), travel for two geng (approximately 20 nautical miles) by navigating S195°W; that is, the compass needle should point towards Gui Ding (towards southwest).

Entry 49

At the Nansha Islands, departing from Sin^4 Gao^1 (Jinghong Island) to arrive at

Hho^2 Log^8 Mui (Nanhua Reef), travel for four geng (approximately 40 nautical miles) by navigating 180°S; that is, the compass needle should point towards Zi Wu (towards due south).

Entry 50

Setting out from the Nansha Islands, leaving Hho^2 Log^8 Mui (Nanhua Reef) and arriving at Lag^8 Mui^2 (Liumen Reef), one should make a voyage for one geng (approximately 10 nautical miles) by navigating N307.5°W; that is, the compass needle should point towards the middle line between Qian Xun and Chen Xu (towards northwest).

Entry 51

At the Nansha Islands, departing from Lag^8 Mui^2 (Liumen Reef) and traveling for four geng (approximately 40 nautical miles) by navigating S165°E, with the compass needle pointing towards Ren Bing (towards southeast) will bring you to $Ddang^2$ $Ziang^1$ (Nanhai Reef).

Entry 52

At the Nansha Islands, leaving Lag^8 Mui^2 (Liumen Reef) to arrive at Zio^5 Bua^2 (Bisheng Reef), travel for two geng (approximately 20 nautical miles) by navigating N307.5°W; that is, the compass needle should point towards the middle line between Qian Xun and Chen Xu (towards northwest).

Entry 53

At the Nansha Islands, set sail from Zio^5 Bua^2 (Bisheng Reef) and arrive at Zio^1 Vu^5 (Yongshu Reef), navigate N37.5°W to travel for four geng (approximately 40 nautical miles); that is, the compass needle should point towards the central line between Qian Xun and Si Hai (towards northwest).

Entry 54

Set out from the Nansha Islands, departing from Zio^1 Vu^5 (Yongshu Reef) to arrive at $Ddua^1$ $Ddang^2$ $Song^4$ (Dongjiao Reef), travel for four geng (approximately 40 nautical miles) by navigating 195°S; that is, the compass needle should point towards Gui Ding (towards south).

Entry 55

Set out from the Nansha Islands, departing from *Zio^5 Bua^2* (Bisheng Reef) to arrive at *Ddua^1 Ddang^2 Song^4* (Dongjiao Reef), navigate W262.5° and travel for four geng (approximately 40 nautical miles); that is, the compass needle should point towards the middle line between Jia Geng and Mao You (towards west).

Entry 56

Set out from the Nansha Islands, leaving *Ui^2 Dua^1 Ve^3* (Taiping Island) to arrive at *Lao^2 Gu^2 Lao^2* (Daxian Reef), and navigating S240°W to travel for three geng (approximately 30 nautical miles); that is, the compass needle should point towards Yin Shen (towards southwest).

Entry 57

Set out from the Nansha Islands, leaving *Lao^2 Gu^2 Lao^2* (Daxian Reef) to arrive at *Hho^2 Lang^6 Mui^2* (Nanhua Reef), you should travel for five geng (approximately 50 nautical miles) by navigating S165°E; that is, the compass needle should point towards Ren Bing (towards southeast).

Entry 58

Set out from the Nansha Islands, leaving *Sin^4 Gao^1* (Jinghong Island) to arrive at *Zio^5 Bua^2* (Bisheng Reef), and navigating S213.5°W to travel for four geng (approximately 40 nautical miles); the compass needle should point towards the middle line between Chou Wei and Gen Kun (towards southwest).

Entry 59

Set out from the Nansha Islands, departing from *Lao^2 Gu^2 Lao^2* (Daxian Reef) to arrive at *Zio^1 Vu^5* (Yongshu Reef), you should travel for four geng (approximately 40 miles) by navigating S240°W; the compass needle should point towards Yin Shen (towards southwest).

Entry 60

Set out from the Nansha Islands, leaving *Nise Zio* (Ranqingdong Reef) and sailing to *Vo^2 Mi^6 Dua^4* (Wumie Reef), you should travel for about four geng (approximately 40 miles) by navigating S172.5°; the compass needle should point towards the middle line between Zi Wu and Ren Bing (towards south).

Entry 61

Set out from the Nansha Islands, depart from $Hih^7 Di^6$ (Zhongye Island), navigate S210°W and travel for one geng (approximately 10 nautical miles), you will arrive at $Hih^7 Dua^4$ (Tiexian Island); that is, the compass needle should point towards Chou Wei (towards southwest).

Entry 62

Set out from the Nansha Islands, leaving $Hih^7 Di^6$ (Zhongye Island) to arrive at $Siu^3 Vi^1$ (Zhubi Reef), you should travel for two geng (approximately 20 nautical miles) by navigating S225°W with the compass needle pointing towards Gen Kun (towards southwest).

Entry 63

Set out from the Nansha Islands, leaving $Siu^3 Vi^1$ (Zhubi Reef) to arrive at $Ui^2 Dua^1 Ve^3$ (Taiping Island), you should voyage for four geng (approximately 40 nautical miles) by navigating S135°E; that is, the compass needle should point towards Qian Xun (towards southeast).

Entry 64

Set out from the Nansha Islands, setting sail from $Hhu^2 Lin^2$ (Xianbin Reef), navigating S105°E to travel for three geng (approximately 30 nautical miles) will bring you to $Ddang^1 Hao^2 Id^7 Din^1$ (Pengbo Shoal); that is, the compass needle should point towards Yi Xin (towards southeast).

Entry 65

At the Nansha Islands, leaving $Ziao^3 Gia^3 Di^6$ (Nanwei Island) to arrive at $Dai^1 Hao^2 Id^7 Din^1$ (Riji Reef), you should travel for two geng (approximately 20 nautical miles) by navigating N285°W; that is, the compass needle should point towards Yi Xin (towards northwest).

Entry 66

Set out from the Nansha Islands, setting sail from $Hih^7 Di^6$ (Zhongye Island)

and arriving at $E^5 \, Da^1$ (Nanyue Island), you should navigate S150°E and travel for two geng (approximately 20 nautical miles) with the compass needle pointing towards Si Hai (towards southeast).

Entry 67

Set out from the Nansha Islands, leaving $E^5 \, Da^1$ (Nanyue Island) and arriving at $Ui^2 \, Dua^1 \, Ve^3$ (Taiping Island), travel for two geng (approximately 20 nautical miles) by navigating 180°S with the compass needle pointing towards Zi Wu (towards due south).

Entry 68

At the Nansha Islands, depart from $Hhong^2 \, Sao^3$ (Xiyue Island) to arrive at $Dua^1 \, Bai^2$ (Changtan Bank), navigate S120°E to travel for one geng (approximately 10 nautical miles); that is, the compass needle should point towards Chen Xu (towards southeast).

Entry 69

At the Nansha Islands, leaving $Hhu^2 \, Lin^2$ (Xianbin Reef) and arriving at $Ddui^5 \, Dad^7$ (Ren'ai Reef), you should voyage for two geng (approximately 20 nautical miles) by navigating 270°W; that is, the compass needle should point towards Mao You (towards west).

Entry 70

At the Nansha Islands, leaving $Ngin^2 \, Bia^3$ (Anda Reef) and navigating S127°E to travel for five geng (approximately 50 nautical miles) will bring you to $Ziao \, Shua$ (Xian'e Reef); that is, the compass needle should point towards the middle line between Qian Xun and Chen Xu (towards southeast).

Entry 71

Set out from the Nansha Islands, departing from $Hhong^2 \, Sao^3$ (Xiyue Island) and arriving at $Ddoi^1 \, Da^1 \, Di^6$ (Nanyue Island), navigate S225°W and travel for three geng (approximately 30 nautical miles) with the compass needle pointing towards Gen Kun (towards southwest).

Entry 72

Set out from the Nansha Islands, setting sail from Siu^3 Vi^1 (Zhubi Reef) and arriving at $Diang^1$ $Uang^2$ (Shuanghuang Cay), travel for two geng (approximately 20 nautical miles) by navigating S120°E; that is, the compass needle should point towards Chen Xu (towards southeast).

Entry 73

At the Nansha Islands, leaving Hih^7 Di^6 (Zhongye Island) and arriving at $Diang^1$ $Uang^2$ (Shuanghuang Cay), navigate S165°E to travel for two geng (approximately 20 nautical miles) with the compass needle pointing towards Ren Bing (towards southeast).

Entry 74

Set out from the Nansha Islands, leaving $Diang^1$ $Uang^2$ (Shuanghuang Cay) and arriving at Ui^2 Dua^1 Ve^3 (Taiping Island), you should travel for two geng (approximately 20 nautical miles) by navigating S165°E with the compass needle pointing towards Ren Bing (towards southeast).

Entry 75

At the Nansha Islands, setting out from $Ddoi^1$ Da^1 (Nanyue Island) and traveling for three geng (approximately 30 nautical miles) by navigating S120°E with the compass needle pointing towards Chen Xu towards southeast, you can arrive at $Ngin^2$ Bia^3 (Anda Reef).

Entry 76

At the Nansha Islands, leaving $Ddang^2$ Gim^1 (Yangxin Cay) and arriving at $Ngin^2$ Bia^3 (Anda Reef), you should navigate S150°E to travel for two geng (approximately 20 nautical miles); that is, the compass needle should point towards Si Hai (towards southeast).

Entry 77

Set out from the Nansha Islands, depart from $Ngin^2$ Bia^3 (Anda Reef) and arrive at Gu^2 Eh^7 (Niu'e Reef), you should travel for two geng (approximately 20 nautical miles) by navigating S195°W with the compass needle pointing towards Gui Ding (towards southwest).

Entry 78

Set out from the Nansha Islands, leaving $Mag^8\ Gia^4$ (Siling Reef) to arrive at $Sim^1\ Huan^1$ (Yuya Shoal), you should travel for two geng (approximately 20 nautical miles) by navigating S240°W with the compass needle pointing towards Yin Shen (towards southwest).

Entry 79

Set out from the Nansha Islands, setting sail from $Nam^2\ Mid^8\ Di^6$ (Hongxiu Island) and arriving at $Sin^4\ Gao^1\ Ddao^2$ (Jinghong Island), navigate S165°E to travel for two geng (approximately 20 nautical miles); that is, the compass needle should point towards Ren Bing (towards southeast).

Entry 80

At the Nansha Islands, departing from $Sin^3\ Gao^1$ (Jinghong Island) and traveling for five geng (approximately 50 nautical miles) by navigating S195°W with the compass needle pointing towards Gui Ding (towards southwest) will bring you to $Lag^8\ Mui^2$ (Liumen Reef).

Entry 81

At the Nansha Islands, leaving $Og^7\ Lang^6\ Mui^2$ (Nanhua Reef) to arrive at $Bua^4\ Gi^1$ (Boji Reef), navigate S165°E to travel for four geng (approximately 40 nautical miles); that is, the compass needle should point towards Ren Bing (towards southeast).

Entry 82

At the Nansha Islands, depart from $Guang^1\ Se^1\ Gia^3$ (Guangxingzai Reef) to arrive at $Ddua^1\ Guang^1\ Se^1$ (Guangxing Reef), you should travel for one geng (approximately 10 nautical miles) by navigating 270°W with the compass needle pointing towards Mao You (towards west).

Entry 83

At the Nansha Islands, leaving $Ddua^1\ Guang^1\ Se^1$ (Guangxing Reef) and making a voyage for two geng (approximately 20 nautical miles) by navigating S135°E with the compass needle pointing towards Qian Xun (towards southeast), you can arrive at Zio^5 $Gong^1$ Li^2 (Danwan Reef).

Entry 84

At the Nansha Islands, setting sail from $Ddua^1$ $Guang^1$ Se^1 (Guangxing Reef) and traveling for four geng (approximately 40 nautical miles) by navigating 360°N will bring you to $Hhai^3$ Hao^3 Dua^4 (Baijiao Reef); that is, the compass needle should point towards Zi Wu (towards north).

Entry 85

Set out from the Nansha Islands, depart from $Hhong^2$ Sao^3 (Xiyue Island) and arrive at Hih^7 Di^6 (Zhongye Island), navigate 270°W to travel for four geng (approximately 40 nautical miles); that is, the compass needle points towards Mao You (towards west).

Entry 86

At the Nansha Islands, leaving $Ziao^3$ Gia^3 Di^6 (Nanwei Island) to arrive at Be^5 Di^6 Gia^3 (Panshi Island) at the Xisha Islands, navigate N22.5°E; that is, the compass needle should point towards the middle line between Gui Ding and Chou Wei (towards northeast).

Entry 87

Set out from the Nansha Islands, leaving $Nise$ Zio (Ranqingdong Reef) and arriving at Vo^2 Mi^6 Dua^4 (Wumie Reef), travel for five geng (approximately 50 nautical miles) by navigating S157.5°E with the compass needle pointing towards the middle line between Ren Bing and Si Hai (towards southeast).

Entry 88

Set out from the Nansha Islands, set sail from $Ddan^1$ Dad^7 (Nantong Reef) and make a voyage for ten geng (approximately 100 nautical miles) by navigating N15°E; that is, the compass needle should point towards Gui Ding (towards northeast), with wind blowing north, you can arrive at $Hhai^3$ Hao^3 Dua^4 (Baijiao Reef).

Entry 89

Set out from the Nansha Islands, leaving $Ngou^5$ Be^6 Yi^1 (Huanglu Reef) and arriving at $Hhai^3$ Hao^3 Dua^4 (Baijiao Reef), you should travel for seven geng (approximately 70 nautical miles) by navigating 7.5°N; that is, the compass needle should point towards the middle line between Zi Wu and Gui Ding (towards north) with wind blowing north.

Entry 90

Set out from the Nansha Islands, depart from Ang^2 Sao^3 Dua^4 Bai^2 (Changtan Bank) and arrive at Hou^4 Gui (Kugui Reef), navigate S202.5°W to travel for two geng (approximately 20 nautical miles); that is, the compass needle should point towards the middle line between Gui Ding and Chou Wei (towards southwest).

Entry 91

Set out from the Xisha Islands, leaving Bua^4 Lou^1 (Zhongjian Island) to arrive at $Gong^4$ Se^5 Dua^1 (Gongshi Reef) at the Nansha Islands, you should travel for twenty-eight geng (approximately 280 nautical miles) by navigating S135°E, with the compass needle pointing towards Qian Xun (towards southeast).

Entry 92

Setting out from the Xisha Islands, leaving Da^1 $Huan^1$ (Langhua Reef) and sailing for Nai^6 Lo^2 (Beizi Island) at the Nansha Islands, navigate E157.5°S and travel for about twenty-eight geng (approximately 280 nautical miles); that is, the needle on the compass should point towards the central line between Si Hai and Ren Bing (towards southeast).

Entry 93

Sailing at the Nansha Islands from the north of Nai^6 Lo^2 Gag^7 (Yongdeng Shoal) to $Gong^4$ Se^5 Dua^1 (Gongshi Reef), navigate S255°W for one geng (approximately 10 nautical miles); that is, the compass needle should point towards Jia Geng (towards southeast).

Entry 94

At the Nansha Islands, departing from Nam^2 Nai^6 Lo^2 Gag^7 (Lesi Shoal) for

$Gong^4$ Se^5 Dua^1 (Gongshi Reef), you will sail N285°W with the compass needle pointing towards Yi Xin (towards northwest).

Entry 95

At the Nansha Islands, leaving $Diang^1$ Di^6 Dua^1 Gia (the Shuangzi Islands) by navigating S160°E, with the compass needle pointing towards between Ren Bing and Si Hai (towards southeast) for two geng (approximately 20 nautical miles), you will arrive at Hih^7 $Ddao^2$ Dua^4 Bai^2 (Tiezhi Reef), which lies close to Hin^2 $Ddin^5$ Dua^1 (Meijiu Reef).

Entry 96

Setting off at the Nansha Islands from Hhu^2 Lin^2 (Xianbing Reef) and navigating 360°N with the compass needle pointing towards Zi Wu (due north) for four geng (approximately 40 nautical miles), you will arrive at $Hhao^1$ $Ddin^2$ (Houteng Reef). When sailing back, navigate E165°S; that is, the compass needle should point towards the central line between Si Hai and Ren Bing (towards southeast).

Entry 97

Sailing at the Nansha Islands from Na^4 $Hong^2$ (Mahuan Island) to $Ngou^5$ $Hhuang^1$ (Wufang Reef), navigate S165°E with the compass needle pointing towards Ren Bing (towards southeast) for one geng (approximately 10 nautical miles). When sailing back, you should navigate N15°E; that is, the compass needle should point towards Gui Ding (towards northeast).

Entry 98

Setting off at the Nansha Islands from $Hhong^2$ Sao^3 (Xiyue Island) and navigating S180° with the compass needle pointing to Zi Wu (towards due south) for one geng (approximately 10 nautical miles), you will arrive at $Hhue^3$ Ai^1 (Huo'ai Reef).

Entry 99

Sailing at the Nansha Islands and leaving $Hhue^3$ Ai^1 (Huo'ai Reef) for Da^1 Gag^7 (Sanjiao Reef), you should navigate S135°E with the compass needle pointing towards Qian Xun (towards southeast) for four geng (approximately 40 nautical miles). When sailing back, navigate N345°W with the compass needle pointing towards Ren Bing (towards northwest).

Entry 100

Setting off at the Nansha Islands from $Ddui^5 Dad^7$ (Ren'ai Reef) and navigating S157.50°E, with the compass needle pointing towards the central line between Ren Bing and Si Hai (towards southeast) for two geng (approximately 20 nautical miles), you will arrive at $Diang^1 Dda^1$ (Xinyi Reef). When sailing back, navigate N7.5°E with the compass needle pointing towards the central line between Zi Wu and Gui Ding (towards northeast).

Entry 101

Sailing at the Nansha Islands from $Diang^1 Dda^1$ (Xinyi Reef) to $Ziao\ Shua$ (Xian'e Reef), you should navigate 277.5°W with the compass needle pointing towards the central line between Yi Xin and Mao You (towards west) for two and a half geng (approximately 25 nautical miles).

Entry 102

When sailing at the Nansha Islands from $Ddui^5 Dad^7$ (Ren'ai Reef) to $Ziao\ Shua$ (Xian'e Reef), navigate S202.5°W with the compass needle pointing towards the central line between Gui Ding and Chou Wei (towards southwest) and sail for two geng (approximately 20 nautical miles).

Entry 103

At the Nansha Islands, leaving $Ddui^5 Dad^7$ (Ren'ai Reef) for $Ngou^5 Hhuang^1$ (Wufang Reef), navigate N15°E with the compass needle pointing towards Gui Ding (northeast) for four geng (approximately 40 nautical miles). When sailing back, navigate S165°E; that is, the compass needle should point towards Ren Bing (towards southeast).

Entry 104

At the Nansha Islands, leaving $Ang^2 Sao^3 Dua^4 Bai^2$ (Changtan Bank) for $Ang^2 Sao^3 Di^6$ (Xiyue Island), navigate S97.50°E with the compass needle pointing towards the central line between Yi Xin and Mao You (towards southeast) for one geng (approximately 10 nautical miles). For a return voyage, navigate N300°W with the compass needle pointing towards Chen Xu (towards northwest).

Entry 105

Sailing at the Nansha Islands from $Na^4\ Hong^2$ (Mahuan Island) to $Hhao^1\ Ddin^2$ (Houteng Reef), navigate S97.5°E with the compass needle pointing towards the central line between Yi Xin and Mao You (towards southeast) for one and a half geng (approximately 15 nautical miles). When sailing back, navigate N315°W with the compass needle pointing towards Qian Xun (towards northwest).

Entry 106

At the Nansha Islands, navigate S150°E with the compass needle pointing towards Si Hai (towards southeast) for four geng (approximately 40 nautical miles) when sailing from $Hhao^1\ Ddin^2$ (Houteng Reef) to $Hhu^2\ Lin^2$ (Xianbing Reef). When sailing back, navigate N360°; that is, the compass needle should point towards Zi Wu (towards due north).

Entry 107

Setting off at the Nansha Islands from $Hhu^2\ Lin^2$ (Xianbing Reef) and navigating S105°E with the compass needle pointing towards Yi Xin (towards southeast) for three geng (approximately 30 nautical miles), you will arrive at $Ddang^1\ Hao^2\ Id^7\ Din^1$ (Pengbo Shoal). When sailing back, navigate N315°W; that is, the compass needle should point towards Qian Xun (towards northwest).

Entry 108

Sailing at the Nansha Islands from $Hhu^2\ Lin^2$ (Xianbing Reef) to $Na^4\ Hong^2$ (Mahuan Island), you should navigate N352.5°W; that is, the compass needle should point towards the central line between Ren Bing and Zi Wu (towards northwestward) for four geng (approximately 40 nautical miles). Sailing back, navigate S142.5°E with the compass needle pointing towards the central line between Qian Xun and Si Hai (towards southeast).

Entry 109

At the Nansha Islands, setting off from $Hhu^2\ Lin^2$ (Xianbing Reef) and navigating E165°S with the compass needle pointing towards Ren Bing (southeast) for four geng (approximately 40 nautical miles) will bring you to $Zio^5\ Liang^2$ (Jianzhang Reef). When sailing back, you should navigate N7.5°E, that is, the compass needle should point towards the central line between Zi Wu and Gui Ding (towards northeast).

Entry 110

Sailing at the Nansha Islands from Hhu^2 Lin^2 (Xianbing Reef) to $Ddui^5$ Dad^7 (Ren'ai Reef), you should navigate 270°W with the compass needle pointing towards Mao You (towards west) for one and a half geng (approximately 15 nautical miles). While sailing back, navigate N15°E with the compass needle pointing towards Gui Ding (towards northeast).

Entry 111

Navigate S165°E with the compass needle pointing towards Ren Bing (southeast) for four geng (approximately 40 nautical miles) when leaving $Ngou^5$ $Hhuang^1$ (Wufang Reef) for $Ddui^5$ Dad^7 (Ren'ai Reef). When sailing back, you should navigate N15°E with the compass needle pointing towards Gui Ding (towards northeast).

Entry 112

At the Nansha Islands, setting out from Hih^7 Di^6 (Zhongye Island) by navigating S135°E with the compass needle pointing towards Qian Xun (towards southeast) for two geng (approximately 20 nautical miles) will bring you to $Ddang^2$ Gim^1 Di^6 Gia^3 (Yangxin Shoal).

Entry 113

Setting off at the Nansha Islands from $Ddang^2$ Gim^1 (Yangxin Shoal) to $Ngin^2$ $Ddia^3$ (Anda Reef), navigate S135°E with the compass needle pointing towards Qian Xun (southeast) for two geng (approximately 20 nautical miles). When sailing back, you should navigate N345°W; that is, the compass needle should point towards Ren Bing (towards northwest).

Entry 114

Leaving $Ngin^2$ $Ddia^3$ (Anda Reef) at the Nansha Islands by navigating S142.5°E with the compass needle pointing towards the central line between Qian Xun and Si Hai (towards southeast) for six geng (approximately 60 nautical miles), you will arrive at *Ziao Shua* (Xian'e Reef). Navigate N345°W with the compass needle pointing towards Ren Bing (towards northwest) when sailing back to *Ngin² Ddia³* (Anda Reef).

Entry 115

At the Nansha Islands, setting off from *Hih⁷ Di⁶ Dua¹* (Zhongye Island) and navigating S210°W with the compass needle pointing towards Chou Wei (towards southwest) for one and a half geng (approximately 5 nautical miles), you will arrive at *Siu³ Vi¹ Dua¹* (Zhubi Reef).

Entry 116

Setting off at the Nansha Islands from *Siu³ Vi¹ Dua¹* (Zhubi Reef) to *Ddoi¹ Da¹* (Nanyue Island), you should navigate S127.5°E for two geng (approximately 20 nautical miles); that is, the compass needle should point towards the central line between Chen Xu and Qian Xun (towards southeast).

Entry 117

Navigate S165°E with the compass needle pointing towards Ren Bing (towards southeast) for two geng (approximately 20 nautical miles) at the Nansha Islands when leaving *Hih⁷ Di⁶* (Zhongye Island) for *Diang¹ Uang² Dua⁴ Gia³* (Shuanghuang Cay).

Entry 118

Sailing at the Nansha Islands from *Diang¹ Uang² Dua⁴ Gia³* (Shuanghuang Cay) to *Ui² Dua¹ Ve³* (Taiping Island), navigate S165°E with the compass needle pointing towards Ren Bing (towards southeast) for one geng (approximately 10 nautical miles). When sailing back, navigate N15°E, with the compass needle pointing towards Gui Ding (northeast).

Entry 119

At the Nansha Islands, setting out from *Nise Zio* (Ranqingdong Reef) and sailing S180° with the compass needle pointing towards Zi Wu (towards due south) for four geng (approximately 40 nautical miles) will bring you to *Vo² Mi⁶ Dua⁴* (Wumie Reef).

Entry 120

Navigate S127.5°E with the compass needle pointing between Chen Xu and Qian Xun (towards southeast) for three geng (approximately 30 nautical miles) at the Nansha Islands when leaving $Vo^2\ Mi^6\ Dua^4$ (Wumie Reef) for $Mag^8\ Gia^4$ (Siling Reef). Navigate N15°E with the compass needle pointing towards Gui Ding (towards northeast) when sailing back.

Entry 121

At the Nansha Islands, sailing for $Sim^1\ Huan^1$ (Yuya Shoal) from $Mag^8\ Gia^4$ (Siling Reef), you should navigate S247.5°W with the compass needle pointing towards the central line between Jia Geng and Yin Shen (towards southwest) for two geng (approximately 20 nautical miles).

Entry 122

Setting off at the Nansha Islands from $Guang^1\ Se^1\ Gia^3$ (Guangxingzai Reef) and sailing 270°W with the compass needle pointing towards Mao You (towards due west) for one geng (approximately 10 nautical miles) will bring you to $Ddua^1\ Guang^1\ Se^1$ (Guangxing Reef).

Entry 123

Sailing off at the Nansha Islands from $Ddua^1\ Guang^1\ Se^1$ (Guangxing Reef) to $Zio^5\ Gong^1\ Li^2$ (Danwan Reef), you should navigate S142.5°E with the compass needle pointing towards the central line between Si Hai and Qian Xun (towards southeast) for two geng (approximately 20 nautical miles). When sailing back, navigate N360°; that is, the compass needle should point towards Zi Wu (towards due north).

Entry 124

Navigate S210°W with the compass needle pointing towards Chou Wei (towards southwest) for six geng (approximately 60 nautical miles) at the Nansha Islands when leaving $Ddan^1\ Dad^7$ (Nantong Reef) for $Vag^8\ Gue^1\ Dua^4$ (Nanping Reef).

Entry 125

Leaving $Sin^4\ Gao^1\ Dua^4$ (Huajiao Reef) and arriving at $Lag^8\ Mui^2$ (Liumen

Reef) at the Nansha Islands, you should navigate S195°W with the compass needle pointing towards Gui Ding (towards southwest) for five geng (approximately 50 nautical miles).

Entry 126

At the Nansha Islands, sailing for *Bua^4 Gi^1* (Boji Reef) from *Hho^2 Na^4 Mui^2* (Nanhua Reef), you should navigate S165°E with the compass needle pointing towards Ren Bing (towards southeast) for four geng (approximately 40 nautical miles). Navigate N15°E with the compass needle pointing towards Gui Ding (towards northeast) when sailing back.

Entry 127

Setting off at the Nansha Islands from *Lag^8 Mui^2* (Liumen Reef) and sailing S157.5°E with the compass needle pointing towards the central line between Ren Bing and Si Hai (towards southeast) for four geng (approximately 40 nautical miles), you will get to *Bua^4 Gi^1* (Boji Reef).

Entry 128

Navigate N300°W with the compass needle pointing towards Chen Xu (northwest) for two geng (approximately 20 nautical miles) at the Nansha Islands when leaving *Lag^8 Mui^2* (Liumen Reef) for *Zio^5 Bua^2* (Bisheng Reef). When sailing back, navigate S135°E; that is, the compass needle should point towards Qian Xun (towards southeast).

Entry 129

When sailing from *Lag^8 Mui^2* (Liumen Reef) to *Hhai^3 Hao^3 Dua^4* (Baijiao Reef) at the Nansha Islands, navigate S247.5°W with the compass needle pointing towards the central line between Jia Geng and Yin Shen (towards southwest) for three geng (approximately 30 nautical miles).

Entry 130

Sailing at the Nansha Islands from *Hho^2 Na^4 Mui^2* (Nanhua Reef) to *Ddang^2 Ziang^1* (Nanhai Reef), you should navigate S195° W with the compass needle pointing towards Gui Ding (towards southwest) for four geng (approximately 40 nautical miles).

Entry 131

When setting off at the Nansha Islands from *Ddang² Ziang¹* (Nanhai Reef) to *Hhai³ Hao³ Dua⁴* (Baijiao Reef), you should navigate N307.5°W; that is, the compass needle should point towards between Chen Xu and Qian Xun (towards northwest).

Entry 132

Sailing at the Nansha Islands from *Hhai³ Hao³ Dua⁴* (Baijiao Reef) to *Ddia³ Gai⁴ Di⁶* (Anbo Cay), you should navigate S240°W with the compass needle pointing towards Yin Shen (towards southwest) for four geng (approximately 40 nautical miles).

Entry 133

Navigate N330°W with the compass needle pointing towards Si Hai (towards northwest) for five geng (approximately 50 nautical miles) if you set off at the Nansha Islands from *Hhai³ Hao³ Dua⁴* (Baijiao Reef) to *Ddang² Song⁴ Gia³* (Huayang Reef).

Entry 134

Setting out at the Nansha Islands from *Ddang² Song⁴ Gia³* (Huayang Reef) by navigating S262.5°W with the compass needle pointing towards the central line between Jia Geng and Mao You (towards southwest) for one geng (approximately 10 nautical miles) will bring you to *Ddua¹ Ddang² Song⁴* (Dongjiao Reef).

Entry 135

Sailing at the Nansha Islands from *Ddua¹ Ddang² Song⁴* (Dongjiao Reef) to *Long⁶ Pi¹ Gia³* (Zhongjiao Reef), navigate N300°W with the compass needle pointing towards Chen Xu (towards northwest) for two geng (approximately 20 nautical miles).

Entry 136

Set sail at the Nansha Islands, departing from *Long⁶ Pi¹ Gia³* (Zhongjiao Reef) by navigating 270°W with the compass needle pointing towards Mao You (towards due west) for one geng (approximately 10 nautical miles), you will arrive at $Ddua^1$ $Long^6 Pi^1$ (Xijiao Reef).

Entry 137

At the Nansha Islands, leaving $Ziao^3 Gia^3 Di^6$ (Nanwei Island) for $Dai^1 Hao^2 Id^7 Din^1$ (Riji Reef), you should navigate 277.5°W for two geng (approximately 20 nautical miles); that is, the compass needle should point towards between Yi Xin and Mao You (towards west).

Entry 138

At the Nansha Islands, sailing from $Zio^5 Bua^2$ (Bisheng Reef) to $Zio^1 Vu^5$ (Yongshu Reef), navigate N322.5°W with the compass needle pointing towards the central line between Qian Xun and Si Hai (towards northwest) for four geng (approximately 40 nautical miles).

Entry 139

At the Nansha Islands, departing from $Zio^1 Vu^5$ (Yongshu Reef) to arrive at $Ddang^2 Song^4 Gia^3$ (Huayang Reef), navigate 180°S to travel for four geng (approximately 40 nautical miles), that is, the compass needle should point towards Zi Wu (towards due south).

Entry 140

Leaving $Zio^1 Vu^5$ (Yongshu Reef) for $Ddua^1 Ddang^2 Song^4$ (Dongjiao Reef) at the Nansha Islands, you should navigate 180°S for four and a half geng (approximately 45 nautical miles); that is, the compass needle should point towards the central line between Zi Wu and Ding Gui (towards southwest).

Entry 141

Setting off at the Nansha Islands from $Ddang^2 Song^4 Gia^3$ (Huayang Reef) to $Siah^7 Gue^1 Dua^4$ (Chigua Reef), one should navigate N60°E with the compass needle pointing towards Yin Shen (towards northeast) for nine and a half geng (approximately 95 nautical miles).

Entry 142

Sailing at the Nansha Islands from $Lao^2 Gu^2 Lao^2$ (Daxian Reef) to $Siah^7 Gue^1$

Dua^4 (Chigua Reef), navigate S127.5°E with the compass needle pointing towards the central line between Qian Xun and Chen Xu (towards southeast) for three geng (approximately 30 nautical miles). When sailing back, navigate 352.5°N; that is, the compass needle should point towards the central line between Ren Bing and Zi Wu (towards northwest).

Entry 143

Sailing at the Nansha Islands from $Nam^2\ Id^7\ Dua^4$ (Nanxun Reef) to $Lao^2\ Gu^2\ Lao^2$ (Daxian Reef), you should voyage for two geng (approximately 20 nautical miles) by navigating S255°W with the compass needle pointing towards Jia Geng (towards southwest).

Entry 144

At the Nansha Islands, when leaving $Ddang^2\ Ziang^1$ (Nanhai Reef) for $Ddua^1\ Guang^1\ Se^1$ (Guangxing Reef), you should navigate 180°S with the compass needle pointing towards Zi Wu (towards due south) for two geng (approximately 20 nautical miles). Navigate N30°E with the compass needle pointing towards Chou Wei (towards northeast) when sailing back.

Entry 145

Sailing at the Nansha Islands from $Hho^2\ Log^8\ Mui$ (Nanhua Reef) to $Sim^1\ Huan^1$ (Yuya Shoal), navigate S127.5°E with the compass needle pointing towards the central line between Qian Xun and Chen Xu (towards southeast). Travel for three geng (approximately 30 nautical miles). When sailing back, navigate N352.5°W; that is, the compass needle should point towards the central line between Ren Bing and Zi Wu (towards northwest).

Entry 146

Set sail from $Ddoi^1\ Da^1\ Di^6$ (Nanyue Island) to $Ngin^2\ Ddia^3$ (Anda Reef) at the Nansha Islands, you should navigate S127.5°E with the compass needle pointing towards the central line between Qian Xun and Chen Xu (towards southeast) for three geng (approximately 30 nautical miles). When sailing back, navigate N352.5°W; that is, the compass needle should point towards the central line between Ren Bing and Zi Wu (towards northwest).

Entry 147

Set sail at the Nansha Islands from Da^1 Gag^7 (Sanjiao Reef) and navigate N285°W to travel for three geng (approximately 30 nautical miles), the compass needle should point towards Yi Xin (towards northwest), you will arrive at $Ngin^2$ $Ddia^3$ (Anda Reef).

Entry 148

At the Nansha Islands, departing from $Diang^1$ Mui^2 (Meiji Reef) and arriving at $Ngin^2$ $Ddia^3$ (Anda Reef), you should voyage for four geng (approximately 40 nautical miles) by navigating N300°W with the compass needle pointing towards Chen Xu (towards northwest)

Entry 149

Leaving at the Nansha Islands from Ang^2 Sao^3 Dua^4 Bai^2 (Changtan Bank) for Hih^7 Di^6 (Zhongye Island), you should navigate N277.5°W for three geng (approximately 30 nautical miles); that is, the compass needle should point towards the central line between Yi Xin and Mao You (towards northwest).

Entry 150

Sailing for Gao^1 Bu^6 (Bolan Reef) from $Ngin^2$ $Ddia^3$ (Anda Reef) at the Nansha Islands, you should navigate N300°W with the compass needle pointing towards Chen Xu (towards northwest) for one geng (approximately 10 nautical miles).

Entry 151

At the Nansha Islands, when sailing for $Ddui^5$ Dad^7 (Ren'ai Island) from Da^1 Gag^7 (Sanjiao Reef), navigate S120°E with the compass needle pointing towards Chen Xu (towards southeast) for four geng (approximately 40 nautical miles)

Entry 152

At the Nansha Islands, sailing for Lag^8 Mui^2 (Liumen Reef) from Lao^2 Gu^2 Lao^2 (Daxian Reef), navigate S172.5°E with the compass needle pointing towards the central line between Ren Bing and Zi Wu (towards southeast) for six geng (approximately 60 nautical miles)

Entry 153

At the Nansha Islands, departing from $Lao^2\ Gu^2\ Lao^2$ (Daxian Reef) and navigating S202.5°W to travel for five and a half geng (approximately 55 nautical miles); that is, the compass needle should point towards the central line between Gui Ding and Chou Wei (towards southwest), you will arrive at $Zio^5\ Bua^2$ (Bisheng Reef),

Entry 154

Set sail at the Nansha Islands and depart from $Lao^2\ Gu^2\ Lao^2$ (Daxian Reef) by navigating S240°W with the compass needle pointing towards Yin Shen (towards southwest) for four geng (approximately 40 nautical miles), you will reach $Zio^1\ Vu^5$ (Yongshu Reef).

Entry 155

Sailing at the Nansha Islands for $Lag^8\ Mui^2$ (Liumen Reef) from $Hho^2\ Log^8\ Mui$ (Nanhua Reef), you should travel for two geng (approximately 20 nautical miles) by navigating N292.5°W with the compass needle pointing towards the central line between Chen Xun and Yi Xin (towards northwest).

Entry 156

Sailing for $Ziao\ Shua$ (Xian'e Reef) at the Nansha Islands from $Diang^1\ Mui^2$ (Meiji Reef), you should navigate S187.5°W for two geng (approximately 20 nautical miles); that is, the compass needle should point between Zi Wu and Gui Ding (towards southwest).

Entry 157

At the Nansha Islands, set off for $Ddang^2\ Gim^1\ Di^6\ Gia^3$ (Yangxin Cay) from $Hou^4\ Gui$ (Kugui Reef) by navigating 180°S with the compass needle pointing towards Zi Wu (towards due south) for one geng (approximately 10 nautical miles).

Entry 158

Sailing at the Nansha Islands for $Nise\ Zio\ Du\ Gia$ (Ranqing East Reef) from

*Nam*² *Mid*⁸ (Hongxiu Island), you should travel for two geng (approximately 20 nautical miles) by navigating S135°E with the compass needle pointing towards Qian Xun (towards southeast).

Entry 159

Sail for *Nam*² *Id*⁷ *Dua*⁴ *Gia*³ (Nanxun Reef) from *Nam*² *Mid*⁸ (Hongxiu Island) at the Nansha Islands, you should navigate N277.5°W with the compass needle pointing towards the central line between Yi Xin and Chen Xu (towards northwest). Traveling for half a geng (approximately 5 nautical miles), two shoals are in sight.

Entry 160

At the Nansha Islands, leaving *Nam*² *Mid*⁸ *Di*⁶ (Hongxiu Island) and arriving at *Nam*² *Id*⁷ *Dua*⁴ *Gia*³ (Nanxun Reef), navigate N273°W for one geng (approximately 10 nautical miles); that is, the compass needle should point between Mao You and Yi Xin (northwestward).

Entry 161

At the Nansha Islands, leave *Nam*² *Mid*⁸ (Hongxiu Island) and on a return way, on the way there are two shoals. Navigate N345°W – S165°E with the compass needle pointing towards Ren Bing (towards northwest and southeast). There is a pass accessible to ships between the two shoals.

Entry 162

At the Nansha Islands, setting out from *Sin*⁴ *Gao*¹ *Di*⁶ (Jinghong Island) and arriving at *Siah*⁷ *Gue*¹ *Dua*⁴ (Chigua Reef), navigate 180°S with the compass needle pointing towards Zi Wu (towards due south) for one geng (approximately 10 nautical miles).

Entry 163

Setting off at the Nansha Islands from *Sin*⁴ *Gao*¹ *Di*⁶ (Jinghong Island) and navigating N352.5°W for one and a half geng (approximately 15 nautical miles) with the compass needle pointing towards the central line between Zi Wu and Ren Bing (towards northwest) will bring you to *Nam*² *Id*⁷ *Dua*⁴ *Gia*³ (Nanxun Reef).

Entry 164

Sailing at the Nansha Islands for $Hho^2\ Log^8\ Mui$ (Nanhua Reef) from $Vo^2\ Mi^6\ Dua^4$ (Wumie Reef), navigate S240°W with the compass needle pointing towards Yin Shen (towards southwest) for three geng (approximately 30 nautical miles).

Entry 165

At the Nansha Islands, setting out from $Ui^2\ Dua^1\ Ve^3$ (Taiping Island) to $Nam^2\ Id^7\ Dua^4\ Gia^3$ (Nanxun Reef), travel for one geng (approximately 10 nautical miles) by navigating S202.5°W with the compass needle pointing between Gui Ding and Chou Wei (towards southwest).

Entry 166

At the Nansha Islands, departing from $Ang^2\ Sao^3\ Dua^4\ Bai^2$ (Changtan Bank) and sailing for $Gong^4\ Se^5\ Dua^1$ (Gongshi Reef), navigate N307.5°W to voyage for three geng (approximately 30 nautical miles); that is, the compass needle should point between Chen Xu and Qian Xun (towards northwest).

Entry 167

Sailing for $Id^7\ Dua^4$ (Lusha Reef) at the Nansha Islands from $Diang^1\ Mui^2$ (Meiji Reef), one should travel for two geng (approximately 20 nautical miles) by navigating N337.5°W with the compass needle pointing between Si Hai and Ren Bing (towards northwest).

Entry 168

Sailing for $Hhue^3\ Ai^1$ (Huo'ai Reef) from $Id^7\ Dua^4$ (Lusha Reef) at the Nansha Islands, navigate N337.5°W for four geng (approximately 40 nautical miles); that is, the compass needle should point between Si Hai and Ren Bing (towards northwest).

Entry 169

Leaving $Hhue^3\ Ai^1$ (Huo'ai Reef) for $Hih^7\ Di^6$ (Zhongye Island) at the Nansha Islands, one should navigate N292.5°W with the compass needle pointing towards the central line between Yi Xin and Chen Xu (towards northwest) for three geng (approximately 30 nautical miles).

Entry 170

At the Nansha Islands, sailing 180°S with the compass needle pointing towards Zi Wu (towards due south), departing from *Guang*^{1} *Se*^{1} (Guangxing Reef) and traveling for two geng (approximately 20 nautical miles) will bring you to *Zio*^{5} *Gong*^{1} *Li*^{3} (Danwan Reef). When sailing back, navigate N15°E; that is, the compass needle should point towards Gui Ding (towards northeast).

Entry 171

Set sail at the Nansha Islands, departing from *Ddang*^{2} *Song*^{4} (Dongjiao Reef) and arriving at *Ziao*^{3} *Gia*^{3} *Di*^{6} (Nanwei Island), travel for four geng (approximately 40 nautical miles) by sailing S262.5°W with the compass needle pointing between Jia Geng and Mao You (towards southwest).

Entry 172

Setting off at the Nansha Islands from *Siu*^{3} *Vi*^{1} (Zhubi Reef) to *Ddoi*^{1} *Da*^{1} *Di*^{6} (Nanyue Island), navigate S112.5°E for two geng (approximately 20 nautical miles); that is, the compass needle should point between Chen Xu and Yi Xin (towards southeast).

Entry 173

Sailing for *Ngin*^{2} *Ddia*^{3} (Anda Reef) at the Nansha Islands from *Ddoi*^{1} *Da*^{1} *Di*^{6} (Nanyue Island), navigate S126°E for two and a half geng (approximately 25 nautical miles); that is, the compass needle should point between Chen Xu and Qian Xun (towards southeast).

Entry 174

At the Nansha Islands, navigate S142.5°E with the compass needle pointing between Ren Bing and Si Hai (towards southeast) for five geng (approximately 50 nautical miles) when sailing for *Lag*^{8} *Mui*^{2} (Liumen Reef) from *Lao*^{2} *Gu*^{2} *Lao*^{2} (Daxian Reef).

Entry 175

Sailing at the Nansha Islands for *Ziao Shua* (Xian'e Reef) from *Diang*^{1} *Mui*^{2}

(Meiji Reef), navigate S187.5°W for two and a half geng (approximately 25 nautical miles) with the compass needle pointing towards the central line between Zi Wu and Gui Ding (towards southwest).

Entry 176

Sailing at the Nansha Islands for $Zio^5\ Bua^2$ (Bisheng Reef) from $Lao^2\ Gu^2\ Lao^2$ (Daxian Reef), one should travel for four geng (approximately 40 nautical miles) by navigating S187.5°W; that is, the compass needle should point towards the middle line between Zi Wu and Gui Ding (towards southwest).

Entry 177

At the Nansha Islands, departing from $Lag^8\ Mui^2$ (Liumen Reef) by navigating S168°E with the compass needle pointing between Ren Bing and Zi Wu (towards south) for four and a half geng (approximately 45 nautical miles), you will reach $Ddang^2\ Ziang^1$ (Nanhai Reef).

Entry 178

Leaving $Hhue^3\ Ai^1$ (Huo'ai Reef) for $Hou^4\ Gui$ (Kugui Reef) at the Nansha Islands, navigate W277.5° for two geng (approximately 20 nautical miles); that is, the compass needle should point towards the central line between Yi Xin and Mao You (towards west).

Entry 179

Set out at the Nansha Islands, sailing for $Hih^7\ Di^6$ (Zhongye Island) from $Ang^2\ Sao^3\ Dua^4\ Bai^2$ (Changtan Bank) you should voyage for two geng (approximately 20 nautical miles) by navigating S255°W with the compass needle pointing towards Jia Geng (towards southwest).

Entry 180

Setting off at the Nansha Islands, departing from $Hhong^2\ Sao^3$ (Xiyue Island) and navigating S120°E with the compass needle pointing towards Chen Xu (towards southeast) for four geng (approximately 40 nautical miles), you will arrive at $Ngou^5\ Hhuang^1$ (Wufang Reef).

Entry 181

Sailing for *Diang*[1] *Dda*[1] (Xinyi Reef) at the Nansha Islands from *Diang*[1] *Mui*[2] (Meiji Reef), navigate S135°E with the compass needle pointing towards Qian Xun (towards southeast) for four geng (approximately 40 nautical miles).

Entry 182

Sailing at the Nansha Islands for *Ngou*[5] *Hhuang*[1] (Wufang Reef) from *Ddui*[5] *Dad*[7] (Ren'ai Reef), one should travel for four geng and a half (approximately 45 nautical miles) by navigating N15°E with the compass needle pointing towards Gui Ding (towards northeast).

Entry 183

At the Nansha Islands, departing from *Lo*[2] *Hong*[2] (Mahuan Island) and arriving at *Ngou*[5] *Hhuang*[1] (Wufang Reef), navigate S172.5°E for one and a half geng (approximately 15 nautical miles); that is, the compass needle should point towards the central line between Zi Wu and Ren Bing (towards southeast).

Entry 184

At the Nansha Islands, leaving *Ngou*[5] *Hhuang*[1] (Wufang Reef) for *Ddui*[5] *Dad*[7] (Ren'ai Island), navigate S165°E with the compass needle pointing towards Ren Bing (towards southeast) for four and a half geng (approximately 45 nautical miles).

Entry 185

At the Nansha Islands, leaving *Ngou*[5] *Hhuang*[1] *Hao* (Wufangtou Reef) for *Bua*[4] *Lou*[1] *Dua*[4] (Banlu Reef), you should voyage for two geng (approximately 20 nautical miles) by sailing S135°E with the compass needle pointing towards Qian Xun (towards southeast).

Entry 186

At the Nansha Islands, set sail from *Ngou*[5] *Hhuang*[1] (Wufang Reef) and navigate S120°E with the compass needle pointing towards Chen Xu (towards southeast) for four geng (approximately 40 nautical miles), you will arrive at *Hhu*[2] *Lin*[2]

(Xianbin Reef).

Entry 187

Sailing at the Nansha Islands for $Sim^1 Huan^1$ (Yuya Shoal) from $Hho^2 Log^8 Mui^2$ (Nanhua Reef), navigate S120°E with the compass needle pointing towards Chen Xu (towards southeast) for four geng (approximately 40 nautical miles).

Entry 188

Setting off at the Nansha Islands from $Ddang^2 Gim^1$ (Yangxin Cay) to $Ddoi^1 Da^1$ (Nanyue Island), you should navigate S255°W for one geng (approximately 10 nautical miles); that is, the compass needle should point towards Jia Geng (southwest).

Entry 189

Sailing for $Lag^8 Ai$ (Lu'an in Vietnam) from $Dai^1 Hao^2 Id^7 Din^1$ (Riji Reef) at the Nansha Islands, you should navigate N315°W with the compass needle pointing towards Qian Xun (towards northwest) for twenty-two geng (approximately 220 nautical miles).

Entry 190

Leaving $Hhue^3 Ai^1$ (Huo'ai Reef) for $Ddoi^1 Da^1$ (Nanyue Island) at the Nansha Islands, navigate S255°W with the compass needle pointing towards Jia Geng (towards southwest) for two and a half geng (approximately 25 nautical miles).

Entry 191

At the Nansha Islands, sailing for $Hhue^3 Ai^1$ (Huo'ai Reef) from $Log^8 Sa^1$ (Lusha Reef), navigate N339°W for four geng (approximately 40 nautical miles); that is, the compass needle should point northwest between Si Hai and Ren Bing.

Entry 192

Sailing at the Nansha Islands for $Log^8 Sa^1$ (Lusha Reef) from the northeastern $Diang^1 Mui^2$ (Meiji Reef), navigate N337.5°W for two geng (approximately 20 nautical miles); that is, the compass needle should point towards the central line between Ren Bing and Si Hai (towards northwest).

Entry 193

At the Nansha Islands, departing from *Diang*[1] *Uang*[2] (Shuanghuang Cay) and arriving at *Ui*[2] *Dua*[1] *Ve*[3] *Ddang*[1] (Dunqian Cay), one should sail for two geng (approximately 20 nautical miles) by navigating S142.5°E with the compass needle pointing towards the middle line between Qian Xun and Si Hai (towards southeast).

3 The Origins and Legends of the Folk Names of the South China Sea Islands in Su Deliu Version and Peng Zhengkai Version of *Genglubu*

3.1 Navigational Routes towards *Ddang¹ Hhai³* (the Xisha Islands)

1. *Dua¹ Ham²* (大潭), Tanmen Port, a fishing port, is situated in Qionghai City, Hainan province.

2. In *Genglubu* — *The Chinese Fishermen's Navigation and Exploration Record of the South China Sea*, *Ddang¹ Hhai³* (东海) is the common folk name of the Xisha Islands given by the fishermen of Hainan. It usually appears on the initial page of various versions of the *Genglubu*. Geographically, this *Ddang¹ Hhai³* is totally different from Donghai (the East China Sea) though they are similarly pronounced in Chinese. Every year when winter starts with the northeast monsoons, the fishermen of Hainan sail off to the Xisha waters, which is their first fishing destination. The word 东 (dong), meaning "east", is a specialized directional term used by the fishermen of Hainan.

3. *Da¹ Di⁶* (三峙) is the pronunciation in Hainan dialect and its official name is Nandao Island. The fishermen of Hainan named Nandao Island *Da¹ Di⁶*, which means "the third island", because it lies just after Beidao Island and Zhongdao Island, as well as in the middle of the Qilian Islands.

4. *Gan¹ Ddao¹* (干豆) is the folk name of Beidao Island. The island's name—*Gan¹ Ddao¹*, which means "dried beans", was given by a fisherman of Hainan because of a legend concerning a man who picked up many bags of dried beans on the reef. In addition, Beidao Island looks like a bean from a distance. Alternatively, according to Prof. Han Zhenhua (韩振华), a well-known expert in South China Sea studies, when the Portuguese first came to China, they passed by Beijiao Reef lying to the north of the Xisha Islands and thought that it was Cantao or Canto (Guangdong), which was translated into Chinese *Gandou*.

5. The fishermen of Hainan traditionally call the Yongle Islands $Zio^5 Ddo^2$ (石塘). In the early Ming Dynasty, $Zio^5 Ddo^2$ was given the official name of the Yongle Islands. Zhudi (1360 – 1424) was the Emperor Chengzu of the Ming Dynasty, whose reign title was Yongle, after which $Zio^5 Ddo^2$ was named. During his reign (1402 – 1424), he ordered the senior general Zheng He to make seven voyages to the Western Seas (Southeast Asia, west of Brunei and the Indian Ocean) on diplomatic missions. Zheng He led a fleet of more than 200 ships carrying well over 27,000 men on each voyage. The seven voyages to the Western Seas greatly promoted the economic and cultural exchanges between China and the countries in Asia and Africa.

6. $Yi^1 Huan^1$ (二圈 or 二筐), whose official name is Yuzhuo Reef, is one of the four basket-like circular reefs scattered among the Yongle Islands. The largest one is $Ddua^1 Huan^1$ (大圈, Huaguang Reef) commonly named "big basket" by the fishermen of Hainan, and the smallest one is $Huan^1 Gia^3$ (圈仔, Lingyang Reef), commonly called "small basket". Between the largest basket and smallest basket are the two middle baskets, which were named $Yi^1 Huan^1$, meaning "the first middle basket" and $Da^1 Huan^1$, meaning "the second middle basket", respectively. In Hainan dialect, the two characters 筐 (kuang) and 圈 (quan) are homonyms, both pronounced huan.

7. $Va^1 Du^4$ (猫注), in Hainan dialect, is the pronunciation of three folk names—猫注, 猫峙 and 猫驻 for Yongxing Island, the official name. $Va^1 Du^4$ is the most convenient and suitable place to anchor in the Xisha waters. The word for island 岛 (dao) is usually replaced by the word 峙 (zhi) by the fishermen of Hainan, so $Va^1 Du^4$ was given the name of "anchor island" 锚峙. In Chinese, the character 锚 (mao) means "anchor" and has the same sound as 猫 (mao), which means "cat". Probably, the character 锚 was miswritten as 猫 because they have similar sound and form. On the other hand, the island looks like a cat squatting. For these two reasons, Yongxing Island also received the folk name of "cat island". Here the three characters 峙 (zhi), 驻 (zhu) and 注 (zhu) in Hainan dialect are homophones——having similar sounds but differences in form and meaning. As an aside, there are very few cats on the island.

Shidao Island, situated on the same circular reefs as Yongxing Island, has three folk names too. These folk names are all pronounced $Va^1 Du^4 Gia^3$, but the characters which compose the names are different: 猫峙仔, 猫注仔 and 猫驻仔, which are all similar in pronunciation and form. The character 仔 (gia) in Hainan

3 The Origins and Legends of the Folk Names of the South China Sea Islands in Su Deliu Version and Peng Zhengkai Version of *Genglubu*

dialect serves as a suffix meaning "small", and it is often used together with an opposing word which means "large or big" to form a contrasting or relational idea, such as the close bond between father and son. For instance, here $Va^1 Du^4$ （猫峙） is big, while $Va^1 Du^4 Gia^3$ （猫峙仔） is small, and both are closely situated, so that such English names as "big cat island" and "small cat island" can be given respectively. In the *Genglubu* there are numerous such cases of folk names for the South China Sea islands.

8. $E^5 Di^6$ （下峙）, also commonly named $E^5 Boi^6 Ddao^2$ （下八岛）, or $Dai^1 Boi^6 Ddao^2$ （西八岛） in Hainan dialect, is located to the southwest of the Xisha Islands and refers specifically to the Yongle Islands. The character 下 (xia) is a directional word particularly used by the fishermen of Hainan, which refers to "west" or "south". Here it can be rendered into "west island". The character 峙 (zhi) in Hainan dialect means "an island jutting up from the ocean, towering and erect".

$E^5 Di^6$ actually has a corresponding name called $Zio^5 Ddo^2$ （石塘, See 5 above）. Here it needs mentioning the Xuande Islands, the official name which is traditionally called $Zio^1 Di^6$ （上峙） or $Zio^1 Sid^7 Ddao^2$ （上七岛） or $Ddang^1 Sid^7 Ddao^2$ （东七岛） by the fishermen of Hainan. The Xuande Islands lie to the northeast of the Xisha Islands and they are seven small islands and shoals. Here the character 上 (shang), as apposed to 下 (xia), also used as a special directional word by the fishermen means "east" or "north". Therefore, $E^5 Di^6$ can be translated into "east island" because it is situated to the northeast of the Xisha Islands.

9. $Hiag^7 Siu^3$ （曲手） is a circular hand-like reef, curving 150° like an arm located between Jinqing Island and Shiyu Island. The fishermen of Hainan traditionally call Quanfu Island $Suan^2 Pu^4 Di^6$ （全富峙） or $Hiag^7 Siu^3$.

10. The fishermen of Hainan traditionally call a sea passage between islands or reefs "gate" or "river". Among the circular reefs to the southwest of the Yongle Islands, there are four passages between $Suan^2 Pu^4 Di^6$ whose official name is Quanfu Island, the largest island there, and Jinqing Island. Jinqing Island is close to the fourth pass, so it was given the folk name of $Di^4 Giang^1$ （四江）, $Di^4 Giang^1 Mui^2$ （世江门）, or $Di^4 Giang^1 Di^6$ （四江峙）, meaning "the fourth river" or "the fourth river gate" by the fishermen. Here the two characters 四 (si) and 世 (shi) in the Hainan dialect are homophones. The character 四 was miswritten as 世.

11. The official name of $Ngin^2 Di^6$ （银峙） is Yinyu Bank. $Ngin^2 Di^6$ is the folk name given by the fishermen of Hainan according to a legend which tells that there was once plenty of silver scattered on the bank a long time ago. Yinyu Bank,

a small bank occupying an area of 0.01 square kilometers, lies to the northeast of Yagong Island, and is roughly a nautical mile from it. There is a deep pit around the circular bank. The pit is too deep to see its bottom, the water there looks dark blue, and its temperature is relatively low, so the fishermen commonly call it "dragon pit".

12. Va^1 $Hheng^1$ (猫兴) is the folk name of Dongdao Island, meaning "plenty of lush trees" in Hainan dialect. The characters 猫 (mao) and 巴 (ba) are homophones in Hainan dialect. The island was given its official name Dongdao Island (东岛) because it lies to the east of the Xisha Islands. The characters 东 means "east" and 岛 means "island". The island is the second largest of the Xisha Islands.

13. Bua^4 Lou^1 (半路) or Bua^4 Lou^1 Di^6 (半路峙) is the folk name of Zhongjian Island, which is situated nearly at the midpoint between the Xisha Islands and the Nansha Islands. The fishermen of Hainan think they have made half a voyage from the Xisha Islands to the Nansha Islands when they reach this island, so they named it Bua^4 Lou^1, or Bua^4 Lou^1 Di^6, meaning "half-way island" based on its navigational distance. It was officially named after the warship *Zhongjian* in commemoration of the Xisha Islands being taken over by the Chinese government in 1946.

14. The fishermen of Hainan have a traditional and common recognition about the directions of the South China Sea waters. They tend to regard east or northeast as "tou" (头), meaning "beginning" or "head", and "west" or "southwest" as "wei" (尾), meaning "end" or "tail". Additionally, they think that the spot close to their home is "tou" (头), while that far away is "wei" (尾). Because Jinyin Island lies to the westernmost part of the Yongle islands, the fishermen traditionally call it Vue^3 Di^6 (尾峙) or Vue^3 $Ddao^2$ (尾岛), both meaning "tail island". The island was given the name of Jinyin (金银), which means "gold and silver" because of the following two stories: one story goes that a lot of coins were discovered on the island; the other story goes that the sea around the island was rich in abalone and other kinds of rare seafood, so the fishermen often have good fishing harvests there.

15. Be^5 Di^6 Gia^3 (白石仔) is the folk name of Panshi Island, which is a circular reef. At the north of this reef, there is a low, flat cay full of white sand, but it is not large. Therefore, the fishermen of Hainan gave the island the names Be^5 Di^6 Gia^3, Be^5 Siu^1 Gia^3 (白树仔), meaning "white island with white tree and white reef" respectively.

3 The Origins and Legends of the Folk Names of the South China Sea Islands in Su Deliu Version and Peng Zhengkai Version of *Genglubu*

16. *Ang² Sao³ Mui²* （红草门） refers to the pass between the Qilian Islands and Yongxing Island. In the southern part of the Qilian Islands, from the south to the north lie Nansha Sand, Zhongsha Sand, and Beisha Sand, and the fishermen of Hainan gave each of them such folk names as *Ang² Sao³ Id⁷* （红草一）, *Ang² Sao³ Yi¹* （红草二） and *Ang² Sao³ Da¹* （红草三）, meaning "red grass 1, red grass 2 and red grass 3" respectively because red purslane, the fishermen call it red grass, grows on the three sandbars.

17. *Diang¹ Pan²* （双帆） or *Ziam¹ Zio⁵* （尖石） are the folk names of the Gaojian Rocks, which is the official name. The Gaojian Rocks are the only two basalt rocks formed by volcanic eruption in the Xisha Islands, rising high above the sea surface and shaped like two pagodas. Seen from a distance, they look like two sails; thus, they got the name *Diang¹ Pan²* which means "twin sails".

18. *Dun² Ngam² Vue³* （船岩尾） is the folk name of Xisha Sand Bank. It lies at the western end of the circular reef of Zhaoshu Island and the westernmost part of the Qilian Islands. It was named *Dun² Ngam² Vue³* （船岩尾）, *Dun² Am⁴ Vue³* （船暗尾）, or *Dun² Ham⁴ Vue³* （船坎尾） after its location by the fishermen of Hainan. *Dun² Ngam² Vue³* means "the end or tail of a boat or ship". Here the sand is compared to a boat or a ship. In each of the three Chinese folk names of Xisha Sand Bank, the middle character 岩 （yan）, 暗 （an） and 坎 （kan） are homophones in the Hainan dialect and they are usually pronounced the same as *am*.

19. *Lao⁵ Sou¹ Mui²* （老粗门） is a sea passage between Shanhu Island and Ganquan Island at the Xisha Islands. *Lao⁵ Sou¹ Ddao²* （老粗岛） is the folk name of Shanhu Island. The width of *Lao⁵ Sou¹ Mui²* is 2,400 meters and its depth is 2 meters in most part, but the deepest part reaches 45 meters. Here there is no living coral, only the remains of corals can be found at the bottom. All the vessels from Hainan Island sail through the passage or the gate first to get to Shanhu Island, and then arrive in the Yongle Islands.

20. *Da¹ Ha¹* （三脚） is the folk name of Chenhang Island which is located among the Yongle Islands. Together with Guangjin Island, Chenhang Island is 2,800 meters away from the main island—Jinqing Island, one of the Yongle Islands. Flat in the middle part, surrounded by sands, Chenhang Island looks like a triangle with wave edges of 0.43 km². Although there are wells in Chenhang Island, the water in the wells is not drinkable. In addition, this island was given the name Chenhang in memory of warship *Chenhang* at the end of the Qing Dynasty.

3.2　Navigational Routes towards *Bag⁷ Hhai⁸* (the Nansha Islands)

1. In *Genglubu*, *Bag⁷ Hhai³* (北海) is the folk name of the Nansha Islands. Traditionally, for the fishermen of Hainan, the center of China is very far away in the north. In this sense, "bei" (北) has the connotation of faraway distance or remoteness in their mind. For this reason, they commonly called a faraway place the north, and thus imagined the faraway continent in the north, as a northern mountain. Since the Nansha Islands are very far away from them, the fishermen gave them the name *Bag⁷ Hhai³*.

2. There are four basket-like circular reefs scattered among the Yongle Islands. The largest one is *Ddua¹ Hiang¹* or *Ddua¹ Huan¹*, commonly named big basket by the fishermen of Hainan, and the smallest one is *Hiang¹ Gia³* or *Huan¹ Gia* (Lingyang Reef), commonly called small basket. Between the largest basket and smallest basket are the two middle-sized baskets which were named *Yi¹ Hiang¹* or *Yi¹ Huan¹* (Yuzhuo Reef), meaning "first middle basket" and *Da¹ Hiang¹* or *Da¹ Huan¹* (Langhua Reef), meaning "second middle basket", respectively. In Hainan dialect, the characters 筐, 圹, and 圈 are homonyms, pronounced *huan*.

3. There are two different folk names given by the fishermen of Hainan for the Shuangzi Islands: *Diang¹ Di⁶* (双峙) and *Nai⁶ Lo²* (耐/奈罗). *Diang¹ Di⁶* was the name given to the two islands—Beizi Island and Nanzi Island. *Nai⁶ Lo²* also refers to the same two islands.

Interestingly, the name *Nai⁶ Lo²* derives from a legend concerning these two islands. It goes that a long time ago, a fisherman and his very young son were stranded on Beizi Island beause of adverse weather conditions. Because they had been there for such a long time, the boy felt his life was boring and lonesome, so he kept asking his father to take him home. The father tried to comfort him by repeating the word *nailuo* which means "be patient" in Hainan dialect. Therefore, the island was given the name of *Nai⁶ Lo²*, meaning "patience island".

4. *Ang² Sao³ Dua⁴* (红草线), also known as *Nam² Nai⁶ Lo² Gag⁷* (南奈罗角), is the folk name of Lesi Shoal, which is the official name. It is situated between N11°19′–N11°22′, E114°35′–E114°39′, and composed of a group of underwater stabilizing reefs, looking like a long belt from a distance. So the fishermen of Hainan also gave it the name of *Ang² Sao³ Dua⁴* or *Hhong² Sao³ Dua¹ Bai²* (红草

3 The Origins and Legends of the Folk Names of the South China Sea Islands in Su Deliu Version and Peng Zhengkai Version of *Genglubu*

线排), meaning "a long reef or shoal belt".

5. *Hih^7 Di^6* (铁峙), the folk name of Zhongye Island, is situated on the circular reef of the Zhongye Islands. *Hih^7 Di^6* is situated close to the other three reefs, which appear one after another and from a distance look like an iron chain. Thus, these reefs were given the name of iron chain. Because Zhongye Island is located near the iron chain reefs, it is commonly called *Hih^7 Di^6*, meaning "iron island" by the fishermen of Hainan. Right after the victory of the Anti-Japanese War in 1946, the island was taken over by the warship *Zhongye* sent by the Chinese government, and so the island was officially named Zhongye Island after this warship.

6. *Hhong^2 Sao^3* (红草) is the folk name of Xiyue Island. There is no tree on the island, but only wild grass grows. Because the grass there looks red in color, the fishermen of Hainan call it *Hhong^2 Sao^3* or *Ang^2 Sao^3 Di^6* (红草峙), meaning red grass or red grass island. Here *Hhong^2 Sao^3* is not the same as the *Ang^2 Sao^3* (Nansha Cay) at the Xisha Islands because the former is an island while the latter is a sand bank.

7. (*Ang^2 Sao^3*) *Dua^4 Bai^2* [(红草) 线排] is the folk name of Changtan Bank which is located to the west of Xiyue Island. The fishermen of Hainan named this island red grass belt because there the underwater sand is dark red in color, looking like red grass from a distance. In addition, it lies to the northeast of Daoming Bank and Reefs, a long shoal stretching along the direction of northeast to southwest that includes Mengzi Reef. Therefore, it was named Changtan, meaning "long bank".

8. When the fishermen of Hainan sail towards the Nansha Islands, their first stop is *Diang^1 Di^6* (the Shuangzi Islands), their second stop is *Hih^7 Di^6* (Zhongye Island) and Reefs, and their third stop is the Daoming Bank and Reefs. As the only island among the Daoming Bank and Reefs, Nanyue Island was given the folk name *Ddoi^1 Da^1 Di^6* (第三峙) or *Ddoi^1 Da^1* (第三), which means "the third or the third island". The Chinese fishermen have settled down on the island for fishing production since the Song Dynasty. They dug wells, built houses and temples, and even planted trees on the island.

9. *Lo^2 Hong^2* (锣孔 or 罗孔) or *Ddua^1 Lo^2 Hong^2* (大罗孔) is the folk name of Mahuan Island. It is a green island lying at the center of a circular reef. Seen from a distance, it looks like a hole on a big copper gong, so it was named *Lo^2 Hong^2*, meaning "gong hole". Here the character 锣 was miswritten as 罗. Mahuan Island is bigger than Feixin Island, which lies nearby, so it was also given

another folk name by the fishermen, $Ddua^1 Lo^2 Hong^2$, meaning "big gong hole". The official name of this island is Mahuan Island, named after Zheng He's translator. Zheng He was a senior general who made seven voyages to the Western Seas during the Yongle reign of Chengzhu Emperor (1360 – 1424) of the Ming Dynasty.

10. $Hhue^3 Ai^1$ (火艾) is the folk name of Huo'ai Reef. In Hainan dialect, a torch (火把) is pronounced $Hhue^3 Ai^1$ and it is often written as 火艾 or 火哀. Huo'ai Reef looks like a torch from a distance, so the fishermen of Hainan gave it the name $Hhue^3 Ai^1$, meaning torch reef. The characters 艾 (ai) and 哀 (ai) are homophones.

11. $Hou^4 Gui$ (裤归) is the folk name of Kugui Reef and it refers to the two reefs lying north and south, more than three nautical miles away from Yangxin Cay in the northeast. It is underwater at flood tide and above water at ebb tide. The two reefs are clearly on the same reef plate looking like a seat of trousers, so it was given the folk name $Hou^4 Gui$, meaning "trousers" by the fishermen of Hainan.

12. Sanjiao Reef is about five kilometers long from east to west. It is a complete circular reef with no passages. Because it is triangular in shape, the fishermen of Hainan customarily call it $Da^1 Gag^7$ (三角), meaning "triangle" or $Da^1 Gag^7 Ziao^1$ (三角礁), meaning "triangle reef".

13. $Diang^1 Mui^2$ (双门) is the folk name of Meiji Reef. In the southern part of Meiji Reef, there are two passages accessible to ships, so the fishermen of Hainan gave it the folk name $Diang^1 Mui^2$, meaning "two gates". Here is the area where margarita snails and giant clams, as well as species of holothurian (sea cucumber) are plentiful. Meiji Reef is one of the main fishing grounds of the fishermen of Hainan.

14. $Ngou^5 Hhuang^1$ (五风) is the folk name of Wufang Reef. On the plate of the circular reef, there stand five reef platforms oriented towards different directions. The fishermen of Hainan named the five platforms: $Ngou^5 Hhuang^1 Hao$ (五方头), meaning "head" because it lies at the head of the northwest of the circular reef; $Ngou^5 Hhuang^1 Bag$ (五方北), meaning "north" because it lies at the end of the north of the circular reef; $Ngou^5 Hhuang^1 Dai$ (五方西), meaning "west" because it lies at the end of the western part of the circular reef; $Ngou^5 Hhuang^1 Nam$ (五方南), meaning "south" because it lies at the end of the southern part of the circular reef; and $Ngou^5 Hhuang^1 Vue^3$ (五方尾), meaning "tail" because it lies at the southwest end of the circular reef. $Ngou^5 Hhuang^1$ means there are rocks in five different places. In Hainan dialect, the characters 风 (feng) and 方 (fang)

3 The Origins and Legends of the Folk Names of the South China Sea Islands in Su Deliu Version and Peng Zhengkai Version of *Genglubu*

are homophones and they both are pronounced *huang*.

15. *Ddui^5 Dad^7* (断节) is the folk name of Ren'ai Reef and it lies roughly 14 nautical miles to the southeast of Meiji Reef. Ren'ai Reef is about 15 kilometers from north to south and 5.6 kilometers from east to west. The northern part of the reef is relatively complete while the southern part is made up of several small reefs which are not connected. Therefore, the fishermen of Hainan customarily call it *Ddui^5 Dad^7*, meaning "segments" or "broken joints". It is also called *Ddui^5 Dad^7 Dua^4* (断节线) because there is an underwater sand belt in the "segmented" areas.

16. Xian'e Reef is the official name, and its folk name is *Ziao Shua* (鸟串). The reef lies about 25 nautical miles to the west of Xinyi Reef. It is a circular reef, 7.4 kilometers long from north to south and 4.6 kilometers wide from east to west. Most of the reef is underwater at flood tide, but some areas are exposed at flood tide. The entire reef emerges at ebb tide. The reef is completely circular and has no passages through it. Seen from a distance, Xian'e Reef looks like a huge beak, so the fishermen of Hainan gave it the name *Ziao Shua* (鸟嘴), meaning bird's mouth. In Hainan dialect, the characters 串 (chuan) and 嘴 (zui) are both pronounced *shua*. Therefore, 鸟嘴 (niao zui) is miswritten as 鸟串 (niao chuan).

17. *Diang^1 Hiao^1* (双挑) or *Diang^1 Dda^1* (双担) is the folk name of Xinyi Reef. On the northern and southern ends of the reef there is a long belt. The fishermen of Hainan named it *Diang^1 Hiao^1* or *Diang^1 Dda^1* because it looks like a shoulder pole stretching across the sea surface if it is seen from a distance.

18. *Gu^2 Sia^1 Eng^1* (牛车英) is the folk name given by the fishermen of Hainan for Niuchelun Reef, which is the official name. It is situated to the southwest of Xianbin Reef, about 19 nautical miles away from the northeast of Xinyi Reef. It is submersed at flood tide. When it emerges at ebb tide as a round reef in shape, it looks like a wooden wheel of a bullock cart. Here the character 英 (ying) is an onomatopoeia, evoking the sound of wooden-wheel bullock cart.

19. *Ha^1 Buad^7* (脚坡 or 脚钵) is the folk name given by the fishermen of Hainan for Haikou Reef, which is the official name. The reef is completely circular and has no passages through it. It is 2.6 kilometers long and 1.8 kilometers wide. There is a lagoon around the circular reef which emerges at ebb tide, looking like a foot basin, so the fishermen customarily call Haikou Reef *Ha^1 Buad^7* which mean "foot basin". In Hainan dialect, the characters 坡 (po) and 钵 (bo) are homophones. Actually, 钵 is miswritten as 坡.

20. *Zio^5 Liang^2* (石龙) is the folk name of Jianzhang Reef, which is the offi-

cial name. On the reef there is a cave which is usually called $Zio^5 \ Ddong^5$ （石洞）, meaning "stone cave" by the fishermen of Hainan. In Hainan dialect, 洞（dong）is often pronounced 笼（long）and thus 石洞 is also called 石笼, meaning "stone cage". However, 石笼 was miswritten as 石龙, meaning "stone dragon" because 笼（long）and 龙（long）are homophone variants.

21. $Hhu^2 \ Lin^2$ （鱼鳞）is the folk name of Xianbin Reef, the latter is the official name. On the southeastern and northwestern parts of the reef, standing above the water line, there are masses of rocks which resemble fish scales, so the fishermen named it $Hhu^2 \ Lin^2$ （鱼鳞）, meaning "fish scales".

22. （$Ddang^1 \ Hao^2$）$Id^7 \ Din^1$ ［（东头）乙辛］is the folk name of Pengbo Shoal, which is the official name. It is actually a circular reef which is 2 kilometers in diameter and it emerges at ebb tide. There is a lagoon with a sandy bottom, 29 – 32 meters deep and it has no passage. The fishermen of Hainan traditionally call it $Ddang^1 \ Hao^2 \ Id^7 \ Din^1$, meaning "east end" based on the direction of the compass needle when a ship navigates there, which points towards Yi Xin (towards east by south) on the compass.

23. A horseshoe crab（鲎）is a sea crustacean that has a long tail like a rattan. At ebb tide, pieces of prismatic rocks that look like horseshoe crab eggs emerge at Houteng Reef. Thus, the reef was given the folk name $Hhao^1 \ Ddin^2$ （鲎藤）, meaning "horseshoe crab rattan" by the fishermen of Hainan, and this folk name became its official name Houteng Reef, too.

24. $Hhai^3 \ Gong^1$ （海公）is the folk name of Banyue Reef, which is the official name. The fishermen of Hainan commonly bestowed the title of 公（gong）to those big, tall, and strong marine creatures which are objects of veneration. A whale is so huge that it is regarded as "sea gong". In this sense, they compared Banyue Reef to $Hhai^3 \ Gong^1$ （Sea Gong）as it resembles a whale. Banyue Reef is circular but incomplete, forming a half-moon shape. Therefore, it was officially named Banyue Reef, which means "half moon". Therefore, Banyue Reef, which is called $Hhai^3 \ Gong^1$ by the fishermen, demonstrates the feature of Chinese fishermen's belief and culture.

25. $Ngin^2 \ Bia^3$ （银饼）or $Ngin^2 \ Ddia^3$ （银锅）is the folk name of Anda Reef, which is the official name. This reef plate is like an immense pot or disc in shape. A legend goes that long time ago, the forefathers of the fishermen salvaged silver out of the plate-shaped lagoon; thus they gave it the name.

26. $Bua^4 \ Lou^1 \ Dua^4$ （半路线）or $Bua^4 \ Lou^1$ （半路）is the folk name of Banlu

3 The Origins and Legends of the Folk Names of the South China Sea Islands in Su Deliu Version and Peng Zhengkai Version of *Genglubu*

Reef, which is the official name. It is situated in the Nansha Islands right between Wufang Reef and Xianbin Reef, 25 nautical miles away from each other. This is how the folk name *Bua⁴ Lou¹* (Banlu Reef) was derived. The character 线 (xian) in Hainan dialect shows that there is a sand belt in the center of the reef. *Bua⁴ Lou¹* is the shortened form of *Bua⁴ Lou¹ Dua⁴*. Here the folk name is not the same as that *Bua⁴ Lou¹* (Zhongjian Island) at the Xisha Islands. The former is a sand belt while the latter is an island.

27. Wufangtou Reef, one of five reefs among the group of the Wufang Reefs, and it was given this name because it is located to the northeastern end of the circular reefs (See 14 above).

28. *Ddang² Ddia³* (铜锅) is the folk name of Yangxin Cay. It is only 100-meter diameter cay. At its center, there is a 1.4-kilometer oval reef plate resembling a very large copper pot. A legend goes that a long time ago, some fishermen discovered a lot of gold on the cay. Because there was so much gold, they suspected it was copper rather than gold, after which it was named *Ddang² Ddia³* (铜锅), which means "copper pot". In addition, it was given the official name after Yangxin, an important government official during the reign of Chengzu (1402 – 1424) in the Ming Dynasty.

29. *Siu³ Vi¹* (丑未) is the folk name of Zhubi Reef, which is the official name. According to the fishermen of Hainan, the area of Zhubi Reef is a very good fishing ground, especially rich in margarita snails. It was said that the first fishermen who had successfully arrived at Zhubi Reef departed from Tiexian Reef and arrived there, with the compass needle pointing towards *Siu³ Vi¹*, one of the directional points on the ancient Chinese compass, thus it got the folk name *Siu³ Vi¹* in Hainan dialect. In this way they can remember where the place is or the destination for fishing.

30. *Hih⁷ Di⁶ Dua⁴ Bai²* (铁峙线排), also known as *Hih⁷ Di⁶ Dua¹ Bai²* (铁峙沙排), is the folk name of Tiezhi Reef, which is the official name. This reef is not a large shoal close to *Hih⁷ Di⁶* (Zhongye Island). The characters 沙 (sha), or 线 (xian), or 线排 (xianpai) is used as the special folk words referring to a shoal in Hainan dialect.

31. *Diang¹ Uang²* (双黄/双王), is also known as the folk name of Shuanghuang Cay. The latter is the official name. It is composed of two separate cays. One is small, and the other large. Seen from a distance, they resemble two yolks in shape, and thus it was named *Diang¹ Uang²* by the fishermen of Hainan. In Hainan

dialect, the characters 黄 (huang), 王 (wang) are both pronounced $Uang^2$. For this reason, 双黄 (shuang huang) and 双王 (shuang wang) are homophone variants.

32. $Hih^7 Dua^4$ (铁线) is the folk name of Tiexian Reef, which is the official name. It is situated in the western part of the Zhongye Islands. Actually, there is an array of three reefs lying in the direction of northeast and southwest, so it was traditionally called $Hih^7 Dua^4$, meaning "an array of iron reefs" by the fishermen of Hainan.

33. The reef rocks on Taiping Island are naturally yellow in color, and shaped like a horse, so the fishermen of Hainan gave it the folk name $Ui^2 Dua^1 Ve^3$ (黄山马) or $Ui^2 Dua^1 Ve^3 Di^6$ (黄山马峙), meaning "a yellow horse island". The island was also named after the warship *Taiping* that was sent by the Chinese government to the Nansha Islands to take over the island after the Anti-Japanese War in 1946.

34. $Gu^2 Eh^7$ (牛轭) is the folk name of Niu'e Reef. It lies in the northeastern end of the Jiuzhang Banks and Reefs and it is the largest one among the group. It looks like a yoke when it emerges at ebb tide. Thus, it was given the name $Gu^2 Eh^7$, meaning "yoke".

35. $Lao^2 Gu^2 Lao^2$ (劳牛劳), also known as $Liu^2 Bu^6 Liu^2$ (流不流 or 刘牛刘), is the folk name of Daxian Reef, which is the official name. It is a circular reef, near which treacherous currents rapidly flow underwater, making a continuous sound caused by waves crashing against the rocks, but the water seems to flow slowly and appears motionless. Thus, the reef was given the name $Lao^2 Gu^2 Lao^2$ and $Liu^2 Bu^6 Liu^2$, meaning motionless or static, by the fishermen of Hainan. In Hainan dialect, the three characters 刘 (liu)、劳 (lao) and 流 (liu) are homophones and 牛 (niu) and 不 (bu) are also homophonic variants. For this reason, the name 劳牛劳 (laoniulao) was miswritten as 刘牛刘 (liuniuliu) and 流不流 (liubuliu).

36. $Nam^2 Id^7$ [南(忆)乙] or $Nam^2 Id^7 Di^6$ (南乙峙) is the folk name of Hongxiu Island, which is the official name. A legend goes that when the forefathers of the fishermen of Hainan first arrived at the island, they mistook it as the southernmost island of the South China Sea. Then in order to remember it, they gave it the name $Nam^2 Id^7$, meaning "to remember it". The characters 忆 and 乙 are homophones, so 南忆 (nanyi) was miswritten as 南乙 (nanyi). In addition, its official name was named after Yang Hongxiu, who was Deputy Captain of the Chinese warship *Zhongye* sent by the Chinese government to take over the South China Sea

3 The Origins and Legends of the Folk Names of the South China Sea Islands in Su Deliu Version and Peng Zhengkai Version of *Genglubu*

Islands in 1946.

37. *Sin⁴ Gao¹* （称钩） is the folk name of Jinghong Island which is the official name. It is one of the two islands of the Jiuzhang Banks and Reefs. It was given the folk name *Sin⁴ Gao¹*, meaning "hook" because the island has a curved tail resembling a hook. In addition, Jinghong Island, as the official name, was named after Wang Jinghong, an assistant leader of Zheng He who made seven voyages to the Western Seas during the reign of Emperor Chengzu (1402 – 1424) of the Ming Dynasty.

38. *Sin⁴ Gao¹ Dua⁴* （称钩线） is the folk name of Huajiao Reef, which is situated in the westernmost end of the Jiuzhang Banks and Reefs. It was given this folk name because the shape of its shoal looks like a small steelyard hook.

39. *Mag⁸ Gia⁴* （目镜）, also known as *Mag³ Gia⁴* （眼镜）, is the folk name of Siling Reef, which is the official name. It is a circular reef about 15 kilometers long from east to west. The whole reef emerges at ebb tide. On the reef, there is a lagoon separated into two smaller ones by a 60-centimeter high cay; one is in the east, the other is in the west; the two cays look very much like a pair of glasses. Thus, this reef was given the name *Mag⁸ Gia⁴* or *Mag³ Gia⁴*, meaning "a pair of glasses" by the fishermen of Hainan. In Hainan dialect, the character 目 (mu) has the same meaning as 眼 (yan), which means "eyes".

40. *Sim¹ Huang¹* ［深匡（筐）］, or *Sim¹ Huan¹* （深圈） is the folk name of Yuya Shoal. It is a deep lagoon around the reefs and so deep that its bottom can hardly be fathomed, and it is easily accessible to ships from all directions, without the need to look for deep water passes. Therefore, this shoal was named *Sim¹ Huang¹*, which means "deep basket".

41. *Vo² Mi⁶ Dua⁴* （无乜线） refers to Wumie Reef. The former is the folk name, and the latter is the official name. In the waters around this reef, there are few marine products or seafood, so the fishermen of Hainan seldom caught any fish there. For this reason, they named this reef *Vo² Mi⁶* （无乜）, which means "nothing or none". At this reef, there is an underwater shoal stretching like a long belt, so Wumie Reef was also named *Vo² Mi⁶ Dua⁴* （无乜线） by the fishermen of Hainan.

42. *Nise Zio* （女青石 or 染青石） is the folk name of Ranqingdong Reef. It was given the name because it lies to the east of Ranqing Reef. The character 东 (dong) means "east". On the other hand, the water around the area is as blue green as paint, so it was named *Nise Zio* （染青石） after the color. In its two folk

names, the character 染 (ran) was probably miswritten as 女 (nv) and 汝 (ru).

43. Bua^4 Gi （簸箕） or Po^1 Gi^1 （坡箕） is the folk name of Boji Reef, which is the official name. Its reef plate is not so large and is relatively round. There are many small rocks scattered in its central area, and it resembles a dustpan as a whole from a distance. Thus, it was given this name.

44. $Ddang^2$ $Ziang^1$ （铜章 or 铜钟） is the folk name of Nanhai Reef which is the official name. It is a complete circular reef and has passes through it. It was named after its formation or shape because it looks like a copper bell. Here, in the Hainan dialect, the characters 章 (zhang) and 钟 (zhong) are homophones, and the latter 铜钟 was probably miswritten as the former 铜章.

45. $Hhai^3$ Hao^3 Dua^4 （海口线） is the folk name of Baijiao Reef, which is the official name. It is the longest and the largest reef plate of the South China Sea. At the bottom of the plate, there is a long and wide sand belt looking like a very wide river mouth stretching into sea. Therefore, it was given the folk name based on this fact.

46. The people of Tanmen, Qionghai, Hainan usually regard Venus as a twinkling star. Guangxing Reef and Guangxingzai Reef are at the same latitude. When they sail at night, the fishermen can see the two reefs, their position on the compass and Venus on the same line, which is a good aid to navigation. Besides, the former is large and in the east, and the latter is small and in the west. For this reason, the fishermen of Hainan gave them such folk names as $Ddua^1$ $Guang^1$ Se^1 （大光星） which means "a big twinkling star" and $Guang^1$ Se^1 Gia^3 （光星仔） which means "a small twinkling star".

47. Zio^5 $Gong^1$ Li^3 ［石公篱（离）］, or Zio^5 $Gong^1$ Li^2 （石公里） is the folk name of Danwan Reef which is the official name. The fishermen of Hainan commonly venerate a huge rock above the sea as Zio^5 $Gong^1$, meaning "stone god". There are several protruding rocks surrounding Danwan Reef, forming something resembling a bamboo fence. Thus, the fishermen call it Zio^5 $Gong^1$ Li^3, which means "stone god fence". In Hainan dialect, the characters 篱, 离 and 里 are homophones, so 石公篱 was miswritten as 石公里 and 石公离.

48. $Ngou^5$ Be^6 Yi^1 （五百二 or 五百弍） is the folk name of Huanglu Reef. As for the origin of the folk name, there are two legends. One legend states that long time ago a fisherman caught a rare hawksbill that weighed 520 jin (equal to 260 kg). The other legend recounts that a fisherman happened to pick up 520 tin ingots. Obviously $Ngou^5$ Be^6 Yi^1 was named after numbers. Here the characters 弍 (er) and

3 The Origins and Legends of the Folk Names of the South China Sea Islands in Su Deliu Version and Peng Zhengkai Version of *Genglubu*

二（er）both means "two" and they are homophones.

49. *Ddan^1 Zid^7*（丹积）or *Ddan^1 Dad^7*（丹节 or 单节）is the folk name of Nantong Reef which is the official name. The reef is completely circular and has no passage, but actually its rocks are segmented with only one section of the rock above the sea, so it was given the name *Ddan^1 Dad^7*（单节）, which means "one segment" or "a single segment". In Chinese, the characters 单 and 丹 are homophones, so are the characters 节 and 积 in Hainan dialect. As a result, the characters 单节 were miswritten as 丹节 or 丹积.

50. *Vag^8 Gue^1 Dua^4*（墨瓜线）is the folk name of Nanping Reef, the official name. This area is abundant in sea cucumbers which are as black as ink and look like cucumbers in shape, so the fishermen of Hainan called sea cucumber *Vag^8 Gue^1*（墨瓜）, meaning "black sea cucumber". Besides, because there is a long shoal at the bottom, it was given another folk name, *Vag^8 Gue^1 Dua^4*, which means "black sea cucumber belt".

51. *Og^7 Log^7 Mui^2*（恶落门）is the folk name of Nanhua Reef which is the official name. Beside the reef there is a passage, it is wide inside of it and narrow outside of it. Its mouth faces southeast and is sheltered from the wind. In addition, the front of the mouth connects in such a zigzag channel that it is very difficult for vessels to enter the passage. Thus, it was given the name *Og^7 Log^7 Mui^2*（恶落门）, which means that "it is difficult for vessels to get through the passage". In the dialect of Hainan, the character 恶（e）means "difficult" and 落（luo）and 扐（le）means "enter". 恶落门 was miswritten as 荷扐门 and 阿落门.

52. *Lag^8 Mui^2*（六门）is the folk name of Liumen Reef, which is the official name. This atoll is oval in shape. It was given the name *Lag^8 Mui^2* because there are six channels or "gates" that have access to the lagoon of this reef in its southwest.

53. *Zio^5 Bua^2*（石盘）is the folk name of Bisheng Reef. Bisheng Reef is its official name. It was given the folk name by the fishermen of Hainan because the reef plate resembles an immense millstone in shape.

54. *Zio^1 Vu^5*（上戊 or 尚戊 or 上武）is the folk name of Yongshu Reef. Yongshu Reef is the official name. Here, the character 戊（wu）may refer to a mound. Yongshu Reef looks like a large mound above the sea from a distance, and thus it was given this folk name. In this entry, the characters 上戊（shangwu）, 尚戊（shangwu）and 上武（shangwu）are homophone variants.

55. *Ddang^2 Song^4*（铜铳）, also known as *Ddua^1 Ddang^2 Song^4*（大铜铳）,

is the folk name of Dongjiao Reef. The fishermen of Hainan usually call gun powder weapons 铳 (chong). A legend goes that once the fisherman found some bronze artillery pieces on the reef, so it was named *Ddang² Song⁴*, meaning "bronze guns". Compared with Huayang Reef to the east, Dongjiao Reef is bigger, so it was also given the folk name *Ddua¹ Ddang² Song⁴* （大铜铳） by the fishermen. Besides, the official name of *Ddang² Song⁴* is Dongjiao Reef, which is an atoll located in the east of the Yinqing Reefs, thus it was named Dongjiao Reef.

56. *Long⁶ Pi¹* （窿鼻 or 弄鼻 or 龙鼻） is the folk name of Xijiao Reef and the latter is the official name. In the dialect of Hainan, the characters 弄 (nong), 窿 (long) and 龙 (long) are homophones. The character 窿 (long) means "expose" and its extended meaning is "very big or huge". 窿鼻 is actually miswritten as 弄鼻 and 龙鼻. Xijiao Reef was given the folk name *Long⁶ Pi¹* because it looks like a nose with flared nostrils. Compared with the relatively small Zhongjiao Reef nearby, *Long⁶ Pi¹* (Xijiao Reef) was also given *Ddua¹ Long⁶ Pi¹* （大龙鼻 or 大弄鼻） as its second folk name.

57. *Ziao³ Gia³ Di⁶* （鸟仔峙） is the folk name of Nanwei Island. It was given this name because many birds inhabit on the island. In the dialect of Hainan, 鸟 (niao), meaning "bird", is usually called *Ziao³ Gia³* （鸟仔） which means "small bird". Thus, the island was called *Ziao³ Gia³ Di⁶*, which means "bird island". In addition, the official name is derived from Luo Zhuoying （罗卓英）, whose pseudonym was Ciwei （慈威）, and he was the governor of Guangdong Province in 1946 when the island was taken over by the Chinese fleet.

58. (*Dai¹ Hao²*) *Id⁷ Din¹* [（西头）乙辛] is the folk name of Riji Reef; the latter is the official name. The reef lies to the west of the Nansha Islands, and sailing from Nanwei Island to Riji Reef, the compass needle points towards Yi Xin (towards west). Thus, it was named *Dai¹ Hao² Id⁷ Din¹* which means "west Yi Xin", and it is one of the settlements of the Chinese fishermen at the Nansha Islands.

59. *Nam² Id⁷ Di⁶ Gia³* （南乙峙仔）, also known as *Nam² Id⁷ Dua¹ Gia³* （南乙沙仔）, is the folk name of Nanxun Reef; the latter is the official name. It is located to the west of Hongxiu Island and is a much smaller shoal than the latter. In the dialect of Hainan, *Di⁶ Gia³* （线仔 or 沙仔） refers to a small shoal.

60. *Log⁸ Sa¹* （禄沙） is the folk name of Lusha Reef, the latter being its official name. It is a coral reef situated to the northeast of Sanjiao Reef where there is a shoal, the bottom of which comes out at ebb tide. For this reason, it was also given the name *Id⁷ Dua⁴* （一线）, meaning "a long shoal" by the fishermen of Hainan.

3 The Origins and Legends of the Folk Names of the South China Sea Islands in Su Deliu Version and Peng Zhengkai Version of *Genglubu*

61. *Ui² Dua¹ Ve³ Ddang¹* (黄山马东), also known as *Ve³ Ddang¹* (马东), is the folk name of Dunqian Cay, the latter being the official name. It is situated to the east of Taiping Island, thus, it got the folk name *Ve³ Ddang¹* (马东). On the other hand, the rocks on Taiping Island are naturally yellow and are also horse-shaped. So the fishermen of Hainan named this island *Ui² Dua¹ Ve³ Ddang¹*, meaning "a yellow horse island". In addition, its official name is Dunqian Cay, named after Li Dunqian, Captain of the Chinese warship *Zhongye*, which was sent by the Chinese government to take over the South China Sea in 1946.

62. *Gao³ Ziang¹* (九章) is the folk name of the Jiuzhang Bank and Reefs. In the area, there are a lot of treacherous reefs which make it difficult for vessels to sail through. In the dialect of Hainan, 九 (jiu) usually means "a lot of or many". Here, both the characters 章 (zhang) and 障 (zhang) mean "difficulties" or "obstacles" and they are homophones.

63. *Ddang² Song⁴ Gia³* (铜铳仔) is the folk name of Huayang Reef, the latter being the official name. Compared with *Ddang² Song⁴* (Dongjiao Reef), Huayang Reef is smaller in size. In the dialect of Hainan, the character 仔 (gia) means "small", so Huayang Reef was given the folk name *Ddang² Song⁴ Gia³* by the fishermen of Hainan. Geographically, the former is located to the east of the latter.

64. *Gong⁴ Se⁵ Dua¹* (贡士沙) is the folk name of Gongshi Reef located in the northeast part of the Shuangzi Reefs in the Nansha Islands, and apart one nautical mile from Beizi Island. Gongshi Reef is in a shape of triangle and full of submerged shoals with no water gate. The shoals rise from the sea when tiding and are submerged when ebbing.

65. *Nai⁶ Lo² Gag⁷* (奈罗角), also known as *Nai⁶ Lo² Gog⁷* (奈罗谷), the folk name of Yongdeng Shoal, is located 16 nautical miles northeast of the Shuangzi Islands. It is a sunken, medium-sized deep-sea atoll. Looking like a spindle, it covers an area of 64 square kilometers. It forms a complex atoll together with Lesi Shoal.

66. *Hin² Ddin⁵ Dua¹* (犬殿沙) or *Vue² Gao³* (梅九), officially known as Meijiu Reef, is located about 2 nautical miles southwest of Tiezhi Reef. It is a V-shaped reef in the middle of the Zhongye Reefs, with an eastward opening. Meijiu Reef is under the jurisdiction of Sansha City, Hainan province.

67. *Ddia³ Gai⁴ Di⁶* (锅盖峙) is the folk name of Anbo Cay, the latter being the official name. It is about 300 meters long and 140 meters wide, with an area of

about 0.02 square kilometers and an altitude of about 2 meters. Overgrown with weeds, it has no trees and is short of fresh water. The shape of the cay is like a pot cover, so Chinese fishermen call it $Ddia^3$ Gai^4 Di^6, meaning "pot cover" in Hainan dialect.

68. $Long^6$ Pi^1 Gia^3 (弄鼻仔) is the folk name of Zhongjiao Reef. It is relatively smaller than Xijiao Reef nearby, which was given the folk name $Long^6$ Pi^1 (龙鼻) because it looks like a nose with flared nostrils, so gaining the name $Long^6$ Pi^1 Gia^3.

69. $Siah^7$ Gue^1 Dua^4 (赤瓜线) is the folk name of Chigua Reef, the latter being the official name. It is a submerged reef in the Jiuzhang Banks and Reefs, located at the southwest end of the atoll. The outer ring of the reef has brown volcanic rocks and the inner ring is white coral reef. The fishermen of Hainan usually call it "chigua belt" because the place produces abundant sea cucumbers.

70. Gao^1 Bud^8 (高佛) or Gao^1 Bu^6 (高不), the folk name of Bolan Reef which is the official name. It is located to the northern side of the Zhenghe Reefs, elliptical in shape, about 1.8 kilometers long and 1.3 kilometers wide. It submerges with rising tide and emerges with the ebb.

4 Tables

4.1 Table of the Information about the South China Sea Islands in Su Deliu and Peng Zhengkai Versions of *Genglubu*

（苏德柳本和彭正楷本《更路簿》南海诸岛中英文信息一览表）

序号 No.	标准中文名称 Official Chinese Names	汉语拼音 Chinese Pinyin	标准英文名称 Official English Names	原英文名称 Original English Names	渔民名称（俗名）Chinese Fishermen's Folk Names	渔民名称读音 Pronunciation of the Folk Names	地理坐标 Geographical Coordinates	
							北纬（N）	东经（E）
1	西沙群岛	Xīshā Qúndǎo	The Xisha Islands	Paracel Islands	东海	Ddang¹ Hhai³	—	—
2	南岛	Nán Dǎo	Nandao Island	South Island	三峙，三岛	Da¹ Di⁶，Da¹ Ddao²	16°57′	112°20′
3	北礁	Běi Jiāo	Beijiao Reef	North Reef	干豆，刚豆	Gan¹ Ddao¹，Gang¹ Ddao¹	17°05′	111°30′
4	永乐群岛	Yǒnglè Qúndǎo	The Yongle Islands	Crescent Chain (Group)	西八岛，下八岛下峙，石塘，石棠	Dai¹ Boi⁶ Ddao²，E⁵ Boi⁶ Ddao²，E⁵ Di⁶，Zio⁵ Ddo²，Zio⁵ Ho²	15°46′ – 17°07′	111°11′ – 112°06′

111

（续表）

序号 No.	标准中文名称 Official Chinese Names	汉语拼音 Chinese Pinyin	标准英文名称 Official English Names	原英文名称 Original English Names	渔民名称（俗名）Chinese Fishermen's Folk Names	渔民名称读音 Pronunciation of the Folk Names	地理坐标 Geographical Coordinates	
							北纬（N）	东经（E）
5	宣德群岛	Xuāndé Qúndǎo	The Xuande Islands	Amphitrite Group	上七岛，东七岛，上峙	$Zio^1\ Sid^7\ Ddao^2$, $Ddang^1\ Sid^7\ Ddao^2$, $Zio^1\ Di^6$	16°43' – 17°00'	112°10' – 112°54'
6	玉琢礁	Yùzhuó Jiāo	Yuzhuo Reef	Vuladdore Reef	二筐，二塘，二圈，㳀圈，二㧍	$Yi^1\ Hiang^1$, $Yi^1\ Ddo^2$, $Yi^1\ Huan^1$, $Si^4\ Huan^1$, $Yi^1\ Huang^4$	16°19' – 16°22'	111°57' – 112°06'
7	浪花礁	Lànghuā Jiāo	Langhua Reef	Bombay Reef	三匡，三圈，三㧍	$Da^1\ Huang^1$, $Da^1\ Hiang^1$, $Da^1\ Huan^1$, $Da^1\ Huang^4$	16°01' – 16°05'	112°26' – 112°36'
8	羚羊礁	Língyáng Jiāo	Lingyang Reef	Antelope Reef	筐仔，圈仔，筐仔峙，筐仔首，圈岛	$Hiang^1\ Gia^3$, $Huan^1\ Gia^3$, $Hiang^1\ Gia^3\ Di^6$, $Hiang^1\ Gia^3\ Hao^2$, $Huan^1\ Ddao^2$	16°28'	111°35'
9	永兴岛	Yǒngxīng Dǎo	Yongxing Island	Woody Island	猫注，猫住，吧注，猫岛，把岛	$Va^1\ Du^4$, $Va^1\ Du^4$, $Ba^5\ Du^4$, $Va^1\ Ddao^2$, $Be^4\ Ddao^2$	16°50'	112°20'
10	晋卿门	Jìnqīngmén	Jinqing Pass	—	四江门	$Di^4\ Giang^1\ Mui^2$	16°27'	111°44'

(续表)

序号 No.	标准中文名称 Official Chinese Names	汉语拼音 Chinese Pinyin	标准英文名称 Official English Names	原英文名称 Original English Names	渔民名称(俗名) Chinese Fishermen's Folk Names	渔民名称读音 Pronunciation of the Folk Names	地理坐标 Geographical Coordinates	
							北纬(N)	东经(E)
11	晋卿岛	Jìnqīng Dǎo	Jinqing Island	Drumond Island	四江,四江岛,世江峙	Di⁴ Giang¹, Di⁴ Giang¹ Ddao², Di⁴ Giang¹ Di⁶	16°28′	111°44′
12	华光礁	Huáguāng Jiāo	Huaguang Reef	Discovery Reef	大筐,大圈,大圈头,大圈,大圲,大圈尾	Ddua¹ Hiang¹, Ddua¹ Ddo², Ddua¹ Huan¹, Ddua¹ Huan¹ Hao², Ddua¹ Huan¹ Hao², Ddua¹ Huang¹, Ddua¹ Huang⁴, Ddua¹ Huan¹ Vue³	16°09′ – 16°17″	111°34′ – 111°49′
13	银屿	Yín Yǔ	Yinyu Island	Observation Bank	银峙	Ngin² Di⁶	16°35′	111°42′
14	鸭公岛	Yāgōng Dǎo	Yagong Island	—	鸭公屿,鸭公岛	A⁶ Gong¹ Yi³, A⁶ Gong¹ Ddao²	16°34′	111°41′
15	东岛	Dōng Dǎo	Dongdao Island	Lincoln Island	猫兴,猫兴峙,巴兴,吧兴,猫英,把兴,爸兴	Va¹ Hheng¹, Va¹ Hheng¹ Di⁶, Ba² Hheng¹, Ba⁵ Hheng¹, Va¹ Eng¹, Be³ Hheng¹, Pa² Hheng¹	16°40′	112°44′

(续表)

序号 No.	标准中文名称 Official Chinese Names	汉语拼音 Chinese Pinyin	标准英文名称 Official English Names	原英文名称 Original English Names	渔民名称（俗名）Chinese Fishermen's Folk Names	渔民名称读音 Pronunciation of the Folk Names	地理坐标 Geographical Coordinates	
							北纬（N）	东经（E）
16	中建岛	Zhōngjiàn Dǎo	Zhongjian Island	Triton Island	半路，半路峙，半路岛，螺岛	Bua⁴ Lou¹，Bua⁴ Lou¹ Di⁶，Bua⁴ Lou¹ Ddao²，Lo² Ddao²	15°47′	111°12′
17	金银岛	Jīnyín Dǎo	Jinyin Island	Money Island	尾峙，尾岛	Vue³ Di⁶，Vue³ Ddao²	16°27′	111°31′
18	盘石屿	Pánshí Yǔ	Panshi Island	Passu Keah	白树仔，白峙仔	Be⁵ Siu¹ Gia³，Be⁵ Di⁶ Gia³	16°02′ – 16°05′	111°45′ – 111°50′
19	红草门	Hóngcǎomén	Hongcao Pass	—	红草门	Ang² Sao³ Mui²	16°53′	112°21′
20	高尖石	Gāojiānshí	the Gaojian Rocks	Pyramid Rocks	尖石，双帆	Ziam¹ Zio⁵，Diang¹ Pan²	16°35′	112°38′
21	西沙洲	Xī Shāzhōu	Xisha Sand Bank	West Sand	船岩尾，船坎尾，船嵌尾，船暗尾	Dun² Ngam² Vue³，Dun² Hiam² Vue³，Ham⁴ Vue³，Dun² Am⁴ Vue³	16°59′	112°13′
22	老粗门	Lǎocūmén	Laocu Pass	—	老粗门，老粗大门	Lao⁵ Sou¹ Mui²，Lao⁵ Sou¹ Ddua¹ Mui²	16°31′	111°35′

(续表)

序号 No.	标准中文名称 Official Chinese Names	汉语拼音 Chinese Pinyin	标准英文名称 Official English Names	原英文名称 Original English Names	渔民名称（俗名） Chinese Fishermen's Folk Names	渔民名称读音 Pronunciation of the Folk Names	地理坐标 Geographical Coordinates	
							北纬（N）	东经（E）
23	珊瑚岛	Shānhú Dǎo	Shanhu Island	Pattle Island	老粗岛，老粗峙	Lao⁵ Sou¹ Ddao², Lao⁵ Sou¹ Di⁶	16°32′	111°36′
24	琛航岛	Chēnháng Dǎo	Chenhang Island	Duncan Island	三脚，大三脚岛，三脚岛，三脚大峙，三脚峙	Da¹ Ha¹, Ddua¹ Da¹ Ha¹ Ddao², Da¹ Ha¹ Ddao², Da¹ Ha¹ Ddua¹ Di⁶, Da¹ Ha¹ Di⁶	16°27′	111°43′
25	全富岛	Quánfù Dǎo	Quanfu Island	—	全富峙，全富，曲手，全副	Suan² Pu⁴ Di⁶, Suan² Pu⁴, Hiag⁷ Siu³, Suan² Pu⁵	16°35′	111°40′
26	南沙洲	Nán Shāzhōu	Nansha Sand	South Sand	红草一，红草，红草岛，红草角	Ang² Sao³ Id⁷, Ang² Sao³, Ang² Sao³ Ddao², Ang² Sao³ Gag⁷	16°56′	112°21′
27	中沙洲	Zhōng Shāzhōu	Zhongsha Sand	Middle Sand	红草二	Ang² Sao³ Yi¹	16°56′	112°21′
28	北沙洲	Běi Shāzhōu	Beisha Sand	North Sand	红草三	Ang² Sao³ Da¹	16°56′	112°20′

(续表)

序号 No.	标准中文名称 Official Chinese Names	汉语拼音 Chinese Pinyin	标准英文名称 Official English Names	原英文名称 Original English Names	渔民名称(俗名) Chinese Fishermen's Folk Names	渔民名称读音 Pronunciation of the Folk Names	地理坐标 Geographical Coordinates	
							北纬 (N)	东经 (E)
29	南沙群岛	Nánshā Qúndǎo	The Nansha Islands	Spratly Islands	北海，长沙	Bag^7 Hhai^3，Siang^2 Sa^1	—	—
30	双子群礁	Shuāngzǐ Qúnjiāo	The Shuangzi Islands	The Two Islands, North Danger. Cay, North Danger Reef	双峙，奈罗，双峙沙仔	Diang^1 Di^6，Nai^6 Lo^2，Diang^1 Di^6 Dua^1 Gia	11°23' – 11°28'	114°19' – 114°25'
31	道明群礁	Dàomíng Qúnjiāo	The Daoming Islands	Loaita Bank and Reefs	—	—	10°40' – 10°55'	114°19' – 114°37'
32	乐斯暗沙	Lèsī Ànshā	Lesi Shoal	Lys Shoal	红草线，红草沙排，洪草沙排，南奈罗角	Ang^2 Sao^3 Dua^4，Ang^2 Sao^3 Dua^4 Bai^2，Ang^2 Sao^3 Hhong^2 Sao^3 Dua^1 Bai^2，Dua^1 Bai^2，Nam^2 Nai^6 Lo^2 Gag^7	11°19' – 11°22'	114°35' – 114°39'

4 Tables

（续表）

序号 No.	标准中文名称 Official Chinese Names	汉语拼音 Chinese Pinyin	标准英文名称 Official English Names	原英文名称 Original English Names	渔民名称（俗名）Chinese Fishermen's Folk Names	渔民名称读音 Pronunciation of the Folk Names	地理坐标 Geographical Coordinates	
							北纬（N）	东经（E）
33	中业岛	Zhōngyè Dǎo	Zhongye Island	Thitu Island	铁峙，铁岛，铁峙沙	Hih⁷ Di·⁶，Hih⁷ Ddao²，Hih⁷ Di·⁶ Dua¹	11°03'	114°17'
34	西月岛	Xīyuè Dǎo	Xiyue Island	West York Island	红草峙，红草	Ang² Sao³ Di·⁶，Hhong² Sao³	11°05'	115°02'
35	长滩	Cháng Tān	Changtan Bank	—	（红草）线排，沙排	(Ang² Sao³) Dua⁴ Bai²，Dua¹ Bai²	10°55' – 11°09'	114°37' – 114°49'
36	南钥岛	Nányuè Dǎo	Nanyue Island	Loaita Island/ South Island of Hors	第三，第三峙，第三岛，下三	Ddoi¹ Da¹，Ddoi¹ Di·⁶，Ddoi¹ Da¹ Ddao¹，E⁵ Da¹	10°40'	114°25'
37	马欢岛	Mǎhuān Dǎo	Mahuan Island	Nanshan Island	大罗孔，罗孔，罗孔岛，罗孔峙，锣孔，那孔	Ddua¹ Lo² Hong²，Lo² Hong²，Lo² Hong² Ddao²，Lo² Hong² Di·⁶，Lo² Hong²，Na⁴ Hong²	10°44'	115°48'
38	火艾礁	Huǒ'ài Jiāo	Huo'ai Reef	Balagtas Reef/ Irving Reef	火哀	Hhue³ Ai¹	10°53'	114°56'

(续表)

序号 No.	标准中文名称 Official Chinese Names	汉语拼音 Chinese Pinyin	标准英文名称 Official English Names	原英文名称 Original English Names	渔民名称（俗名） Chinese Fishermen's Folk Names	渔民名称读音 Pronunciation of the Folk Names	地理坐标 Geographical Coordinates	
							北纬 (N)	东经 (E)
39	库归礁	Kùguī Jiāo	Kugui Reef	—	裤归，裤归线仔，裤归沙仔，裤归，裤归沙仔	Hou⁴ Gui, Hou⁴ Gui Dua⁴ Gia³, Hou⁴ Gui Dua¹ Gia³, Hou⁴ Ddang¹, Hou⁴ Gui, Hou⁴ Dua¹ Gia	10°44′ – 10°46′	114°35′
40	三角礁	Sānjiǎo Jiāo	Sanjiao Reef	Livock Reef/ Irving Reef	三角	Da¹ Gag⁷	10°10′ – 10°13′	115°16′ – 115°19′
41	美济礁	Měijì Jiāo	Meiji Reef	Mischief (South) Reef	双门，双沙	Diang¹ Mui², Diang¹ Sa¹	9°52′ – 9°56′	115°30′ – 115°35′
42	五方礁	Wǔfāng Jiāo	Wufang Reef	Jackson Atoll/ Mischief North Reef	五孔，五风	Ngou⁵ Hong², Ngou⁵ Hhuang¹	10°27′ – 10°32′	115°42′ – 115°48′
43	五方尾	Wǔfāngwěi	Wufangwei Reef	Hamspon Reef	—	—	10°27′	115°44′

(续表)

序号 No.	标准中文 名称 Official Chinese Names	汉语拼音 Chinese Pinyin	标准英文名称 Official English Names	原英文名称 Original English Names	渔民名称（俗名） Chinese Fishermen's Folk Names	渔民名称读音 Pronunciation of the Folk Names	地理坐标 Geographical Coordinates	
							北纬（N）	东经（E）
44	五方南	Wǔfāngnán	Wufangnan Reef	Petch Reef	—	—	10°27′	115°47′
45	五方西	Wǔfāngxī	Wufangxi Reef	Deane Reef	—	—	10°30′	115°43′
46	五方北	Wǔfāngběi	Wufangbei Reef	Hoare Reef	—	—	10°32′	115°44′
47	五方头	Wǔfāngtóu	Wufangtou Reef	Dickinson Reef	—	Ngou[5] Hhuang[1] Hao	10°32′	115°48′
48	仁爱礁	Rén'ài Jiāo	Ren'ai Reef	Second Thomas Shoal	断节，断节线	Ddui[5] Dad[7], Ddui[5] Dad[7] Dua[4]	9°39′ – 9°48′	115°51′ – 115°54′
49	仙娥礁	Xiān'é Jiāo	Xian'e Reef	Alicia Annie Reef	乌串，乌串	Ziao Shua	9°22′ – 9°26′	115°26′ – 115°28′
50	信义礁	Xìnyì Jiāo	Xinyi Reef	First Thomas Shoal	双挑，双担	Diang[1] Hiao[1], Diang[1] Dda[1]	9°20′ – 9°21′	115°54′ – 115°58′
51	牛车轮礁	Niūchēlún Jiāo	Niuchelun Reef	Boxall Reef	牛车英	Gu[2] Sia[1] Eng[1]	9°36′	116°10′

(续表)

序号 No.	标准中文名称 Official Chinese Names	汉语拼音 Chinese Pinyin	标准英文名称 Official English Names	原英文名称 Original English Names	渔民名称（俗名）Chinese Fishermen's Folk Names	渔民名称读音 Pronunciation of the Folk Names	地理坐标 Geographical Coordinates	
							北纬（N）	东经（E）
52	海口礁	Hǎikǒu Jiāo	Haikou Reef	Investigator N. E. Shoal	脚跛	Ha¹ Buad⁷	9°11'	116°27'
53	舰长礁	Jiànzhǎng Jiāo	Jianzhang Reef	Royal Captain Shoal	石龙	Zio⁵ Liang²	9°02'	116°40'
54	仙宾礁	Xiānbīn Jiāo	Xianbin Reef	Sabina Shoal	鱼鳞	Hhu² Lin²	9°43'–9°49'	116°25'–116°37'
55	蓬勃暗沙	Péngbó Ànshā	Pengbo Shoal	Bombay Shoal	东头乙辛	Ddang¹ Hao² Id⁷ Din¹	9°27'	116°56'
56	鲎藤礁	Hòuténg Jiāo	Houteng Reef	Iroquois Reef	蠧藤，号藤	Hhao¹ Ddin² , Hho¹ Ddin²	10°37'	116°10'
57	半月礁	Bànyuè Jiāo	Banyue Reef	Half Moon Shoal	海公	Hhai³ Gong¹	8°54'	116°17'
58	安达礁	Āndá Jiāo	Anda Reef	Eldad Reef	银饼，银饼沙，银锅	Ngin² Bia³ , Ngin² Bia³ Dua¹ , Ngin² Ddia³	10°21'	114°42'
59	半路礁	Bànlù Jiāo	Banlu Reef	Hardy Reef	半路，半路线，伴路	Bua⁴ Lou¹ , Bua⁴ Lou¹ Dua⁴ , Pua⁵ Lou¹	10°08'	116°08'

(续表)

序号 No.	标准中文名称 Official Chinese Names	汉语拼音 Chinese Pinyin	标准英文名称 Official English Names	原英文名称 Original English Names	渔民名称（俗名）Chinese Fishermen's Folk Names	渔民名称读音 Pronunciation of the Folk Names	地理坐标 Geographical Coordinates	
							北纬 (N)	东经 (E)
60	杨信沙洲	Yángxìn Shāzhōu	Yangxin Cay	Lankiam Cay	铜锅，铜金，铜金峙，铜金峙仔	$Ddang^2$ $Ddia^3$, $Ddang^2$ Gim^1, $Ddang^2$ Gim^1 Di^6, $Ddang^2$ Gim^1 Di^6 Gia^3	10°43′	114°32′
61	渚碧礁	Zhǔbì Jiāo	Zhubi Reef	Subi (Soubi) Reef	丑未，丑未沙，丑未线	Siu^3 Vi^1, Siu^3 Vi^1 Dua^1, Siu^3 Vi^1 Dua^4	10°54′ – 10°56′	114°04′ – 114°07′
62	铁峙礁	Tiězhì Jiāo	Tiezhi Reef	—	铁岛线排，铁峙线排，铁峙沙排	Hih^7 $Ddao^2$ Dua^4 Bai^2, Hih^7 Di^6 Dua^4 Bai^2, Hih^7 Di^6 Dua^1 Bai^2	11°05′	114°23′
63	双黄沙洲	Shuānghuáng Shāzhōu	Shuanghuang Cay	—	双黄，双王线仔	$Diang^1$ $Uang^2$, $Diang^1$ $Uang^2$, $Diang^1$ Dua^4 Gia^3	10°42′ – 10°43′	114°19′ – 114°20′
64	铁线礁	Tiěxiàn Jiāo	Tiexian Reef	—	铁线，铁沙，铁峙沙，铁峙线	Hih^7 Dua^4, Hih^7 Dua^1, Hih^7 Di^6 Dua^1, Hih^7 Di^6 Dua^4	11°01′ – 11°04′	114°11′ – 114°16′

(续表)

序号 No.	标准中文名称 Official Chinese Names	汉语拼音 Chinese Pinyin	标准英文名称 Official English Names	原英文名称 Original English Names	渔民名称（俗名）Chinese Fishermen's Folk Names	渔民名称读音 Pronunciation of the Folk Names	地理坐标 Geographical Coordinates	
							北纬（N）	东经（E）
65	太平岛	Tàipíng Dǎo	Taiping Island	Itu Aba Island	黄山马，黄山马峙，黄山马岛	$Ui^2 Dua^1 Ve^3$, $Ui^2 Dua^1 Ve^3 Di^6$, $Ui^2 Dua^1 Ve^3 Ddao^2$	10°23′	114°22′
66	牛轭礁	Niú'è Jiāo	Niu'e Reef	Whitsum Reef	牛轭，牛厄，五厄，牛轭沙，牛轭线	$Gu^2 Eh^7$, $Gu^2 Eg^7$, $Ngou^5 Eg^7$, $Gu^2 Zi^1$, $Gu^2 Eh^7 Dua^1$, $Gu^2 Eh^7 Dua^4$	9°57′ – 10°00′	114°36′ – 114°40′
67	大现礁	Dàxiàn Jiāo	Daxian Reef	Discovery Great Reef	劳牛劳，劳牛劳线，流不流，老牛老，老无老，捞牛捞	$Lao^2 Gu^2 Lao^2$, $Lao^2 Gu^2 Lao^2 Dua^4$, $Lao^5 Gu^2 Lao^2$, $Liu^6 Bu^1 Liu^2$, $Lao^5 Vo^2 Lao^5$, $Lao^2 Gu^2 Lao^2$	10°00′ – 10°08′	113°52′ – 113°53′
68	鸿庥岛	Hóngxiū Dǎo	Hongxiu Island	Namyit Island	南乙，南乙峙，南密，南密峙，南笔，南秘岛，南箕	$Nam^2 Id^7$, $Nam^2 Id^7 Di^6$, $Nam^2 Mid^8$, $Nam^2 Mid^8 Di^6$, $Nam^2 Bid^7$, $Nam^2 Mid^7 Ddao^2$, $Nam^2 Zin^1$	10°11′	114°22′

(续表)

序号 No.	标准中文名称 Official Chinese Names	汉语拼音 Chinese Pinyin	标准英文名称 Official English Names	原英文名称 Original English Names	渔民名称（俗名） Chinese Fishermen's Folk Names	渔民名称读音 Pronunciation of the Folk Names	地理坐标 Geographical Coordinates	
							北纬（N）	东经（E）
69	景宏岛	Jǐnghóng Dǎo	Jinghong Island	Sin Cowe Island	秤钩峙，称钩，称钩峙，称钩岛，称沟，浅沟峙	Sin⁴ Gao¹ Di⁶, Sin⁴ Gao¹ Sin⁴ Gao¹ Di⁶, Sin⁴ Gao¹ Ddao², Sin⁴ Gao¹, Sin³ Gao¹ Di⁶	9°53′	114°20′
70	华礁	Huá Jiāo	Huajiao Reef	Loveless Reef	秤钩线	Sin⁴ Gao¹ Dua⁴	9°51′	114°16′
71	司令礁	Sīlìng Jiāo	Siling Reef	Commodore Reef	目镜，眼镜	Mag⁸ Gia⁴, Mag³ Gia⁴	8°22′– 8°24′	115°11′– 115°17′
72	榆亚暗沙	Yúyà Ànshā	Yuya Shoal	Investigator Shoal	深匡，深圈	Sim¹ Huang¹, Sim¹ Huan¹	8°07′– 8°14′	114°30′– 114°50′
73	无乜礁	Wúmiē Jiāo	Wumie Reef	Pigeon Reef/ Tennent Reef	无乜线，无乜沙	Vo² Mi⁶ Dua⁴, Vo² Mi⁶ Dua¹	8°50′– 8°53′	114°38′– 114°41′
74	染青东礁	Rǎnqīng Dōngjiāo	Ranqing East Reef	Ross Reef	女青石，染青石	Nise Zio	9°54′	114°36′
75	簸箕礁	Bòjī Jiāo	Boji Reef	Erica Reef	簸箕，坡箕，半簸	Bua⁴ Gi¹, Po¹ Gi¹, Bua⁴ Gi¹	8°06′	114°08′

(续表)

序号 No.	标准中文名称 Official Chinese Names	汉语拼音 Chinese Pinyin	标准英文名称 Official English Names	原英文名称 Original English Names	渔民名称（俗名）Chinese Fishermen's Folk Names	渔民名称读音 Pronunciation of the Folk Names	地理坐标 Geographical Coordinates	
							北纬 (N)	东经 (E)
76	南海礁	Nánhǎi Jiāo	Nanhai Reef	Mariveles Reef	铜钟，铜章	Ddang² Ziang¹	7°56' – 8°00'	113°53' – 113°58'
77	柏礁	Bǎi Jiāo	Baijiao Reef	Barque Canada Reef	海口线，海口沙	Hhai³ Hao³ Dua⁴, Hhai³ Hao³ Dua¹	8°04' – 8°17'	113°15' – 113°23'
78	光星仔礁	Guāngxīngzǎi Jiāo	Guangxingzai Reef	Ardasier Reef	光星仔	Guang¹ Se¹ Gia³	7°37'	113°56'
79	光星礁	Guāngxīng Jiāo	Guangxing Reef	Dallas Reef	光星，大光星	Guang¹ Se¹, Ddua¹ Guang¹ Se¹	7°36' – 7°38'	113°45' – 113°50'
80	弹丸礁	Dànwán Jiāo	Danwan Reef	Swallow Reef	石公篱，石公里	Zio⁵ Gong¹ Li², Zio⁵ Gong¹ Li³	7°23'	113°50'
81	皇路礁	Huánglù Jiāo	Huanglu Reef	Royal Charotte Reef	五百二，五百弍	Ngou⁵ Be⁶ Yi¹	6°57'	113°35'
82	南通礁	Nántōng Jiāo	Nantong Reef	Louisa Reef	丹积，丹节	Ddan¹ Zid⁷, Ddan¹ Dad⁷	6°20'	113°14'
83	南屏礁	Nánpíng Jiāo	Nanping Reef	Hayes Reef	墨瓜线	Vag⁸ Gue¹ Dua⁴	5°22'	112°38'

(续表)

序号 No.	标准中文名称 Official Chinese Names	汉语拼音 Chinese Pinyin	标准英文名称 Official English Names	原英文名称 Original English Names	渔民名称（俗名）Chinese Fishermen's Folk Names	渔民名称读音 Pronunciation of the Folk Names	地理坐标 Geographical Coordinates	
							北纬 (N)	东经 (E)
84	南华礁	Nánhuá Jiāo	Nanhua Reef	Cornwallis South Reef	恶落门、荷弄门、荷陆门、荷落门、荷劝门、荷乐门、恶浪门、荷汞门、符劝门、荷浪门、下落门、荷那门、荷方门	$Og^7 Log^7 Mui^2, Hho^2 Long^6 Mui^2, Hho^2 Lag^8 Mui^2, Hho^2 Log^7 Mui^2, Hho^2 Leg^7 Mui^2, Hho^2 Log^8 Mui, Og^7 Lang^6 Mui^2, Hho^2 Log^8 Mui^2, Hho^2 Pu^2 Leg^7 Mui^2, Hho^2 Lang^6 Mui^2, E^5 Log^7 Mui^2, Hho^2 Na^4 Mui^2, Hho^2 Lad^8 Mui^2$	8°40′– 8°46′	114°10′– 114°12′
85	六门礁	Liùmén Jiāo	Liumen Reef	Alison Reef	六门	$Lag^8 Mui^2$	8°46′– 8°50′	113°54′– 114°03′
86	毕生礁	Bìshēng Jiāo	Bisheng Reef	Pearson Reef	石盘	$Zio^5 Bua^2$	8°56′– 8°59′	113°39′– 113°44′

(续表)

序号 No.	标准中文名称 Official Chinese Names	汉语拼音 Chinese Pinyin	标准英文名称 Official English Names	原英文名称 Original English Names	渔民名称（俗名）Chinese Fishermen's Folk Names	渔民名称读音 Pronunciation of the Folk Names	地理坐标 Geographical Coordinates	
							北纬 (N)	东经 (E)
87	永暑礁	Yǒngshǔ Jiāo	Yongshu Reef	Fiery Cross Reef/N. W. Investigator Reef	上戊，尚戊，象武	Zio^1 Vu^5, Zio^1 Vu^5, Sio^5 Vu^3	9°30′–9°40′	112°53′–113°04′
88	东礁	Dōng Jiāo	Dongjiao Reef	East London Reef/East Reef	大铜铳，铜铳	$Ddua^1$ $Ddang^2$ $Song^4$, $Ddang^2$ $Song^4$	8°48′–8°50′	112°34′–112°40′
89	尹庆群礁	Yǐnqìng Qúnjiāo	the Yinqing Reefs	London Reefs	—	—	8°48′–8°55′	112°12′–112°53′
90	西礁	Xī Jiāo	Xijiao Reef	West (London) Reef	大弄鼻，龙鼻，弄鼻	$Ddua^1$ $Long^6$ Pi^1, $Long^6$ Pi^1	8°49′–8°53′	112°12′–112°17′
91	南威岛	Nánwēi Dǎo	Nanwei Island	Spratly Island	鸟仔峙	$Ziao^3$ Gia^3 Di^6	8°39′	111°55′
92	日积礁	Rìjī Jiāo	Riji Reef	Ladd Reef	西头乙辛	Dai^1 Hao^2 Id^7 Din^1	8°39′–8°40′	111°39′–112°42′

(续表)

序号 No.	标准中文名称 Official Chinese Names	汉语拼音 Chinese Pinyin	标准英文名称 Official English Names	原英文名称 Original English Names	渔民名称（俗名） Chinese Fishermen's Folk Names	渔民名称读音 Pronunciation of the Folk Names	地理坐标 Geographical Coordinates	
							北纬 (N)	东经 (E)
93	南薰礁	Nánxūn Jiāo	Nanxun Reef	Gaven Reef	南乙峙仔，南乙沙仔，南乙线仔，南密线仔，南秘线仔，沙仔	Nam² Id⁷ Di⁶ Gia³，Nam² Id⁷ Dua¹ Gia³，Nam² Id Dua⁴ Gia³，Nam² Mid⁸ Dua⁴ Gia³，Nam² Mid⁷ Dua⁴ Gia³，Dua¹ Gia³	10°10′–10°13′	114°13′–114°15′
94	禄沙礁	Lùshā Jiāo	Lusha Reef	Hopps Reef	禄沙，一线	Log⁸ Sa¹，Id⁷ Dua⁴	10°14′	115°22′
95	敦谦沙洲	Dūnqiān Shāzhōu	Dunqian Cay	Sandy Cay	马东，黄山马东，黄山马东峙	Ve³ Ddang¹，Ui² Dua¹ Ve³ Ddang¹，Ui² Dua¹ Ve³ Ddang¹ Di⁶	10°23′	114°28′
96	九章群礁	Jiǔzhāng Qúnjiāo	the Jiuzhang Banks and Reefs	Union Banks & Reefs/Union Tablemount	九章	Gao³ Ziang¹	9°42′–10°00′	114°15′–114°40′
97	华阳礁	Huáyáng Jiāo	Huayang Reef	Cuarteron Reef	铜铳仔	Ddang² Song⁴ Gia³	8°51′–8°52′	112°50′–112°53′

(续表)

序号 No.	标准中文名称 Official Chinese Names	汉语拼音 Chinese Pinyin	标准英文名称 Official English Names	原英文名称 Original English Names	渔民名称（俗名）Chinese Fishermen's Folk Names	渔民名称读音 Pronunciation of the Folk Names	地理坐标 Geographical Coordinates	
							北纬（N）	东经（E）
98	奈罗礁	Nàiluó Jiāo	Nailuo Reef	South Reef	奈罗线仔，奈罗沙仔，下峙沙仔，双峙沙仔，沙仔	Nai⁶ Lo² Dua⁴ Gia³, Nai⁶ Lo² Dua¹ Gia³, E⁵ Di⁶ Dua¹ Gia³, Diang¹ Di⁶ Dua¹ Gia³, Dua¹ Gia³	11°23′	114°19′
99	贡士礁	Gòngshì Jiāo	Gongshi Reef	North Reef	贡士沙，贡士线	Gong⁴ Se⁵ Dua¹, Gong⁴ Se⁵ Dua⁴	11°28′	114°24′
100	北子岛	Běizǐ Dǎo	Beizi Island	North East Cay	奈罗峙，奈罗	Nai⁶ Lo² Di⁶, Nai⁶ Lo²	11°27′	114°22′
101	永登暗沙	Yǒngdēng Ànshā	Yongdeng Shoal	Trident Shoal	奈罗角，奈罗谷	Nai⁶ Lo² Gag⁷, Nai⁶ Lo² Gog⁷	11°23′ – 11°31′	114°38′ – 114°44′
102	安波沙洲	Ānbō Shāzhōu	Anbo Cay	Amboyna Cay	锅盖峙	Ddia³ Gai⁴ Di⁶	7°53′	112°56′
103	中礁	Zhōng Jiāo	Zhongjiao Reef	Central (London) Reef	弄鼻仔	Long⁶ Pi¹ Gia³	8°55′	112°22′
104	赤瓜礁	Chìguā Jiāo	Chigua Reef	Mabini Reef/ Johnson Reef	赤瓜线	Siah⁷ Gue¹ Dua⁴	9°42′	114°17′

(续表)

序号 No.	标准中文名称 Official Chinese Names	汉语拼音 Chinese Pinyin	标准英文名称 Official English Names	原英文名称 Original English Names	渔民名称（俗名） Chinese Fishermen's Folk Names	渔民名称读音 Pronunciation of the Folk Names	地理坐标 Geographical Coordinates	
							北纬（N）	东经（E）
105	舶兰礁	Bólán Jiāo	Bolan Reef	Petley Reef	高佛，高不	Gao¹ Bud⁸, Gao¹ Bu⁶	10°25′	114°35′
106	梅九礁	Méijiǔ Jiāo	Meijiu Reef	—	梅九，大殿沙，大殿沙	Vue² Gao³, Hin² Ddin⁵ Dua¹, Ddua¹ Ddin⁵ Dua¹	11°03′	114°19′
107	中南暗沙	Zhōngnán Ànshā	Zhongnan Shoal	Dreyer Shoal/ Dreyer Bank	长沙线	Dua¹ Sa¹	13°57′	115°24′

说明：

1. 此表中，南海诸岛的信息主要来源于广东省地名委员会《南海诸岛地名资料汇编》，广东省地图出版社1987年版。

2. 从表中信息可以发现，我国南海诸岛"原英文名称"都是西方殖民者命名的，有些英文名称有两个名称，而有些岛礁却没有原英文名称。所以，制定我国南海诸岛的标准英文名称很有必要。本研究旨在达到这一目的。详见贾绍东《南海诸岛名称英译探讨——以苏德柳抄本更路簿为例》，载《南海学刊》2021年第3期，第67–75页。

Notes:

1. Most of the information in the table is derived from the book *The Documents and Materials Compilations of the South China Sea Islands Names* compiled by Guangdong Provincial Committee on Geographical Names and published by Cartographic Publishing House of Guangdong Province in Guangzhou.

2. It can be seen from the table that some of the South China Sea Islands have two original English names, and all the original English names were given by the Western colonists, and some islands don't have English name. For this reason, it is quite necessary for Chinese scholars to conduct research into this issue as to give an official English name to each of the South China Sea Islands. So this research is just for the purpose. For more detailed information, please refer to the article *Exploring the Translation of the Names of the South China Sea Islands: A Case Study of Su Deliu Version of Genglubu* published by the *Journal of South China Sea Studies* in Sept. 2021.

4.2 Table of the Information about the Islands and Places of the Southeast Asian Countries in Su Deliu Version of *Genglubu*

（苏德柳本《更路簿》东南亚（外洋）地名中英文信息一览表）

序号 No.	海南渔民俗名 Folk Names	标准名 Official Names	海南方言读音 Hainan Dialect Pronunciation	英文名 English Names	地理坐标 Geographical Coordinates	备注 Notes
1	尖笔罗，占笔罗山	占婆岛	$Ziam^1 Bi^7 Lo^2$, $Ziam^1 Bi^7 Lo^2 Dua^1$	Champa Island	15°57′ N, 108°31′ E	越南 Vietnam
2	宝峙	白龙尾岛	$Bo^3 Di^6$	Bech Long Vi	20°8′ N, 107°44′ E	越南 Vietnam
3	单峙	汉翁岛，宗岛	$Ddan^1 Di^6$	Hon Ong	15°49′ N, 108°39′ E	越南 Vietnam
4	外罗，外罗山	李山岛/惹岛	$Hhua^1 Lo^2$, $Hhua^1 Lo^2 Dua^1$	Dao Ly Son/ Culao Re	15°22′ N, 109°07′ E	越南 Vietnam
5	新竹，新竹港，新洲	归仁港	$Din^1 Ddiog^7$, $Din^1 Ddiog^7 Gang^3$, $Din^1 Ziu^1$, $Din^1 Ziu^1$	Guy Nhon/ Qui Nhon	13°44′ N, 109°14′ E	越南 Vietnam
6	大佛，烟筒头	华列拉岬	$Ddua^1 Bud^8$, $In^1 Ddong^2 Hao^2$	Cape Varella	12°54′ N, 109°27′ E	越南 Vietnam
7	草峙	昏果岛/老虎岛	$Sao^3 Di^6$	Con Co	17°9′N, 107°2′E	越南 Vietnam

(续表)

序号 No.	海南渔民俗名 Folk Names	标准名 Official Names	海南方言读音 Hainan Dialect Pronunciation	英文名 English Names	地理坐标 Geographical Coordinates	备注 Notes
8	沙记角	巴朗安角（广义市东角）	$Dua^1 Pi^3 Gag^7$	Ba Lang An Mui (Thanh pho Quang Ngai)	15°13′N, 108°56′E	越南 Vietnam
9	枚极/枚松极	笠杯屿/科尼岛	$Mui^2 Geg^8$, $Mui^2 Dong^2 Geg^8$	Cu Lao Coni	13°45′N, 109°17′E	越南 Vietnam
10	珠窝头/窝头	荣桔港（广义省清水县）	$Du^1 O^1 Hao^2$, $O^1 Hao^2$	Dung Quat (east of Thanh Thuy, Thanh pho Quang Ngai)	15°23′N, 108°49′E	越南 Vietnam
11	硬里	广义东	$Nge^5 Li^3$	east of Thanh pho Quang Ngai	15°19′N, 108°52′E	越南 Vietnam
12	洲鸭/鸭洲	富贵岛南	$Ziu^1 A^6$, $A^6 Ziu^1$	south of Phu Quy	10°21′N, 108°56′E	越南 Vietnam
13	洲鸭	富贵岛	$Ziu^1 A^6$	Phu Quy Island	10°31′N, 108°56′E	越南 Vietnam
14	纸碎港/竹竿峙	归仁港北	$Dua^3 Hhui^4 Gang^3$, $Ddiog^7 Go^1 Di^6$	Nuok Island north of Quy Nhon	13°58′N, 109°14′E	越南 Vietnam
15	羊角峙	水牛岛/公周岛	$Io^2 Gag^7 Di^6$	Hon Trau	13°58′N, 109°14′E	越南 Vietnam
16	罗湾头/豚安	巴达兰角	$Lo^2 Uan^1 Hao^2$, $Log^8 An^1$	Cape of Padaran	11°21′N, 109°1′E	越南 Vietnam

(续表)

序号 No.	海南渔民俗名 Folk Names	标准名 Official Names	海南方言读音 Hainan Dialect Pronunciation	英文名 English Names	地理坐标 Geographical Coordinates	备注 Notes
17	马蹄清/牛路青	瓜岛	Ve^3 Lou^1 Seng^1, Gu^2 Lou^1 Se^1	Pulau Gambir	13°36′N, 109°22′E	越南 Vietnam
18	白豆清	瓜岛	Be^5 Ddao^1 Seng^1	Pulau Gambir	13°36′N, 109°22′E	越南 Vietnam
19	白豆清	喹岛	Be^5 Ddao^1 Seng^1	—	13°37′N, 109°20′E	越南 Vietnam
20	云迷/云术	芽庄港	Yun^2 Hiu^2, Yun^2 Dud^8	Port of Nha Trang	12°11′N, 109°14′E	越南 Vietnam
21	云术上门	进入芽庄港的北面水道	Yun^2 Dud^8 Zio^1 Mui^2	northern entrance to Nha Trang	12°48′N, 109°21′E	越南 Vietnam
22	加淅毲/伽南毲	槟绘湾/竹岛	Ge^1 Nam^2 Miao^3, Ge^1 Mam^2 Mao^5	Ben Hoi/Hon Tre	12°21′N, 109°22′E	越南 Vietnam
23	昆仑/昆仑头	昆仑群岛	Hun^1 Lun^2, Hun^1 Lun^2 Hao^2	Con Dao	8°41′N, 106°36′E	越南 Vietnam
24	赤坎（头）/赤埃头	格嘎角	Siah^7 Ham^4 (Hao^2), Siah^7 Ai^1 Hao^2	Ke Ga	10°42′N, 107°59′E	越南 Vietnam
25	西?	绥丰东南岸	Dai^1?	southeast coast of Tuy Phong	11°10′N, 108°42′E	越南 Vietnam
26	覆锅	胡灵山东北	Fog^7 Ddia^3	northeast of Nui Son Linh	10°32′N, 107°40′E	越南 Vietnam

(续表)

序号 No.	海南渔民俗名 Folk Names	标准名 Official Names	海南方言发音 Hainan Dialect Pronunciation	英文名 English Names	地理坐标 Geographical Coordinates	备注 Notes
27	鹤顶（山）	巴地头顿省胡灵山	Hhag^8 Ddeng^3（Dua^1）	Nui Son Linh	10°29′N, 107°31′E	越南 Vietnam
28	外任	湄公河口	Hhua^1 Yim^5	mouth of Mekong River	10°22′N, 107°15′E	越南 Vietnam
29	昆仑仔/小昆仑	大蛋岛/汉蛋岛	Hun^1 Lun^2 Gia^3, Niao^7 Hun^1 Lun^2	Moi Ba Non	8°37′N, 106°8′E	越南 Vietnam
30	丁加宜	丁加奴州	Dden^1 Ge^1 Ngi^2	Trengganu	5°20′N, 103°8′E	马来西亚 Malaysia
31	吉连州	吉兰丹/哥打巴鲁海口	Gid^7 Lin^2 Ziu^1	Kelantan/Kota Bharu	6°12′N, 102°14′E	马来西亚 Malaysia
32	斗磁/草峙	利浪岛/热浪岛	Ddou^3 Se^3, Sao^3 Di^6	Pulau Redang	4°48′N, 103°40′E	马来西亚 Malaysia
33	斗屿	登嘉楼	Ddou^3 Yi^3	Pulau Tenggual	4°48′N, 103°40′E	马来西亚 Malaysia
34	斗峙	瓜拉彭亨港	Ddou^3 Di^6	Kuala Pahang	4°48′N, 103°40′E	马来西亚 Malaysia
35	草磁	大巴兴地岛/停泊岛	Sao^3 Se^3	Pulau Perhentian	5°37′N, 103°4′E	马来西亚 Malaysia
36	前陈	杰马贾岛	Dai^2 Sin^2	Jemaja Island	3°11′N, 106°17′E	马来西亚 Malaysia
37	东竹/上下笁/笁屿	奥尔岛	Ddang^1 Ddiog^7	Pulau Aur	2°27′N, 104°31′E	马来西亚 Malaysia

(续表)

序号 No.	海南渔民俗名 Folk Names	标准名 Official Names	海南方言读音 Hainan Dialect Pronunciation	英文名 English Names	地理坐标 Geographical Coordinates	备注 Notes
38	东西竹/东西竺	奥尔岛（柔佛州东部）	Ddang^1 Dai^1 Ddiog^7, Ddang^1 Dai^1 Dog^7	Pulau Aur (east of Johor)	2°27′N, 104°20′E	马来西亚 Malaysia
39	真磁/真薯/真仕/真峙	薯岛	Zin^1 Se^3, Zin^1 Du^2, Zin^1 Se^6, Zin^1 Di^6	Khoai	8°25′N, 104°51′E	越南 Vietnam
40	武珥	—	Ddai^6 Mao^6	Wallace	9°39′N, 107°23′E	越南 Vietnam
41	武珥/武珥鸭	富贵岛	Ddai^6 Mao^6, Ddai^6 Mao^6 A^6	Phu Quy	10°31′N, 108°56′E	越南 Vietnam
42	东西洞	萨巴特岛	Ddang^1 Dai^1 Ddong^5	Sapate Island	10°6′N, 108°56′E	越南 Vietnam
43	吕宋/宋吕	上腊港	Lu^5 Dang^4, Dang^4 Lu^5	—	10°39′N, 107°46′E	英文名无法找到 English name not available
44	真磁林	潘切东	Zin^1 Se^3 Lim^2	east of Phan Thiet	10°54′N, 108°17′E	越南 Vietnam
45	浅	—	Sin^3	Royal Bisho	9°44′N, 108°39′E	—
46	正路堀地/地盘门岛	西布特岛/雕门岛	Zia^4 Lou^1 Ni^2 Ddi^5, Ddi^5 Bua^2	Tioman Island	2°51′N, 104°6′E	马来西亚 Malaysia
47	地盘仔	斯里布阿岛/西布特岛	Ddi^5 Bua^2 Gia^3	Pulau Seri Buat	2°41′N, 103°54′E	马来西亚 Malaysia

(续表)

序号 No.	海南渔民俗名 Folk Names	标准名 Official Names	海南方言读音 Hainan Dialect Pronunciation	英文名 English Names	地理坐标 Geographical Coordinates	备注 Notes
48	赤礁	大竹岛/巴岛（昆仑西）	Siah^7 Ziao^1	Hon Tre Lon	8°45′N, 106°30′E	越南 Vietnam
49	粗肯	大苏梅岛/克拉岛	Sou^1 Bue^4	Koh Samui/ Kra Island	9°31′N, 99°57′E	泰国湾 Thailand
50	坎后角	金瓯角	Ham^4 Hhao^5 Gag^7	Mui Ca Mau	8°36′N, 104°42′E	越南 Vietnam
51	大横	土周岛/布罗般洋岛	Ddua^1 Hhue^2	Pulau Panjang	9°18′N, 103°28′E	越南 Vietnam
52	小横	威岛	Niao^7 Hhue^2	Ko Wai	9°54′N, 102°55′E	柬埔寨 Cambodia
53	笔架	阁克兰艾岛/大欤岛	Bid^7 Ge^4	Koh Khram Yai	12°15′N, 99°59′E	泰国 Thailand
54	笔架头	三百峰/三百里山	Bid^7 Ge^4 Hao^2	Khao Sam Roi Yod	12°14′N, 99°59′E	泰国 Thailand
55	假薐/假薯	香蕉岛	Ge^3 Se^3, Ge^3 Du^2	Fausse Obi/ Hon Chuoi	8°56′N, 104°31′E	越南 Vietnam
56	势厂门	三百里山东	Di^4 Siang^3 Mui^2	east of Khao Sam Roi Yod	—	泰国 Thailand

(续表)

序号 No.	海南渔民俗名 Folk Names	标准名 Official Names	海南方言读音 Hainan Dialect Pronunciation	英文名 English Names	地理坐标 Geographical Coordinates	备注 Notes
57	陈公峙	阁诺岛	$Ddan^2 Gong^1 Di^6$	Ko Khi Nok	12°30′N, 100°0′E	泰国 Thailand
58	陈公峙	克兰岛	$Ddan^2 Gong^1 Di^6$	Ko Lan	12°55′N, 100°46′E	泰国 Thailand
59	竹仔唇	龙仔厝	$Ddiog^7 Di^6$	Samut Sakhon	13°29′N, 100°16′E	泰国 Thailand
60	眷(万)佛苏	万佛岁/眷武里	$Gin^4 (Van^1) Bud^8 Dou^1$	Chonburi	13°22′N, 100°58′E	泰国 Thailand
61	塔	佛丕府东岸	Pi^3	east coast of Phetcha Buri	13°9′N, 100°4′E	泰国 Thailand
62	东势厂门	克兰岛东	$Dang^1 Di^4 Siang^3 Mui^2$	east of Ko Lan	—	泰国 Thailand
63	乌头厂/乌头浅	帕别角(岛)	$Ziao^3 Hao^2 Siang^3, U^1 Hao^2 Sin^3$	Nong Thale, Krabi Town	13°9′N, 100°4′E	泰国 Thailand
64	茶盘	巴曹岛	$Dde^2 Bua^2$	Pulau Bajau/Koh Kut	11°39′N, 102°34′E	马来西亚 Malaysia
65	将军帽	丁宜岛	$Jiang^1 Gun^1 Mao^4$	Pulau Tinggi	2°18′N, 104°7′E	马来西亚 Malaysia
66	罗汉峙	利马岛	$Lo^2 Hhan^4 Di^6$	Lima Island	1°21′N, 104°18′E	新加坡 Singapore
67	罗汉峙	白石鹤灯	$Lo^2 Hhan^4 Di^6$	Pedra Branca	1°20′N, 104°24′E	新加坡 Singapore
68	赤?	新加坡东	$Siah^7 ?$	east of Singapore	1°18′N, 104°9′E	新加坡 Singapore
69	埠	新加坡港	Pou^4	Port of Singapore	1°15′N, 103°50′E	新加坡 Singapore

(续表)

序号 No.	海南渔民俗名 Folk Names	标准名 Official Names	海南方言读音 Hainan Dialect Pronunciation	英文名 English Names	地理坐标 Geographical Coordinates	备注 Notes
70	锦花峙	棉花岛	$Min^2\ Hhue^1\ Di^6$	Pulau Kapas	5°13′N, 103°16′E	马来西亚 Malaysia
71	竹峙	龙仔厝港外	$Ddiog^7\ Di^6$	outside of Samut Sakhon Port	13°23′N, 100°23′E	泰国 Thailand
72	彭亨港	龙仔厝港口	$Pe^2\ Heng^1\ Gang^3$	Port of Samut Sakhon	13°37′N, 100°18′E	泰国 Thailand
73	赤仔（港口）	小苏梅岛/阁帕岸岛	$Siah^7\ Gia^3\ (Gang^3\ Hao^3)$	Koh Phangan	9°44′N, 100°1′E	泰国 Thailand
74	苏梅	大苏梅岛/阁沙梅	$Dou^1\ Vue^2$	Ko Sa Mui	9°31′N, 99°57′E	泰国 Thailand
75	猫鼠	宋卡港外两岛	$Va^1\ Siu^3$	two islands outside Songkhla	7°13′N, 100°35′E	泰国 Thailand
76	无来有澳	北大年港/班巴帕南港	$Vo^2\ Lai^2\ U^5\ Ao^4$	Port of Ban Pak Phanang	6°55′N, 101°16′E	泰国 Thailand
77	东竹	竹岛（越南西南）	$Ddang^1\ Ddiog^7$	Hon Tre (southwest of Vietnam)	9°44′N, 104°21′E	越南 Vietnam

(续表)

序号 No.	海南渔民俗名 Folk Names	标准名 Official Names	海南方言读音 Hainan Dialect Pronunciation	英文名 English Names	地理坐标 Geographical Coordinates	备注 Notes
78	暹罗港	暹罗货柜码头	Siam² Lo² Gang³	Siam Container Terminal	—	泰国 Thailand
79	粟峙	纳土纳群岛	Diag⁷ Di⁶	Natuna Islands	3°22′N, 106°16′E	印度尼西亚 Indonesia
80	坑仔长	西哈努克港	Hang⁴ Gia³ Ddo²	Sihanoukville	10°39′N, 103°29′E	柬埔寨 Cambodia
81	三角	三角屿/巴兴地群岛	Da¹ Gag⁷	Perhentian Islands	5°54′N, 102°46′E	马来西亚 Malaysia
82	长腰	民丹岛/宾坦岛东	Ddo² Io¹	east of Bintan Island	1°11′N, 104°41′E	新加坡 Singapore
83	长腰	诗务岛/泗务岛	Ddo² Io¹	Pulau Sibu/Baobi	2°13′N, 104°4′E	马来西亚 Malaysia
84	猪姆头	林加岛东部	Ddu¹ Vo³ Hao²	east of Lingga Island	0°17′S, 104°58′E	印度尼西亚 Indonesia
85	猪姆头	诗巫岛/泗务岛	Ddu¹ Vo³ Hao²	Pulau Sibu/Baobi	2°12′N, 104°05′E	马来西亚 Malaysia
86	漫头峙/梦头峙	苏门答腊岛东	Man⁶ Hao² Di⁶, Mang¹ Hao² Di⁶	Saya (east of Sumatra Island)	0°47′S, 104°55′E	印度尼西亚 Indonesia

(续表)

序号 No.	海南渔民俗名 Folk Names	标准名 Official Names	海南方言读音 Hainan Dialect Pronunciation	英文名 English Names	地理坐标 Geographical Coordinates	备注 Notes
87	南梦	巨港灯北	Nam² Mang¹	north of Palembang	1°57′S, 105°7′E	印度尼西亚 Indonesia
88	萘灯	巨港入海口东	I¹ Ddeng¹	eastern mouth of Palembang	2°21′S, 105°4′E	印度尼西亚 Indonesia
89	逼灯	巨港入海口	Beg⁷ Ddeng¹	mouth of Palembang	2°7′S, 105°35′E	印度尼西亚 Indonesia
90	文肚湾/文肚	克卢丁海岸	Vun² Ddou³ Wan¹, Vun² Ddou³	Selat Bangka	2°7′S, 105°35′E	印度尼西亚 Indonesia
91	七星/秤星	—	Sid⁷ Se¹, Sin⁴ Se¹	Seven Island/ Tudju Island	1°18′S, 105°19′E	印度尼西亚 Indonesia
92	鸣禽阴	巨港入海口东	Meng³ Him² Do³	eastern mouth of Palembang	2°21′S, 105°4′E	印度尼西亚 Indonesia
93	旧港	巨港入海口东	Gu¹ Gang³	eastern mouth of Palembang	2°21′S, 105°4′E	印度尼西亚 Indonesia
94	旧港	旧港灯	Gu¹ Gang³	Palembang	2°7′S, 105°35′E	印度尼西亚 Indonesia

(续表)

序号 No.	海南渔民俗名 Folk Names	标准名 Official Names	海南方言读音 Hainan Dialect Pronunciation	英文名 English Names	地理坐标 Geographical Coordinates	备注 Notes
95	新洲港	新加坡	Din^1 Ziu^1 Gang^3	Port of Singapore	1°21′N, 104°18′E	新加坡 Singapore
96	云冒/云昌	高当岛/当岛	Hhun^2 Mao^5, Hhun^2 Sang^1	Koh Tang	10°18′N, 103°8′E	柬埔寨 Cambodia
97	谷远	涛岛/龟岛	Gog^7 Hhui^5	Ko Tao	10°6′N, 99°50′E	泰国 Thailand
98	云冒仔/云昌仔	波林岛	Hhun^2 Mao^5 Gia^3, Hhun^2 Sang^1 Gia^3	Depond Reef/ Kas Prins	9°54′N, 102°58′E	柬埔寨 Cambodia
99	白石盘盏	白礁岛（新加坡海峡与南海交会口）	Be^5 Zio^5 Bua^2 Hhab^8	Pulau Batu Puteh/ Pedra Branca	1°20′N, 104°24′E	新加坡 Singapore
100	铁礁峙/铁盯峙	彭亨州关丹附近	Hih^7 Liam^2 Di^6, Hih^7 Ddiam^1 Di^6	Berhala	3°18′N, 103°34′E	马来西亚 Malaysia
101	佃馬仕	甘馬昔	Gam^1 Ve^3 Se^6	Kemasik	4°28′N, 103°27′E	马来西亚 Malaysia
102	星洲/新州	新加坡港	Se^1 Ziu^1, Din^1 Ziu^1	Port of Singapore	1°16′N, 103°50′E	新加坡 Singapore
103	吧厘	巴厘	Ba^5 Li^3	Bali Island	8°00′S – 9°00′S, 114°00′S – 116°00′E	印度尼西亚 Indonesia
104	廖（疗）门灯	莱茵海峡	Liao^2 (Liao^2) Mui^2 Ddeng^1	Rhio Strait	1°8′N, 104°12′E	印度尼西亚 Indonesia

(续表)

序号 No.	海南渔民俗名 Folk Names	标准名 Official Names	海南方言读音 Hainan Dialect Pronunciation	英文名 English Names	地理坐标 Geographical Coordinates	备注 Notes
105	青峙仔	莱茵海峡南	Se¹ Di⁶ Gia³	south of Rhio Strait	0°44′N, 104°30′E	印度尼西亚 Indonesia
106	佛肚灯	巨港灯东北	Bud⁸ Ddou³ Ddeng¹	northeast of Palembang	1°56′S, 105°7′E	印度尼西亚 Indonesia
107	禽胆灯	巨港灯北	Him² Dda³ Ddeng¹	north of Palembang	2°3′S, 104°54′E	印度尼西亚 Indonesia
108	乙辛灯	克卢丁对岸	Id⁷ Din¹ Ddeng¹	east protruding part of Palembang	2°9′S, 105°19′E	印度尼西亚 Indonesia
109	门上灯	都保里港西南	Mui² Zio¹ Ddeng¹	southwest of Toboali Port	2°57′S, 106°17′E	印度尼西亚 Indonesia
110	三立	三立洋	Da¹ Lib⁸	—	3°18′S, 106°27′E	英文名无法找到 English name not available
111	吉里文/汶	卡里摩爪哇	Gid⁷ Li³ Vun², Vun⁵	Karimun Jawa	5°49′S, 110°11′E	印度尼西亚 Indonesia
112	蚆蜊土	泗水北	Yio¹ Liang² Hou²	north of Surabaya	6°52′S, 112°52′E	印度尼西亚 Indonesia

(续表)

序号 No.	海南渔民俗名 Folk Names	标准名 Official Names	海南方言读音 Hainan Dialect Pronunciation	英文名 English Names	地理坐标 Geographical Coordinates	备注 Notes
113	角砂峙	伊扬岛	Gag^7 Ban^5 Di^6	Iyan Island	6°59′S, 114°10′E	印度尼西亚 Indonesia
114	三门灯	苏民纳县	Da^1 Mui^2 Ddeng^1	Sumenep	7°5′S, 114°16′E	印度尼西亚 Indonesia
115	鸟旧排灯	克桑比兰帕	Ziao^3 Gu^1 Bai^2 Ddeng^1	—	7°40′S, 114°26′E	英文名无法找到 English name not available
116	知心线灯	鹿岛	Dai^1 Dim^1 Dua^4 Ddeng^1	Pulau Menjangan	8°5′S, 114°28′E	印度尼西亚 Indonesia
117	外南行门	外南梦县	Hhua^1 Nam^2 Hhang^2 Mui^2	Banyu Wangi	8°5′S, 114°27′E	印度尼西亚 Indonesia
118	笳箩马/加箩马	外南梦	Gia^1 Lo^2 Ve^3, Ge^1 Lo^2 Ve^3	Sobo Banyu Wangi	8°15′S, 114°22′E	印度尼西亚 Indonesia
119	青鱼头	登巴萨南	Se^1 Hhu^2 Hao^2	south of Kota Denpasar	8°50′S, 115°4′E	印度尼西亚 Indonesia
120	浮罗啷郁	苏比岛	Pu^2 Lo^2 Li^5 Ud^7	Subi	2°55′N, 108°48′E	印度尼西亚 Indonesia

(续表)

序号 No.	海南渔民俗名 Folk Names	标准名 Official Names	海南方言读音 Hainan Dialect Pronunciation	英文名 English Names	地理坐标 Geographical Coordinates	备注 Notes
121	宏午峦	纳土纳岛行政首府拉奈	Hhong^2 Ngou^5 Luan^2	Ranai	3°95′ N, 108°20′ E	印度尼西亚 Indonesia

说明:

1. 为便于翻译,避免在译文中出现不必要的注释,译者编排的"苏德柳本《更路簿》东南亚(外洋)地名中英文信息一览表"供读者方便查阅。上述表中的信息主要参考了李文化团队文化研究成果《苏德柳簿第四篇至第八篇东南亚更路数字化分析》(目前尚未发表),以及李文化等发表的论文《数字人文方法下的〈郑和航海图〉暹罗湾考地名》(《图书馆杂志》2021年第8期)和李彩霞的《苏承芬本〈更路簿〉外洋地名考证》(《海南大学学报(人文社科版)》2019年第2期)。在此特别说明,一并致以衷心感谢。

2. 此表中有三个海南渔民所命名的俗名(古地名)与其中文标准名称及英语名称,即吕宋/宋吕,三立,乌旧排灯,目前无法考证,也无研究结果,故无法给出正确的官方中英文名称。

Notes:

1. This table was made so as to provide more information for readers and avoid unnecessary annotations in the translated version. The information in the table is mainly derived from the following literature: *The Digital Analysis of the Navigation Routes of Part IV – VIII of Su Deliu Version of Genglubu* by Li Wenhua and his research team (unpublished); Li Wenhua, et al. *The Research on the Name of Siam Bay in Zheng He Nautical Chart from the Perspective of Digital Humanities*, Library Journal, 2021 (8); Li Caixia. *Textual Research into Alien Countries' Toponyms in Su Chengfen's Geng Lu Bu*, Humanities & Social Sciences Journal of Hainan University, 2019 (1). I would like to express my special thanks for the authors.

2. In the table there are a few undefined folk names or ancient names of the islands such as 吕宋/宋吕, 三立, 乌旧排灯 given by the fishermen of Hainan, and they are related with the navigation routes between Malaysia and Indonesia and Singapore in Su Deliu Version of *Genglubu*. Until now little research into them has been done, so no literature can be found to acquire the information about their geographical coordinates and their official Chinese and English names. For this reason, their Hainan dialect pronunciation is used for the translated version.

4.3 Table of the Information about the Places along the Coast of Hainan Island to the Coast of Guangdong in Su Deliu Version of *Genglubu*

（苏德柳本《更路簿》海南岛沿岸至广东省沿岸地名中英文信息一览表）

序号 No.	海南渔民俗名 Hainan Fishermen's Folk Name	标准名 Official Name	海南方言读音 Hainan Dialect Pronunciation	英文名 English Name	地理坐标 Geographical Coordinates	备注 Notes
1	大潭、大坛	潭门港	Dua^1 Ham^2	Tanmen Port	19°24′N, 110°63′E	海南省琼海市 Qionghai City, Hainan Province
2	单人峙	—	Ddan^1 Nang^2 Di^6	—	—	目前尚无考证和研究成果 No information can be found
3	铜钱、铜鼓	铜鼓岭/角	Ddang^2 Zi^2, Ddang^2 Gou^3	Mount Tonggu	19°65′N, 111°06′E	海南省文昌市龙楼镇 Longlou Town, Wenchang City, Hainan Province
4	南行丁	—	Nam^2 Hhang^2 Liao^3	—	—	目前尚无考证和研究成果 No information can be found
5	七洲洋	七洲列岛	Sid^7 Ziu^1 Io	the Qizhou Islands	19°52′N – 20°N, 111°11′E – 111°17′E	文昌市东部 east of Wenchang City
6	南亭门、鲁万山、老万山、东姜山	（大）万山岛	Nam^2 Heng^2 Mui^2, Lu^3 Van^1 Dua^1, Lao Van^1 Dua^1, Ddang^1 Gio^1 Dua^1	Dawanshan Island	21°95′N, 113°74′E	位于今广东省珠海市东南 southeast of Zhuhai City, Guangdong Province

（续表）

序号 No.	海南渔民俗名 Hainan Fishermen's Folk Name	标准名 Official Name	海南方言读音 Hainan Dialect Pronunciation	英文名 English Name	地理坐标 Geographical Coordinates	备注 Notes
7	北峙，北土峙	北土岛	Bag^7 Di^6, Bag^7 Se^6 Di^6	Beishi Island	19°59′N, 110°16′E	七洲列岛之一 One of the islands of Qizhou Islands
8	大澳门	大澳渔村	Dua^1 Ao^4 Mui^2	Da'ao Fishing Village	—	位于广东省阳江市东平镇东南 Southeast of Dongping Town, Yangjiang City, Guangdong Province
9	大洲	燕窝岛	Dua^1 Ziu^1	Yanwo Island	18°68′N, 110°49′E	海南省万宁市东南 southeast of Wanning City, Hainan Province
10	赤奸（仔）	—	Siah^7 Hho^3（Gia^3）	—	—	目前尚无考证和研究成果 No information can be found
11	陵水	陵水角	Leng^2 Dui^3	Lingshui Cape	18°23′N, 110°2′E	陵水 Lingshui County
12	宇林，榆林	榆林港	Yi^2 Lim^2, Yi^2 Lim^2	Yulin Port	18°12′N, 109°32′E	三亚 Sanya City
13	堂山	—	Tang^2 Dua^1	—	—	目前尚无考证和研究成果 No information can be found

(续表)

序号 No.	海南渔民俗名 Hainan Fishermen's Folk Name	标准名 Official Name	海南方言读音 Hainan Dialect Pronunciation	英文名 English Name	地理坐标 Geographical Coordinates	备注 Notes
14	梨海山，梨头山，南海黎母大山	白虎角	Li² Hhai³ Dua¹, Li² Hao² Dua¹	Mount Limu	18°30′N, 108°41′E	海南省三亚市 Sanya City, Hainan Province

说明：

1. 此表中有四个海南渔民俗名（古地名），如单人峙、南行丁、赤好（仔）、垒山等。关于它们的中文标准名称及地理坐标目前尚无考证和研究成果，故无法翻译，在此选用海南渔民方言特别标出。译文中用海南渔民方言读音。

2. 关于"南亭门"有两种说法：一说是南亭门属于广东省东莞市，详见简根齐、吴昊《海南渔民〈更路簿〉地名命名考》，载《社会科学战线》2021年第6期；另一说是指今广东省珠海市东南大海中大万山岛，详见许盘清、安俊丽、曹树基《航线与星程：文昌七洲洋与西沙七洲洋的地理位置》，载《中国历史地理论丛》2022年第37卷第1期。

3. 关于"梨海山"有学者推测是指今海南省三亚市白虎角，也有学者认为"梨海山"或"南海黎母大山"是指海南的黎母山，是海南岛海拔最高的山，中心在今五指山和乐东县交界处，可能作为海南岛的标志，详见简根齐、李旷远《郑和船队从广东至西沙群岛海域的航线和地名辨析》，载《吉林大学社会科学学报》2020年第1期。译文采用前者。

Notes:

1. In this tables there are four folk names or ancient names such as 单人峙, 南行丁, 赤好（仔）, 垒山, whose information about their geographical coordinate and official Chinese name is not available at present. So their Hainan dialect pronunciation is only employed for the translated version.

2. In terms of Nan Ting Men, there are two opinions of it. The first is that this place may belong to Dongguan City, Guangdong Province. For details, please refer to Yan Genqi, et al. *On the Toponym in the Hainan Fishermen's Genglubu*, Social Science Front, 2021 (6). The second is that it may be Dawanshan Island, in the southeast of Zhuhai City, Guangdong Province. For details, please refer to Xu Panqing, et al. *Routes and Mileages: Geographical Location of Wenchang Qizhouyang and Xisha Qizhouyang*, Journal of Chinese Historical Geography, 2022 (1).

3. In terms of the geographical location of Li Hai Shan, opinions vary. Xu Panqing, et al. (2022) think that it may refer to Baihu Cape, Sanya City, Hainan Province while Yan Genqi, et al. (2020) believe that it may refer to Mount Limu, the highest in Hainan Island, and its center is on the border of Wuzhi City and Ledong County, and it is regarded as a sign of Hainan Island. For details, please refer to Yan Genqi, et al. *On the Route and Toponym of the Voyage by Zheng He Fleet from Guangdong to Xisha Waters*, Jilin University Journal Social Sciences Edition, 2020 (1). The first opinion is preferably adopted in the translated text.

Postscript

In 2014, it was the first time that I came into contact with *Genglubu* when I was writing an article on how to translate Chinese introductory texts concerning intangible cultural heritage of Hainan. In the fall of the following year when I supervised a postgraduate student who specialized in MTI at Hainan University and began to prepare for writing a translation research report, she was then struggling to search for suitable materials, and just at that time, a book *An Arcane Book about the South China Sea: Cultural Interpretations of the South China Sea Voyage Book by Fishermen of Hainan* (*the Arcane Book*) (《南海天书——海南渔民〈更路簿〉文化诠释》), written by Prof. Zhou Weiming and Prof. Tang Lingling was newly published. After reading the book, I had a better understanding of *Genglubu*, so I recommended it to the student, who took an interest in it, too. Then she chose Chapters 4 and 5 of the book as the source text for her Chinese-English translation research. In spite of the fact that the translation was very difficult for her to do, with our joint efforts, it was completed. After the defense, the translated text and the thesis were very positively commented by my colleagues, which further stirred my interest in the translation studies of *Genglubu*. In October 2020, I applied to Guangdong Planning Office of Philosophy and Social Sciences for a research project entitled *Probing into Translating the South China Sea Genglubu Based on Su Deliu and Peng Zhengkai Versions*. It was approved.

Up to now, little translation research into *Genglubu* has been conducted, and only a few publications in this field have come out because, compared with other texts, it has its unique characteristics including Hainan dialect, the folk names or pet names of the South China Sea islands, culture-loaded items regarding marine navigational routes and ancient compass terminology, which makes the translation very difficult. Therefore, in the course of translation, before putting pen on paper, the translators had to study a lot of literature, do extensive consultation, and take advice from experts and experienced fishermen. By doing so, we are able to fully comprehend each of the South China island folk names given by the fishermen of Hainan, to clearly know the folk name of each island concerning all the marine navigational routes in some Southeast Asian countries (Vietnam, Cambodia, Thailand,

Indonesia, Malaysia, Singapore) and their specific geographic coordinates, to get familiar with the ancient compass function as to how it worked properly to take the navigational routes, and to understand the folk names corresponding to their official English names. Here what should be particularly mentioned in Su Version is that several islands along the routes of some Southeast Asian countries (Vietnam, Cambodia, Thailand, Indonesia, Malaysia, Singapore) have more than one folk name, and in other cases, one specific folk name was given to two or three different islands. These phenomena have brought about the problem in determining their exact locations. As a result, it's quite hard for the translators to determine which is which. In addition, the Hainan dialect pronunciation and spelling of the islands as well as their origins and legends are not so easy to translate. Perhaps this is the reason why few translators are willing to gnaw on this hard bone. However, with more than two years of unremitting efforts, we have finally succeeded in cracking down this hard bone.

We had made task arrangements for each team member before the project was approved. As the project leader, in addition to being responsible for the project's overall planning, drafting, proofreading, and writing the preface and postscript for the translation research, I have finished translating the most parts of Su Version, including Part I, Part II, Part III, Part V, Part VI, Part VII, and sections 1 – 4 of Part IV. I have made three tables —Table of the Information about the South China Sea Islands in Su Deliu and Peng Zhengkai Versions of *Genglubu*; Table of the Information about the Islands and Places of the Southeast Asian Countries in Su Deliu Version of *Genglubu* and Information Table of the Places along the Coast of Hainan Island to the Coast of Guangdong in Su Deliu Version of *Genglubu*. My colleagues, Associate Prof. Wu Suzhen and Associate Prof. Zhai Qiulan, have translated Peng Version and Sections 5 – 12 of Part IV in Su Version. Ms. Chen Zhaoyu has provided the translated draft of the preface and postscript of this book.

The completion of this works owes to all parties' cooperation and concerted efforts.

First things first, I would very much like to express my greatest gratitude for the funding of Guangdong Planning Office of Philosophy and Social Sciences, for the contributions made by the anonymous review experts, and the support of relevant departments of Guangzhou College of Applied Science and Technology.

In the second place, my greatest gratitude should go to Prof. Zhou Weimin for writing the foreword to the works. Although he is 90 years old, he was sharp-minded. After having read it over, he agreed to write it with delight.

Thirdly, I would like to express my heartfelt thanks to the professors and experts from Hainan University Prof. Zhang Shuoren, Prof. Qin Xiaohua, Prof. Li Wenhua, and Ms. Chen Hong—for their generous professional guidance in the field of *Genglubu* during the implementation of the project. Ms. Chen Hong spent her spare time giving phonetic notation of Hainan dialect to the all folk names (ancient names) of both the South China Sea Islands and the islands of some Southeast Asian countries.

Next, many thanks should go to Italian American English teacher, Mr. Aymie Michael George who put forward some constructive advice on the revision of the translated text, and to Ms. Hu Xiaoli, a Ph. D. student from School of Economics and Management, South China University of Technology, who helped me with data collection and word processing. Besides, I would like to thank my wife, Ms. Lü Hong who does most housework and helps me a lot with the project.

Finally, I would like to give our special thanks to Ms. Zhang Rui as well as other staff of Sun Yat-sen University Press for their hard work at revising, editing and publishing this book.

This project may be the first attempt to conduct research into the translation of *Genglubu*. There might be some misunderstanding of the original text and mistakes or errors in the English version. I am open to your comments and criticism.

Jia Shaodong
March 26, 2024

1 苏德柳本《更路簿》原文及释义

1.1 立东海更路（西沙更路）①

第1条 自大潭过东海，用乾巽使到十贰时（更），使（驶）半转回乾巽巳亥，约有十五页（更）。

释义：从大潭到东海，航行针向使用单针（乾巽），行驶到十二更，行驶到一半时航行针向转为缝针（乾巽和巳亥的中间线），大概行驶十五更。

第2条 自三峙下干豆，风，三庚（更）收。对西使（驶）。

释义：在西沙，从三峙（南岛）开往干豆（北礁），南风时，航行针向用单针（甲庚）；北风时，航行针向用单针（乙辛），航程三更到达，收帆泊船。向西行驶。

第3条 自三峙下石塘，用艮坤寅申，三庚（更）收。对西南。

释义：在西沙，从三峙（南岛）开往石塘（永乐群岛），航行针向为缝针（艮坤和寅申的中间线），航程三更到达。航行方向对西南。

第4条 自三峙下二圈，用癸丁丑未平，三更半收。对西南。

释义：在西沙，从三峙（南岛）开往二圈（玉琢礁），航行针向为缝针（癸丁和丑未的中间线），航程三更半到达。航向西南。

第5条 自三峙上三圈，用壬丙巳亥平，四更收。对东南。

释义：在西沙，从三峙（南岛）开往三圈（浪花礁），航行针用缝针（壬丙和巳亥的中间线），航程四更到达。航行方向对东南。

第6条 自猫注去干豆，乙辛兼辰戌，四更半收。对西北、北风。

释义：在西沙，从猫注（永兴岛）开往干豆（北礁），航行针用缝针（乙

---

① 说明：1. 为便于英译，对"立东海更路"和"立北海更路"进行了编号。最早的抄本没有编号。

2. 原文释义主要参考了周伟民、唐玲玲《南海天书：海南渔民〈更路簿〉文化诠释》，昆仑出版社2015年版；夏代云：《卢业发、吴淑茂、黄家礼〈更路簿〉研究》，海洋出版社2016年版；王利兵：《南海航道更路经研究：以苏德柳本〈更路簿〉为例》，载《中国边疆史地研究》2016年第2期，第119－134页。在此对所有作者表示衷心感谢。

3. 关于苏德柳本《更路簿》中的南海诸岛俗名（土地名）的起源及其相关信息，请参照"苏德柳本和彭正楷本《更路簿》南海诸岛俗名起源与传说"和"苏德柳本和彭正楷本《更路簿》南海诸岛中英文信息一览表"。

辛和辰戌的中间线），航程四更半到达。如果是北风，航行方向对西北。

第7条 自猫注去下峙曲手，用坤申，四更收。对西南。

释义：在西沙，从猫注（永兴岛）开往下峙（永乐群岛）的曲手，航行针用缝针（艮坤和寅申的中间线），航程四更到达。航行方向对西南。

第8条 自猫注去二圈，用丁未，三更半收。对南。

释义：在西沙，从猫注（永兴岛）开往二圈（玉琢礁），航行针用缝针（癸丁和丑未的中间线），航程三更半到达。航向对南。

第9条 自二圈下下峙，用辰戌，一更收。对西北。

释义：在西沙，从二圈（玉琢礁）开往下峙（永乐群岛），航行针用单针（辰戌），航程一更到达。航向对西北。

第10条 自石塘上二圈，用乙辛辰戌，二更。对东南。

释义：在西沙，从石塘（永乐群岛）开往二圈（玉琢礁），航行针用缝针（乙辛和辰戌的中间线），航程二更就可到达。航向对东南。

第11条 自石塘世江门出，上猫注，用甲庚，六更收。对东。

释义：在西沙，从石塘（永乐群岛）的世江门（晋卿门）出发，开往猫注（永兴岛），航行针用单针（甲庚），航程六更就可到达。航行方向对东。

第12条 自四江去大圈，用乾巽过头，约更半。对东南。

释义：在西沙，从四江（晋卿岛）开往大圈（华光礁），航行针用单针（乾巽稍过一点），航程大约一更半到达。航向对东南。

第13条 自银峙去干豆，用壬丙，三更半收。对北。

释义：在西沙，从银峙（银屿）开往干豆（北礁），航行针用单针（壬丙），航程三更半到达。航行方向对北。

第14条 自猫兴上三圈，用癸丁丑未平，三更半收。对南。

释义：在西沙，从猫兴（东岛）开往三圈（浪花礁），航行针用缝针（癸丁和丑未的中间线），航程三更半到达。航行方向对南。

第15条 自猫注上三圈，用壬丙平，四更。对南。

释义：在西沙，从猫注（永兴岛）开往三圈（浪花礁），航行针用单针（壬丙），航程四更到达。航行方向对南。

第16条 自大圈下去半路，用艮坤加二线丑未，三更。对南。

释义：在西沙，从大圈（华光礁）开往半路（中建岛），航行针用缝针（艮坤加二线丑未），航程三更到达。航行方向对南。

第17条 自二圈去干豆，用乾巽，四更半收。对西北。

释义：在西沙，从二圈（玉琢礁）开往干豆（北礁），航行针用单针（乾巽），航程四更半到达。航行方向对西北。

第 18 条　自尾峙去半路，用癸丁，三更半收。对西南。

释义：在西沙，从尾峙（金银岛）开往半路（中建岛），航行针用单针（癸丁），航程三更半到达。航行方向对西南。

第 19 条　自三圈去半路，用甲庚，六更半收。对西南。

释义：在西沙，从三圈（浪花礁）开往半路（中建岛），航行针用单针（甲庚），航程六更半到达。航行方向对西南。

第 20 条　自二圹（筐）去白峙仔，用丑未，更半收。对南。

释义：在西沙，从二圹（玉琢礁）开往白峙仔（盘石屿），航行针用单针（丑未），航程一更半到达。航行方向对南。

第 21 条　自大圈头下白峙仔，用子午，一更收。对南。

释义：在西沙，从大圈（华光礁）东北边开往白峙仔（盘石屿），航行针用单针（子午），航程一更到达。航行方向对南。

第 22 条　自红草门上双帆，用乾巽，二更收。对东南。

释义：在西沙，从红草门（红草门）开往双帆（高尖石），航行针用单针（乾巽），航程二更到达。航行方向对东南。

第 23 条　自红草门上猫兴，用乙辛，二更收。对东南。

释义：在西沙，从红草门（红草门）开往猫兴（东岛），航行针用单针（乙辛），航程二更就可到达。航行方向对东南。

第 24 条　自白峙仔去半路，用寅申，三更收。对西南。

释义：在西沙，从白峙仔（盘石屿）开往半路（中建岛），航行针用单针（寅申），航程三更可到达收帆。航行方向对西南。

第 25 条　自半路去外罗，用甲庚寅申，十五更收。对西南。

释义：在西沙，从半路（中建岛）去越南中部近海的外罗（李山岛），航行针用缝针（甲庚和寅申的中间线），航程十五更可到达收帆。航行方向对西南。

第 26 条　自二圈下大圈，用寅申，一更收。对西。

释义：在西沙，从二圈（玉琢礁）开往大圈（华光礁），航行针用单针（寅申），航程一更到达。航行方向对西。

第 27 条　自三圈下白峙仔，用甲庚卯酉，五更。对西。

释义：在西沙，从三圈（浪花礁）开往白峙仔（盘石屿），航行针用缝针（甲庚和卯酉的中间线），航程五更到达。航行方向对西。

第 28 条　自白峙仔上三圈，用卯酉，五更收。对东。

释义：在西沙，从白峙仔（盘石屿）开往三圈（浪花礁），航行针用单针（卯酉），航程五更到达。航行方向对东。

第29条 自船岩尾往干豆,用乙卯,四更收。对西。

释义:在西沙,从船岩尾(西沙洲)驶往干豆(北礁),航行针用缝针(乙辛和卯酉的中间线),航程四更到达。航行方向对西。

1.2 立北海更路（南沙更路）①

第1条 自三圹（筐）往北海双峙，用乾巽至半洋潮回巳亥，二十六（更）收。

释义：在西沙，从三圹（浪花礁）开往北海双峙（南沙群岛的双子群礁），航行针用单针（乾巽）航行至一半时，出现半日潮，航行针向用单针转对巳亥，航程二十六更后，到达收帆。

第2条 自白峙仔往双峙，用乾巽，三十八（更）收。

释义：在西沙，从白峙仔（盘石屿）开往双峙（双子群礁），航行针用单针（乾巽），航程三十八（更）到达。

第3条 自双峙去红草线排，用乙辛，二更收。对东。

释义：在南沙，从双峙（双子群礁）开往红草线排（乐斯暗沙），航行针用单针（乙辛），航程二更就可到达。航行方向对东。

第4条 自双峙去铁峙，用巳亥，三更收。对南。

释义：在南沙，从双峙（双子群礁）开往铁峙（中业岛），航行针用单针（巳亥），航程三更到达。航行方向对南。

第5条 自红草下线排，用辰戌，二更收。对西北。

释义：在南沙，从红草（西月岛）开往线排（长滩），航行针用单针（辰戌），航程二更就可到达。航行方向对西北。

第6条 自红草下第三峙，用艮坤，三更收。对西南。

释义：在南沙，从红草（西月岛）开往第三峙（南钥岛），航行针用单针（艮坤），航程三更到达。航行方向对西南。

第7条 自红草上锣孔，用卯酉，五更收。对东。

释义：在南沙，从红草（西月岛）开往锣孔（马欢岛），航行针用单针

---

① 说明：1. 为便于英译，对"立东海更路"和"立北海更路"进行了编号。最早的抄本没有编号。

2. 原文释义主要参考了周伟民、唐玲玲《南海天书：海南渔民"更路簿"文化诠释》，昆仑出版社2015年版；夏代云：《卢业发、吴淑茂、黄家礼〈更路簿〉研究》，海洋出版社2016年版；王利兵：《南海航道更路经研究：以苏德柳本〈更路簿〉为例》，载《中国边疆史地研究》2016年第2期，第119－134页。在此对所有作者表示衷心感谢。

3. 关于苏德柳本《更路簿》中的南海诸岛俗名（土地名）的起源及其相关信息，请参照"苏德柳本和彭正楷本《更路簿》南海诸岛俗名起源与传说"和"苏德柳本和彭正楷本《更路簿》南海诸岛中英文信息一览表"。

4. 第1条中"半洋潮"的另一种解释是指从西沙群岛航行至南沙群岛途中，经过"半路"这一带时，潮汐出现"半日潮"。这也是海南渔民划分西沙群岛和南沙群岛的大概界线。详见阎根齐、吴昊《海南渔民〈更路簿〉地名命名考》，载《社会科学战线》2021年第6期，第142－149页。

（卯酉），航程五更到达。航行方向对东。

  第 8 条　自红草去火襄，用癸丁，二更收。对西南。

  释义：在南沙，从红草（西月岛）开往火襄（火艾礁），航行针用单针（癸丁），航程二更到达。航行方向对西南。

  第 9 条　自红草线排下铁峙，用甲庚，二更收。对西南。

  释义：在南沙，从红草线排（长滩）开往铁峙（中业岛），航行针用单针（甲庚），航程二更到达。航行方向对西南。

  第 10 条　自红草线排去火襄，用乾巽辰戌，二更收。对东南。

  释义：在南沙，从红草线排（长滩）开往火襄（火艾礁），航行针用缝针（乾巽和辰戌的中间线），航程二更到达。航行方向对东南。

  第 11 条　自火襄去裤归，用乙卯，二更收。对西。

  释义：在南沙，从火襄（火艾礁）开往裤归（库归礁），航行针用缝针（乙辛和卯酉的中间线），航程二更到达。航行方向对西。

  第 12 条　自火襄去三角，用乞（乾）巽，三更收。对东南。

  释义：在南沙，从火襄（火艾礁）开往三角（三角礁），航行针用单针（乾巽），航程三更到达。航行方向对东南。

  第 13 条　自三角去双门，用辰戌，二更收。对东南。

  释义：在南沙，从三角（三角礁）开往双门（美济礁），航行针用单针（辰戌），航程二更到达。航行方向对东南。

  第 14 条　自红草去五风，用辰戌，四更收。对东南。

  释义：在南沙，从红草（西月岛）开往五风（五方礁），航行针用单针（辰戌），航程四更到达。航行方向对东南。

  第 15 条　自双门去断节，用乙辛卯酉，二更收。对东。

  释义：在南沙，从双门（美济礁）开往断节（仁爱礁），航行针用缝针（乙辛和卯酉的中间线），航程二更到达。航行方向对东。

  第 16 条　自双门去乌（鸟）串，用壬丙，二更收。对南。

  释义：在南沙，从双门（美济礁）开往乌（鸟）串（仙娥礁），航行针用单针（壬丙），航程二更到达。航行方向对南。

  第 17 条　自双门去双挑，用乾巽，四更收。对东南。

  释义：在南沙，从双门（美济礁）开往双挑（信义礁），航行针用单针（乾巽），航程四更到达收帆。航行方向对东南。

  第 18 条　断节去双挑，用壬丙巳亥，二更收。对东南。

  释义：在南沙，从断节（仁爱礁）开往双挑（信义礁），航行针用缝针（壬丙和巳亥的中间线），航程二更到达收帆。航行方向对东南。

第 19 条 自断节去牛车英，用乙辛辰戌，二更收。对东南。

释义：在南沙，从断节（仁爱礁）开往牛车英（牛车轮礁），航行针用缝针（乙辛和辰戌的中间线），航程二更到达。航行方向对东南。

第 20 条 自断节去五风，用癸丁，五更收。对东北。

释义：在南沙，从断节（仁爱礁）开往五风（五方礁），航行针用单针（癸丁），航程五更到达。航行方向对东北。

第 21 条 自牛车英去脚坡，用乾巽，三更。对东南。

释义：在南沙，从牛车英（牛车轮礁）开往脚坡（海口礁），航行针用单针（乾巽），航程三更到达收帆。航行方向对东南。

第 22 条 自牛车英下断节，用乾巽，二更。对西北。

释义：在南沙，从牛车英（牛车轮礁）开往断节（仁爱礁），航行针用单针（乾巽），航程二更到达。航行方向对西北。

第 23 条 自脚坡去石龙，用卯酉，二更收。对东。

释义：在南沙，从脚坡（海口礁）开往石龙（舰长礁），航行针用单针（卯酉），航程二更到达。航行方向对东。

第 24 条 自石龙去鱼鳞，用子午，四更收。对北。

释义：在南沙，从石龙（舰长礁）开往鱼鳞（仙宾礁），航行针用单针（子午），航程四更到达。航行方向对北。

第 25 条 自脚坡下牛车英（英），用壬丙巳亥，三更收。对西北。

释义：在南沙，从脚坡（海口礁）开往牛车英（牛车轮礁），航行针用缝针（壬丙和巳亥的中间线），航程三更到达。航行方向对西北。

第 26 条 自石龙下脚坡，用乙辛辰戌，二更。对西北。

释义：在南沙，从石龙（舰长礁）开往脚坡（海口礁），航行针用缝针（乙辛和辰戌的中间线），航程二更到达。航行方向对西北。

第 27 条 自鱼鳞去（东头）乙辛，用乙辛加三线卯酉，三更。对东。

释义：在南沙，从鱼鳞（仙宾礁）开往（东头）乙辛（蓬勃暗沙），航行针用缝针（乙辛加三线卯酉），航程三更到达。航行方向对东。

第 28 条 自鱼鳞去号藤，用子午壬丙，五更。对北。

释义：在南沙，从鱼鳞（仙宾礁）开往号藤（鲎藤礁），航行针用缝针（子午和壬丙的中间线），航程五更到达。航行方向对北。

第 29 条 自鱼鳞下断节，用卯酉，二更。对西。

释义：在南沙，从鱼鳞（仙宾礁）开往断节（仁爱礁），航行针用单针（卯酉），航程二更到达。航行方向对西。

第 30 条 自双挑去海公，用乾巽加三线辰戌，三更。对东南。

释义：在南沙，从双挑（信义礁）开往海公（半月礁），航行针用缝针

（乾巽加三线辰戌），航程三更到达。航行方向对东南。

第31条 自双挑去乌（鸟）串，用乙辛加二线卯酉，二更。对西。

释义：在南沙，从双挑（信义礁）开往乌（鸟）串（仙娥礁），航行针用缝针（乙辛加二线卯酉），航程二更到达。航行方向对西。

第32条 自乌（鸟）串下银饼，用壬丙，五更收。对西北。

释义：在南沙，从乌（鸟）串（仙娥礁）开往银饼（安达礁），航行针用单针（壬丙），航程五更到达。航行方向对西北。

第33条 自锣孔去号藤，用卯酉，二更。对东。

释义：在南沙，从锣孔（马欢岛）开往号藤（鲎藤礁），航行针用单针（卯酉），航程二更到达收帆。航行方向对东。

第34条 自锣孔去五风，用壬丙子午，更半收。对南。

释义：在南沙，从锣孔（马欢岛）开往五风（五方礁），航行针用缝针（壬丙和子午的中间线），航程一更半到达。航行方向对南。

第35条 自五风去断节，用壬丙，四更收。对南。

释义：在南沙，从五风（五方礁）开往断节（仁爱礁），航行针用单针（壬丙），航程四更到达。航行方向对南。

第36条 自五风去鱼鳞，用辰戌，四更收。对东南。半路有线一只，名曰半路线。

释义：在南沙，从五风（五方礁）开往鱼鳞（仙宾礁），航行针用单针（辰戌），航程四更到达。航行方向对东南。半路有一个暗沙线排，名叫半路线（半路礁）。

第37条 自五风头去半路线，用乾巽，二更收。对东南。

释义：在南沙，从五风头（五方头）开往半路线（半路礁），航行针用单针（乾巽），航程二更到达。航行方向对东南。

第38条 自铁峙去裤归，用辰戌，二更收。对东南。

释义：在南沙，从铁峙（中业岛）开往裤归（库归礁），航行针用单针（辰戌），航程二更到达。航行方向对东南。

第39条 自铁峙去铜金，用乾巽，二更。对东南。

释义：在南沙，从铁峙（中业岛）开往铜金（杨信沙洲），航行针用单针（乾巽），航程二更到达。航行方向对东南。

第40条 自铁峙去丑未，用艮坤，二更收。对西南。

释义：在南沙，从铁峙（中业岛）开往丑未（渚碧礁），航行针用单针（艮坤），航程二更到达。航行方向对西南。

第41条 自铁峙线仔（排）去丑未，用丑未，二更收。对西南。

释义：在南沙，从铁峙线仔（铁峙礁）开往丑未（渚碧礁），航行针用单针（丑未），航程二更到达，收帆泊船。航行方向对西南。

第 42 条　自铁峙去双王（黄），用壬丙，二更收。对东南。

释义：在南沙，从铁峙（中业岛）开往双王（双黄沙洲），航行针用单针（壬丙），航程二更到达。航行方向对东南。

第 43 条　自铁线去裤归，用乾巽，二更半收。对东南。

释义：在南沙，从铁线（铁线礁）开往裤归（库归礁），航行针用单针（乾巽），航程二更半到达。航行方向对东南。

第 44 条　自丑未去双王，用辰戌，二更收。对东南。

释义：在南沙，从丑未（渚碧礁）开往双王（双黄沙洲），航行针用单针（辰戌），航程二更到达。航行方向对东南。

第 45 条　自丑未去黄山马，用乾巽，三更收。对东南。

释义：在南沙，从丑未（渚碧礁）开往黄山马（太平岛），航行针用单针（乾巽），航程三更到达。航行方向对东南。

第 46 条　自铁峙去第三，用巳亥，二更收。对东南。

释义：在南沙，从铁峙（中业岛）开往第三（南钥岛），航行针用单针（巳亥），航程二更到达。航行方向对东南。

第 47 条　自第三去黄山马，用午丙，二更。对南。

释义：在南沙，从第三（南钥岛）开往黄山马（太平岛），航行针用缝针（子午和壬丙的中间线），航程二更到达。航行方向对南。

第 48 条　自第三去银饼，用乾巽，三更收。对东南。

释义：在南沙，从第三（南钥岛）开往银饼（安达礁），航行针用单针（乾巽），航程三更到达。航行方向对东南。

第 49 条　自裤归上三角，用辰戌，五更收。对东南。

释义：在南沙，从裤归（库归礁）开往三角（三角礁），航行针用单针（辰戌），航程五更到达。航行方向对东南。

第 50 条　自铜金去银饼，用巳亥，二更收。对东南。

释义：在南沙，从铜金（杨信沙洲）开往银饼（安达礁），航行针用单针（巳亥），航程二更到达。航行方向对东南。

第 51 条　自铜金去第三，用甲庚，二更收。对西南。

释义：在南沙，从铜金（杨信沙洲）开往第三（南钥岛），航行针用单针（甲庚），航程二更到达。航行方向对西南。

第 52 条　自银饼去鸟串，用辰戌，五更收。对东南。

释义：在南沙，从银饼（安达礁）开往鸟串（仙娥礁），航行针用单针（辰戌），航程五更到达。航行方向对东南。

第53条　自银饼下黄山马，用卯酉，二更收。对正西。

释义：在南沙，从银饼（安达礁）开往黄山马（太平岛），航行针用单针（卯酉），航程二更到达。航行方向对正西。

第54条　自银饼去牛厄（轭），用癸丁，二更收。对西南。

释义：在南沙，从银饼（安达礁）开往牛厄（牛轭礁），航行针用单针（癸丁），航程二更到达。航行方向对西南。

第55条　自黄山马去丑未，用壬丙巳亥，三更收。对西北。

释义：在南沙，从黄山马（太平岛）开往丑未（渚碧礁），航行针用缝针（壬丙和巳亥的中间线），航程三更到达。航行方向对西北。

第56条　自黄山马去牛厄，用乾巽，三更。对东南。

释义：在南沙，从黄山马（太平岛）开往牛厄（牛轭礁），航行针用单针（乾巽），航程三更到达。航行方向对东南。

第57条　自黄山马去刘牛刘，用寅申，三更。对西南。

释义：在南沙，从黄山马（太平岛）开往刘牛刘（大现礁），航行针用单针（寅申），航程三更到达。航行方向对西南。

第58条　自黄山马去南乙峙，用壬丙，一更。对东南。

释义：在南沙，从黄山马（太平岛）开往南乙峙（鸿庥岛），航行针用单针（壬丙），航程一更，到达收帆。航行方向对东南。

第59条　自南乙峙去秤钩，用子午，二更收。对南。

释义：在南沙，从南乙峙（鸿庥岛）开往秤钩（景宏岛），航行针用单针（子午），航程二更到达收帆。航行方向对南。

第60条　自南乙峙去秤钩峙仔，用壬丙，二更。对东南。

释义：在南沙，从南乙峙（鸿庥岛）开往秤钩峙仔（华礁），航行针用单针（壬丙），航程二更到达。航行方向对东南。

第61条　自牛厄去目镜，用巳亥添四线丙，九更收。对东南。

释义：在南沙，从牛厄（牛轭礁）开往目镜（司令礁），航行针用缝针（巳亥加四线壬丙），航程九更到达。航行方向对东南。

第62条　自目镜去深圹，用寅申，二更收。对西南。

释义：在南沙，从目镜（司令礁）开往深圹（榆亚暗沙），航行针用单针（寅申），航程二更到达。航行方向对西南。

第63条　自目镜去不乜线，用乾巽，三更收。对西北。

释义：在南沙，从目镜（司令礁）开往不乜线（无乜礁），航行针用单针（乾巽），航程三更到达。航行方向对西北。

第64条　自女青石去不乜线，用午丙，五更收。对东南。

释义：在南沙，从女青石（染青东礁）开往不乜线（无乜礁），航行针用缝针（子午和壬丙的中间线），航程五更到达。航行方向对东南。

第65条 自不乜线去深圈，用壬丙，二更收。对东南。

释义：在南沙，从不乜线（无乜礁）开往深圈（榆亚暗沙），航行针用单针（壬丙），航程二更到达。航行方向对东南。

第66条 自深圈去坡箕，用甲庚寅申，二更收。对西南。

释义：在南沙，从深圈（榆亚暗沙）开往坡箕（簸箕礁），航行针用缝针（甲庚和寅申的中间线），航程二更到达。航行方向对西南。

第67条 自坡箕下铜章，用寅申，一更收。对西南。

释义：在南沙，从坡箕（簸箕礁）开往铜章（南海礁），航行针用单针（寅申），航程一更，到达收帆。航行方向对西南。

第68条 自铜章下海口线，用乾巽添辰戌，三更。对西北。

释义：在南沙，从铜章（南海礁）开往海口线（柏礁），航行针用缝针（乾巽和辰戌的中间线），航程三更到达。航行方向对西北。

第69条 自铜章去光星仔，用壬丙巳亥，二更半。对东南。

释义：在南沙，从铜章（南海礁）开往光星仔（光星仔礁），航行针用缝针（壬丙和巳亥的中间线），航行二更半，到达收帆。航行方向对东南。

第70条 自光星仔去大光星，用卯酉，一更收。对正西。

释义：在南沙，从光星仔（光星仔礁）开往大光星（光星礁），航行针用单针（卯酉），航程一更到达。航行方向对正西。

第71条 自光星仔去海口线，用壬丙子午，四更。对西北。

释义：在南沙，从光星仔（光星仔礁）开往海口线（柏礁），航行针用缝针（壬丙和子午的中间线），航程四更到达。航行方向对西北。

第72条 自光星仔去石公里，用乾巽，二更。对东南。

释义：在南沙，从光星仔（光星仔礁）开往石公里（弹丸礁），航行针用单针（乾巽），航程二更到达。航行方向对东南。

第73条 自石公里去五百弍，用丁未，二更半收。对西南。

释义：在南沙，从石公里（弹丸礁）开往五百弍（皇路礁），航行针用缝针（癸丁和丑未的中间线），航程二更半到达。航行方向对西南。

第74条 自五百弍去丹节线，用未添丁，三更。对西南。

释义：在南沙，从五百弍（皇路礁）开往丹节（南通礁），航行针用缝针（丑未和癸丁的中间线），航程三更到达。航行方向对西南。

第75条 自丹节去墨瓜线，用坤未，六更收。对西南。

释义：在南沙，从丹节（南通礁）开往墨瓜线（南屏礁），航行针用缝针（艮坤和丑未的中间线），航程六更到达。航行方向对西南。

第76条 自秤沟（钩）去荷扐门，用午添二线丁，五更。对西南。

释义：在南沙，从秤沟（景宏岛）开往荷扐门（南华礁），航行针用缝针（子午加二线癸丁），航程五更到达。航行方向对西南。

第77条 自秤沟去六门，用单丁，五更收。对西南。

释义：在南沙，从秤沟（景宏岛）开往六门（六门礁），航行针用单针（癸丁），航程五更到达收帆。航行方向对西南。

第78条 自荷扐门去坡箕，用壬丙，四更。对东南。

释义：在南沙，从荷扐门（南华礁）开往坡箕（簸箕礁），航行针用单针（壬丙），航程四更到达收帆。航行方向对东南。

第79条 自六门去坡箕，用巳亥，四更收。对东南。

释义：在南沙，从六门（六门礁）开往坡箕（簸箕礁），航行针用单针（巳亥），航程四更到达。航行方向对东南。

第80条 自荷扐门去铜章，用子午，四更。对正南。

释义：在南沙，从荷扐门（南华礁）开往铜章（南海礁），航行针用单针（子午），航程四更到达收帆。航行方向对正南。

第81条 自荷扐门去深圈，用辰戌，四更收。对东南。

释义：在南沙，从荷扐门（南华礁）开往深圈（榆亚暗沙），航行针用单针（辰戌），航程四更到达，航行方向对东南。

第82条 自六门去铜章，用壬丙，四更收。对东南。

释义：在南沙，从六门（六门礁）开往铜章（南海礁），航行针用单针（壬丙），航程四更到达收帆。航行方向对东南。

第83条 自六门去石盘，用辰戌，二更收。对西北。

释义：在南沙，从六门（六门礁）开往石盘（毕生礁），航行针用单针（辰戌），航程二更到达收帆。航行方向对西北。

第84条 自刘牛刘去六门，用壬丙，五更收。对东南。

释义：在南沙，从刘牛刘（大现礁）开往六门（六门礁），航行针用单针（壬丙），航程五更到达。航行方向对东南。

第85条 自刘牛刘去荷扐门，用巳亥，五更收。对东南。

释义：在南沙，从刘牛刘（大现礁）开往荷扐门（南华礁），航行针用单针（巳亥），航程五更到达收帆。航行方向对东南。

第86条 自刘牛刘去石盘，用癸丁，五更收。对西南。

释义：在南沙，从刘牛刘（大现礁）开往石盘（毕生礁），航行针用单针（癸丁），航程五更到达收帆。航行方向对西南。

第87条 自刘牛刘去秤钩，用辰戌，三更收。对东南。

释义：在南沙，从刘牛刘（大现礁）开往秤钩（景宏岛），航行针用单针

（辰戌），航程三更到达。航行方向对东南。

第88条 自荷扨门去六门，用辰戌，一更。对西北。

释义：在南沙，从荷扨门（南华礁）开往六门（六门礁），航行针用单针（辰戌），航程一更到达。航行方向对西北。

第89条 自刘牛刘去上戊，用寅申，四更。对西南。

释义：在南沙，从刘牛刘（大现礁）开往上戊（永暑礁），航行针用单针（寅申），航程四更到达。航行方向对西南。

第90条 自海口线去铜铳，用巳亥，五更。对西北。

释义：在南沙，从海口线（柏礁）开往铜铳（东礁），航行针用单针（巳亥），航程五更到达。航行方向对西北。

第91条 自铜铳去龙鼻，用乙辛，二更收。对西北。

释义：在南沙，从铜铳（东礁）开往龙鼻（西礁），航行针用单针（乙辛），航程二更到达收帆。航行方向对西北。

第92条 自龙鼻去鸟仔峙，用寅申，二更。对西南。

释义：在南沙，从龙鼻（西礁）开往鸟仔峙（南威岛），航行针用单针（寅申），航程二更到达。航行方向对西南。

第93条 自鸟仔峙去乙辛，用乙辛，二更收。对西北。

释义：在南沙，从鸟仔峙（南威岛）开往（西头）乙辛（日积礁），航行针用单针（乙辛），航程二更到达。航行方向对西北。

第94条 自（西头）乙辛回安南山，用巳亥，廿余更。对西北。

释义：在南沙，从（西头）乙辛（日积礁）开往安南山（越南山脉），航行针用单针（巳亥），航程二十多更到达。航行方向对西北。

第95条 （西头）乙辛与锣汉湾头，乾巽相对，二十二更。对西北。

释义：在南沙，从（西头）乙辛（日积礁）开往锣汉湾头，航行针用单针（乾巽），航程二十二更到达收帆。航行方向对西北。

第96条 自南乙去南乙线仔，用乙辛，一更。对西北。

释义：在南沙，从南乙（鸿庥岛）开往南乙线仔（南薰礁），航行针用单针（乙辛），航程一更到达。航行方向对西北。

第97条 自南乙线仔去刘牛刘，用甲卯，二更半。对正西。

释义：在南沙，从南乙线仔（南薰礁）开往刘牛刘（大现礁），航行针用缝针（甲庚和卯酉的中间线），航程二更半，到达收帆。航行方向对正西。

第98条 自铜金至黄山马，用丑未，二更。对西南。

释义：在南沙，从铜金（杨信沙洲）开往黄山马（太平岛），航行针用单针（丑未），航程二更到达。航行方向对西南。

1 苏德柳本《更路簿》原文及释义

第99条 自铜金去三角,用乙卯,五更收。对东。

释义:在南沙,从铜金(杨信沙洲)开往三角(三角礁),航行针用缝针(乙辛和卯酉的中间线),航程二更到达。航行方向对东。

第100条 自断节下双门,用乾巽巳亥,二更收。对西北。

释义:在南沙,从断节(仁爱礁)开往双门(美济礁),航行针用缝针(乾巽和巳亥的中间线),航程二更到达。航行方向对西北。

第101条 自双门下三角,用壬丙巳亥,二更收。对西北

释义:在南沙,从双门(美济礁)开往三角(三角礁),航行针用缝针(壬丙和巳亥的中间线),航程二更到达。航行方向对西北。

第102条 自海口线上六门,用丁未,三更收。对东北。

释义:在南沙,从海口线(柏礁)开往六门(六门礁),航行针用缝针(癸丁和丑未的中间线),航程三更到达。航行方向对东北。

第103条 自双门去一线,用午丙,二更收。对西北。

释义:在南沙,从双门(美济礁)开往一线(禄沙礁),航行针用缝针(子午和壬丙的中间线),航程二更到达。航行方向对西北。

第104条 自三角下银锅,用乙辛加三线辰戌,三更半。对西南。

释义:在南沙,从三角(三角礁)开往银锅(安达礁),航行针用缝针(乙辛加三线辰戌),航程三更半到达。航行方向对西南。

第105条 自丹节去海口线,北风用癸丁,拾更收。

释义:在南沙,从丹节(南通礁)开往海口线(柏礁),如果是北风,航行针用单针(癸丁),航程十更到达。

第106条 自墨瓜线去浮罗丑未,用寅申加二线坤,二十五更。

释义:在南沙,开往墨瓜线(南屏礁)开往浮罗丑未(马来半岛的浮罗),航行针用缝针(寅申加二线艮坤),航程二十五更到达。

第107条 自墨瓜线去宏武銮,用甲庚,二十五更。西南。

释义:在南沙,开往墨瓜线(南屏礁)开往宏武銮,航行针用单针(甲庚),航程二十五更到达。航行方向对西南。

第108条 往浮罗喇郁,用甲卯,二十五更。

释义:在南沙,开往浮罗喇郁,航行针用缝针(甲庚和卯酉的中间线),航程二十五更到达。

第109条 自红草线排下裤归,用丁未,二更。

释义:在南沙,从红草线排(长滩)开往裤归(库归礁),航行针用缝针(癸丁和丑未的中间线),航程二更到达。

第110条 自丹节去浮罗喇(喇)郁,用甲庚加一线寅申,三十二更。

释义:在南沙,从丹节(南通礁)开往浮罗喇郁,航行针用缝针(甲庚

加一线寅申），航程三十二更可到达。

  第111条 自光星仔去石公里，用子午加三线丙，更半。

  释义：在南沙，从光星仔（光星仔礁）开往石公里（弹丸礁），航行针用缝针（子午加三线壬丙），航程一更半可到达。

  第112条 自石盘去上戊，用乾巽巳亥，四更收。对西北。

  释义：在南沙，从石盘（毕生礁）开往上戊（永暑礁），航行针用缝针（乾巽和巳亥的中间线），航程四更到达。航行方向对西北。

  第113条 自六门去海口线，用艮坤，三更收。三更半。

  释义：在南沙，从六门（六门礁）开往海口线（柏礁），航行针用单针（艮坤），航程三更到达，或三更半到达。

  第114条 自五百贰（弍）去海口线，北风用午丁，七更。

  释义：在南沙，从五百贰（皇路礁）开往海口线（柏礁），如果是北风，航行针用缝针（子午和癸丁的中间线），航程七更到达。

  第115条 自黄山马东去九章，用巳亥，二更收。对东南。

  释义：在南沙，从黄山马东（敦谦沙洲）开往九章（九章群礁），航行针用单针（巳亥），航程二更到达。航行方向对东南。

  第116条 自铜铳仔下大铜铳，用甲卯，二更收。对西。

  释义：在南沙，从铜铳仔（华阳礁）开往大铜铳（东礁），航行针用缝针（甲庚和卯酉的中间线），航程二更到达。航行方向对西。

1.3 其他更路（南洋更路）①

1.3.1 驶船更路定例

如船外罗东过，看水醒三日，且看风面，船身不可贪东。前此舟近西，不可贪西。海水澄清，并有朽木飘流，浅成挑，如见飞鸟（鸭头鸟）方正路。舟过外罗七更是长线，连石塘内，北有全富峙，老粗峙，世江峙，三足峙，又有尾峙。如舟东见此七峙，急急转帆，用甲庚卯酉驶回。见外罗尝且上坔山，白（自）烟筒头到尖笔罗过，舟近山约离一更开妙。到此外，舟身可以倚甲庚驶开为妙。或到七洲洋中，见有流界几分，即是南亭门。若干洋如见尖笔罗，过之可乾巽辰戌针。三更取外罗外过舟，用丙午取烟头大佛，又用丁午八更取罗安头。

1.3.2 大潭往海南岛沿岸、广东沿岸、西沙群岛、中南半岛、南洋群岛更路

1.3.2.1

1. 大坛（潭）对北（广东沿海），丑未相对，浮马十五更。
2. 大坛（潭）与单人峙相对，浮马一更。
3. 铜钱与大坛（潭）相对，甲庚卯酉，四更。
4. 上皆（上屿：宣德群岛？；下屿：永乐群岛？）与（？）峙丑未相对，浮马十六更。
5. 铜钱与南行了甲庚卯酉对，三更。
6. 铜钱与北峙子午对，浮马十更。
7. 或舟在北峙对外一更开，用针三更取铜鼓内过，用丙午取铜鼓是带坡马，北边湾名叫大澳门。
8. 北峙对铜鼓坤未，三更。
9. 北峙与铜钱子午对，十三更。
10. 北峙与干豆乾巽已亥对，十四更。
11. 北峙与大坛（潭）癸丁丑未对，十六更。

---

① 说明：1. 原文取自韩振华等《我国南海诸岛史料汇编》，东方出版社1988年版，第369－381页；广东省地名委员会编：《南海诸岛地名资料汇编》，广东省地图出版社1987年版，第88－95页；周伟民、唐玲玲：《南海天书：海南渔民"更路簿"文化诠释》，昆仑出版社2015年版，第255－281页。

2. 关于苏德柳本《更路簿》中涉及东南亚（南洋）俗名（土地名）的相关信息，请参照附件"苏德柳本《更路簿》东南亚（外洋）地名中英文信息一览表"。

3. 为便于翻译，避免漏译，使译文条理清晰，故对原文的第四篇中12个部分进行了编号。

12. 或舟在铜鼓外约一更零开，用单丁加乙线未，五更取大洲，大洲外过用丁未平取赤好（仔），内过是浮马，南边湾可泊舟。

13. 铜鼓与干豆长沙用乾巽辰戌对，十更。

14. 铜鼓与大坛（潭）癸丁丑未对，十六更。

15. 罗万与铜鼓艮坤丑未对，二十五更。

16. 大洲与干豆乙辛辰戌对，十二更。

17. 大洲与石塘壬丙巳亥对，十五更。

18. 大洲与尖笔罗艮坤丑未对，十八更收。

19. 大洲与单峙丑未对，十八更。

20. 大洲与外罗丑未加乙线丁，贰拾更。

21. 大洲与新竹子午癸丁对，贰十八更。

22. 大洲与大佛子午对，三十六更。

23. 陵水与尖笔罗丑未对，十六更。

24. 陵水与外罗子午癸丁对，十七更收。

25. 宇林与外罗子午对，十四更。

26. 榆林与尖笔罗子午癸丁对，十四更。

1.3.2.2

1. 外罗与大佛子午对，十二更。

2. 外罗与万里长（沙）卯酉甲庚对，十四更。

3. 外罗与草峙乾巽对，十二更。

4. 外罗与沙圯角艮坤寅申对，更余。

5. 外罗与枚极丁未对，十更。

6. 外罗与窝头卯酉对，更余。

7. 外罗与硬里甲庚对，壹更。

8. 外罗与纸秽港竹竿峙子午癸丁对。

9. 外罗与洲鸭子午壬丙对。

10. 外罗与尖笔罗乾巽辰戌对，三更。

11. 外罗与珠窝头卯酉，离更零，此门可近，用单午针。

12. 外罗与干豆寅申对，六更。

13. 外罗与竹竿峙子午癸丁对。

14. 外罗与长沙乙辛卯酉对，七更。

1.3.2.3

1. 马路清与大佛子午壬丙对，四更。

2. 带坡马羊角峙与新竹港子午壬丙对，一更。

3. 羊角峙与白豆清午丙对，二更。

4. 羊角离枚松极零倚即是新竹港,峙内打水十八托,外打水三十托,下边即钓壹。

5. 羊角峙与新竹子午壬丙对,乙更。

1.3.2.4

1. 新洲往大佛,如舟在新洲有一更开,用单丙去大佛四更。

2. 羊角峙去白豆清内外过用午丙针,白豆清南边湾东北风可泊舟,内边坡圮有澳(坳)湾,东北西南风亦可泊舟。

3. 大佛与云述癸丁对,三更。

4. 大佛与云术上门浮马艮坤寅申有牌,内一更。

5. 大佛与洲押午两对。

6. 烟筒头与洲鸭子午癸丁对,十二更。

7. 烟筒头与长沙尾甲寅卯酉对。

8. 大佛打水六十托,用午丁针,三更取加俑藐,大佛山上有烟筒头,浮马内边东北风可泊船。

9. 云术对门外边马(码)头,子午癸丁针取罗汉湾头,五更带坡马。

10. 云述外马(码)头子午壬丙对洲鸭,浮马八更,南边有浅海,南北生甚长,约有二更远。

11. 罗湾头与昆仑坤未对,十七更。

12. 罗湾头与赤埃头甲庚加寅申对,三更。

13. 罗湾头与西甲庚寅申对,一更半。

14. 带坡马赤坎与洲鸭乾巽对。

1.3.2.5

罗湾头往昆仑更路。

1. 如船在罗湾头离半更开,用坤未平,十七更取昆仑。

2. 罗湾头下洋打水有十七八托,正路如昆仑外过。约扣算更鼓,系是看针高底(低),顶头坤未平可见昆仑。或深或浅,打水为定,或有二十余托,又有三四十托,辛酉戌三字。昆仑是浮马,四边不泊舟。

3. 覆锅与鹤顶甲庚对,更零远。

4. 鹤顶与外任甲庚卯酉对,更余收。

5. 昆仑对门有昆仑仔,卯酉对,二更。昆仑甲卯三更见昆仑仔。

1.3.2.6

1. 昆仑与丁加宜艮坤寅申对,三十更。

2. 昆仑与吉连州甲庚寅申对,三十更。

3. 昆仑与斗磁丑未对,二十九更。

4. 昆仑与草磁艮坤寅申对,三十更。

5. 昆仑与前陈子午对壬丙，三十八更。

6. 昆仑与东竹子午癸丁对，三十八更。

7. 船在昆仑南边约一更开，以单酉取真磁，船在北边约一更开，用卯酉加三线甲取真磁，昆仑外过约一更开，以艮坤八更取玳瑁。

8. 用丑未五更见鹤顶山。用寅申十五更取东西洞，外边过有石如瑁。

9. 昆仑一更船开，以癸丁丑未十四更取吕宋，防浅。

10. 昆仑一更开，以丑未十七更真磁林卿（即）浅。

11. 昆仑内过，以坤申拾式（更），有浅不识某名。

12. 用单坤十四更，见宋吕（吕宋）当头。

13. 昆仑内过，以艮放近寅十六更（是）玳瑁。

14. 洲押上昆仑外过用丑艮癸三字，无不差矣，单寅针有山不识其名。

15. 昆仑去地盘驶到路中，打水二十余托，或有四十托，是正路坁地。

16. 用单未四十更取地盘仔，用丁未三十八更取地盘仔。

17. 昆仑西去，打水肆拾托，不远，有赤礁出水。

18. 用庚针八更取真磁，论小峙分金字对坐向。

19. 大昆仑与小昆仑卯酉对，主大昆仑东头。如真磁甲庚八更。

20. 如船在东北头，以丁未三十八更取地盘。

21. 或在昆仑东北一更开，用丑癸十五更取赤坎，真磁对向。

1.3.2.7

1. 真磁与吉连洲丑未对，式十更。

2. 真磁与粗背卯酉对，十八更。

3. 真磁与坎后角壬丙巳亥对，一更。

4. 真磁与大横乾巽对，八更。

5. 真磁与笔架乾巽巳亥对。

6. 大横与小横辰戌对，五更。

7. 假磁与大横乾巽辰戌对。

8. 小横与笔架乾巽辰戌贪对，至式十三更。若是下洋江用乾巽针。

9. 笔架头与势厂门卯酉对。

10. 陈公峙与竹峙癸丁子午对。

11. 眷佛苏与痞甲庚对。

12. 陈公峙与东势厂门卯酉对。

13. 竹峙（与）鸟头厂浅癸丁对坐。

14. 或在真磁内边身以丙巳针式十六更取茶盘。

1.3.2.8

真磁去新州埠头更路。

1. 真磁西势开船，以丙午三十八更取地盘东边过，东南头有不尖三枝似龙角样。

2. （真磁）丙午三更半取东西竹，自中门过。

3. （真磁）以单丙针三更取将军帽（帽），东西幌（帽）带甚长。舟过帽带，以单丁取罗汉峙外，东南头去有白石壹个，有岭，岭上有灯为证。

4. 自中入船，以甲卯针一更半取赤①，又用单酉针式更半取埠泊船。

1.3.2.9

真磁往丁加宜更路。

1. 自真磁外过离一更开，以单丁针二十更取草峙，或见绵花峙，约赤坎在。草峙是浮马，东北风可泊舟。

2. 真磁远看三四只峙，门中打水十四五托，圯地，外过以乙辛辰戌，八更取大横。

3. 真磁与假磁巳亥对，离有三更远，打水十八托。

4. 大横内打水十六托，外过打水二十五，是泥地。以乙辛辰戌三更取小横。

5. 小横南畔打水二十四托，远看作断三四只，西高东底（低），门中流抛开，倚甚急。

6. （小横）以单乾针十更，又乾巽辰戌十五更取笔架，笔架头多尖峰，生甚长，似笔架样，打水式十托。

7. （笔架）以壬丙针取陈公峙，并见内面犁头山。

8. 陈公峙以壬子更取鸟头浅，五更东边过，打水式十托。用单癸丁三更取竹峙，以壬子三更。

1.3.2.10

1. 暹罗港正路，可防错入彭享（亨）港。知欲（欲知）正路，可以子癸针，或单丁亦可。

2. 大横与赤仔是乙辛对，三拾更。

3. 大横与苏梅乙辛卯酉对，三十五更。

4. 大横南离半更开，以庚申对猫鼠，三十一更远。

5. 大横与无来有澳艮坤对坐。

6. 大横与赤仔港口乙辛卯酉对，式十五更。

7. 小横与苏梅是卯酉对，二十更。

8. 小横与无来由澳丑未对。

9. 真薯与东竹壬丙巳亥对，十更。

---

① 疑缺字，大概指新加坡东。

10. 真峙与粟峙壬丙巳亥对，三拾更。

11. 真薯与南离半更开，与大横是乾巽对，七更。

12. 真薯与坑仔长壬丙对，拾七更。

13. 真薯三角癸丁丑未对，弍更。

14. 真薯西，离更半开，与斗峙癸丁对，弍十五更。

15. 假薯与大横乙辛辰戌对，肆更。

16. 假薯与真薯子午壬丙对。

17. 梨海山与宝峙乾巽巳亥对。

18. 梨海山与外罗壬丙对。

19. 上洋有地盘大山，放洋以癸丁丑未十八更，又转单丁二十更见昆仑。

1.3.2.11

1. 舟在东竹，以丙巳八更取长腰外过，石礁甚多，不得依近。

2. 舟在长腰离半更开，以丙午针取猪姆头八更，不可依近，内湾猪母猪仔礁甚多，宜须防忌。

3. 加舟在猪姆头更零开，以单丁三更取漫头峙。

4. 漫头峙用丙巳针七更取南梦，又转单午针三更取荪灯。

5. 逼灯东湾入即是文肚湾，亦可泊舟。如舟在猪母头，以单丙针四更取七星，又转丙午针四更取南梦，转以单午针三更取灯。灯西有石礁一只，壹只出水名鸣禽阻。离坡半更开，流水甚急。

1.3.2.12

猪母头落旧港针路。

1. 如舟在猪姆头，以单丁三更取梦头峙。取小横南畔打水弍十四托，远看断做三只（峙）。

2. 此行不是外过，以癸丁加弍线午丙，山离（离山）一更开，十一更取旧港。

3. 旧港与文肚甲庚寅申坐。

4. 以舟在猪母头一更开，以癸丁针八更取长腰。

5. 加（如）舟在长腰一更开，以壬子七更取东竹。

6. 如舟在新洲港出，以卯酉五更至罗汉（峙），东南边有白石十一尺，自中出舟不得下洋。

7. 东竹与长腰子午对，九更。

1.3.3

1. 自昆仑去真仕，用甲卯，九（更）。

2. 自真仕去大横，用乾巽，六更。

3. 自大横去小横，用辰戌。

4. 自大横去云冒,用乾巽兼巳亥,六(更)。
5. 自小横去云冒,用乙未,二更。
6. 自云冒去谷远,用卯酉,十八更。离三更有云冒仔。

1.3.4
1. 自新州港出,用卯酉更取白石盏盎灯①。
2. 自白石盏灯用壬丙兼二线巳亥取长腰,七更。
3. 自长腰马去猪姆头马,用壬丙,O更②。
4. 自猪姆头去地盘仔,用壬丙,二更收。
5. 自地盘仔去铁镰峙,用壬丙巳亥,三更收。
6. 自铁砧峙内边去斗峙,用子午兼二线壬丙,八更。
7. 斗峙与佁僞仕艮坤相对,斗峙离仕埠约更半远。

1.3.5 自星洲去吧里更路
1. 自疗门灯去青峙仔,用乾巽,四更收。
2. 自青峙仔去猪姆头,用壬丙,乙(柴)更收。
3. 自猪姆头去偈倒峙,用单丁,三更收。东过。
4. 自偈倒峙去秤星,用单乾巽,三更收。西过。
5. 自秤星去佛肚灯,用单丁,三更收。西过,亦见禽胆灯。
6. 自禽胆灯去乙辛灯,用乙辛,二更收。
7. 自乙辛灯去门上灯,用巳亥,七更收。
8. 自门上灯去三立,用壬丙,二更收。
9. 自三立去吉里文,用乾巽辰戌,二十九(更)收。
10. 自吉里汶去蚯蚓上,用乙辛辰戌,十九更收。中断依蚯蚓土向东驶,蚯蚓土了即见角办峙。
11. 自三门灯去鸟旧排灯,用壬丙,三更半收。
12. 自鸟旧排灯东过去知心线灯,用单午,二更半收。
13. 自知心线去外南行门,二边角总有灯看入门,用丁未驶即见笳箩马。
14. 自加箩马去青鱼头,用乾巽辰戌,约五更收。

1.3.6
1. 大洲与尖笔罗坤未对,十八更。
2. 大洲与外罗丁未对,式十一更。
3. 外罗与白豆清午丙对,十一更。

---

① 可能是指初期在海上设置的航标灯。这是在新加坡海上的航行。联系到下一篇自新加坡至印度尼西亚的航行,大海上有航标灯。

② 疑"O更"其中漏字。据考证,是一更。

4. 白豆清与大佛午丙对，四更。
5. 大佛与云述午丁对，四更。
6. 大佛与洲押午丙对。
7. 云述与禄安午丁对，五更。
8. 禄安与昆仑坤未对，十九更。
9. 禄安与洲押，子午对，三更。
10. 昆仑与地盘，三十六更，单丁对。
11. 昆仑与浮罗唎郁，乾巽巳亥对，二十四更。
12. 浮罗唎郁与宏午銮水船头，乾巽巳亥对。
13. 大地盘与东竹壬丙对，三更。
14. 东竹与白石盏灯，午丁对，六更。

2 彭正楷本《更路簿》原文及释义

2.1 立东海更路（西沙更路）[①]

第1条 自尾峙下半路用癸丁加一线子午，二更，向南驶收。

释义：在西沙，从尾峙（金银岛）开往半路（中建岛），航行针用缝针（癸丁加一线子午），航程二更到达，航行方向对南。

第2条 自三圈下半路用甲庚寅申，六更，向西南驶收。

释义：在西沙，从三圈（浪花礁）开往半路（中建岛），航行针用缝针（甲庚和寅申的中间线），航程六更到达，航行方向对西南。

第3条 自半路往干豆用癸丁，五更半，向东北驶收。

释义：在西沙，从半路（中建岛）开往干豆（北礁），航行针用单针（癸丁），航程五更半到达，航行方向对东北。

第4条 自大圈头上往三圈南风用辰戌，三更，向东南驶收。

释义：在西沙，从大圈（华光礁）东北边开往三圈；如果是南风，航行针用单针（辰戌），航程三更到达，航行方向对东南。

第5条 自老粗大门驶出四江门用乾巽辰戌，二更，向东南驶，二边相对。

释义：在西沙，从老粗大门（老粗门）开往四江门（晋卿门），航行针用缝针（乾巽和辰戌的中间线），航程二更到达，航行方向对东南。

第6条 自三脚门上驶往银峙用子午壬丙平，向北驶，二边相见。

释义：在西沙，从三脚（琛航岛）的水道出海口往返银峙（银屿）航行针用缝针（正对子午和壬丙的中间线），航行方向对北。

---

① 说明：1. 为便于英译，对"立东海更路"和"立北海更路"进行了编号。最早的抄本没有编号。

2. 原文及其释义主要参考了周伟民、唐玲玲《南海天书：海南渔民"更路簿"文化诠释》，昆仑出版社2015年版，第611-641页；夏代云：《卢业发、吴淑茂、黄家礼〈更路簿〉研究》，海洋出版社2016年版。在此致以衷心感谢。

3. 关于彭正楷本《更路簿》中南海诸岛俗名（土地名）的起源及其相关信息，详见"苏德柳本和彭正楷本《更路簿》南海诸岛俗名起源与传说"和"苏德柳本和彭正楷本《更路簿》南海诸岛中英文信息一览表"。

第 7 条　自猫注往干豆用辰戌加一线乙辛，三更，向西北驶收。

释义：在西沙，从猫注（永兴岛）开往干豆（北礁），航行针用缝针（辰戌加一线乙辛），航程三更到达，航行方向对西北。

第 8 条　自三峙往猫注子午相对，向南驶收。

释义：在西沙，从三峙（南岛）开往猫注（永兴岛），航行针用单针（子午），航行方向对南。

第 9 条　自红草门上猫兴用乙辛，一更半，向东南驶收。

释义：在西沙，从红草门（红草门）开往猫兴（东岛），航行针用单针（乙辛），航程一更半到达，航行方向对东南。

第 10 条　自四江往猫兴用甲庚，四更半收。

释义：在西沙，从四江（晋卿岛）开往猫兴（东岛），航行针用单针（甲庚），航程四更半到达。

第 11 条　自石塘往大圈用乾巽，一更收。

释义：在西沙，从石塘（永乐群岛）开往大圈（华光礁），航行针用单针（乾巽），航程一更到达。

第 12 条　自干豆往石塘用巳亥，二更收。

释义：在西沙，从干豆（北礁）开往石塘（永乐群岛），航行针用单针（巳亥），航程二更到达。

第 13 条　自猫注往二圈用丁未，二更半收。

释义：在西沙，从猫注（永兴岛）开往二圈（玉琢礁），航行针用缝针（癸丁和丑未的中间线），航程二更半到达。

第 14 条　自船坎尾往干豆用乙辛加卯酉，三更收。

释义：在西沙，从船坎尾（西沙洲）开往干豆（北礁），航行针用缝针（乙辛和卯酉的中间线），航程三更到达。

第 15 条　自红草往石塘用寅申，三更收。

释义：在西沙，从红草（南沙洲）开往石塘（永乐群岛），航行针用单针（寅申），航程三更到达。

第 16 条　自二圈往石塘用乾巽，一更半收。

释义：在西沙，从二圈（玉琢礁）开往石塘（永乐群岛），航行针用单针（乾巽），航程一更半到达。

第 17 条　自二圈往大圈用寅申，一更收。

释义：在西沙，从二圈（玉琢礁）开往大圈（华光礁），航行针用单针（寅申），航程一更到达。

第 18 条　自三圈到奈买驶巳亥到卅更转回壬丙卅更收。

释义：在西沙，从三圈（浪花礁）开往奈买（双子群岛），航行针用单针（巳亥），航程三十更，航行针转回单针（壬丙），航程三十更到达。

2.2 立北海更路（南沙更路）①

第1条 自白峙仔到双峙驶乾巽巳亥，平二十八更收。

释义：在西沙，从白峙仔（盘石屿）开往双峙（双子群礁）航行针用缝针（正对着乾巽和巳亥的中间线），航程二十八更到达。

第2条 自三圈往罗孔用乾巽驶二十八更收。

释义：在西沙，从三圈（浪花礁）开往罗孔（马欢岛）航行针用单针（乾巽），航程二十八更到达。

第3条 自双峙往铁峙驶子午癸丁平二更收。

释义：在南沙，从双峙（双子群礁）开往铁峙（中业岛）航行针用缝针（子午和癸丁的中间线），航程二更到达。

第4条 自下峙沙仔到铁峙沙排驶壬丙二线巳亥，二更收。

释义：在南沙，从下峙沙仔（奈罗礁）开往铁峙沙排（铁峙礁）航行针用缝针（壬丙加二线巳亥），航程二更到达。

第5条 自铁峙到库归驶乙辛辰戌，二更收。

释义：在南沙，从铁峙（中业岛）开往库归（库归礁），航行针用缝针（乙辛和辰戌的中间线），航程二更到达。

第6条 自库归到三角驶乙辛辰戌，五更收。

释义：在南沙，从库归（库归礁）开往三角（三角礁），航行针用缝针（乙辛和辰戌的中间线），航程五更到达。

第7条 自三角到双门驶乾巽，二更收，回驶壬丙。

释义：在南沙，从三角（三角礁）开往双门（美济礁），航行针用单针（乾巽），航程二更到达。返回时航行针用单针（壬丙）。

第8条 自双门到断节驶乙辛卯酉，二更收，回乾戌收。

释义：在南沙，从双门（美济礁）开往断节（仁爱礁），航行针用缝针（乙辛和卯酉的中间线），航程二更到达。返回时航行针用缝针（乾巽和辰戌

---

① 说明：1. 为便于英译，对"立东海更路"和"立北海更路"进行了编号。最早的抄本没有编号。

2. 原文及其释义主要参考了周伟民、唐玲玲《南海天书：海南渔民"更路簿"文化诠释》，昆仑出版社2015年版，第611–641；夏代云：《卢业发、吴淑茂、黄家礼〈更路簿〉研究》，海洋出版社2016年版。在此致以衷心感谢。

3. 关于彭正楷本《更路簿》中南海诸岛俗名（土地名）的起源及其相关信息，详见"苏德柳本和彭正楷本《更路簿》南海诸岛俗名起源与传说"和"苏德柳本和彭正楷本《更路簿》南海诸岛中英文信息一览表"。

的中间线）。

第9条　自断节到牛车英驶乙辛，二更收，回全上条（乾戌）收。

释义：在南沙，从断节（仁爱礁），开往牛车英（牛车轮礁），航行针用单针（乙辛），航程二更到达。返回时航行针用缝针（乾巽与辰戌的中间线）。

第10条　自牛车英到脚拔驶乾巽，三更收，回用壬丙。

释义：在南沙，从牛车英（牛车轮礁）开往脚拔（海口礁），航行针用单针（乾巽），航程三更到达。返回时航行针用单针（壬丙）。

第11条　自脚拔到石龙驶乙辛卯酉，平二更收。

释义：在南沙，从脚拔（海口礁）开往石龙（舰长礁），航行针用缝针（乙辛和卯酉的中间线），航程二更到达。

第12条　自石龙到鱼鳞驶癸丁，四更收。

释义：在南沙，从石龙（舰长礁）开往鱼鳞（仙宾礁），航行针用单针（癸丁），航程四更到达。

第13条　自鱼鳞到五凤驶巳亥，四更收。

释义：在南沙，从鱼鳞（仙宾礁）开往五凤（五方礁），航行针用单针（巳亥），航程四更到达。

第14条　自贡士沙到红草沙排驶乙辛辰戌三更收。

释义：在南沙，从贡士沙（贡士礁）开往红草沙排（长滩），航行针用缝针（乙辛和辰戌的中间线），航程三更到达。

第15条　自沙排到火哀驶乾巽，二更收。

释义：在南沙，从沙排（长滩）开往火哀（火艾礁），航行针用单针（乾巽），航程二更到达。

第16条　自火哀到三角驶乾巽四更收。

释义：在南沙，从火哀（火艾礁）开往三角（三角礁），航行针用单针（乾巽），航程四更到达。

第17条　自红草线排到红草驶乙辛二更收。

释义：在南沙，从红草线排（长滩）开往红草（西月岛），航行针用单针（乙辛），航程二更到达。

第18条　自红草到罗孔驶乙辛卯酉平五更收。

释义：在南沙，从红草（西月岛）开往罗孔（马欢岛），航行针用缝针（乙辛和卯酉的中间线），航程五更到达。

第19条　自罗孔至鲨藤驶乙辛卯酉二更收。

释义：在南沙，从罗孔（马欢岛）开往鲨藤（鲨藤礁），航行针用缝针（乙辛和卯酉的中间线），航程二更到达。

第20条　自红草到五凤驶乙辛辰戌四更收。

释义：在南沙，从红草（西月岛）开往五凤（五方礁），航行针用缝针（乙辛和辰戌的中间线），航程四更到达。

第21条　自五凤至断节驶壬丙四更收。

释义：在南沙，从五凤（五方礁）开往断节（仁爱礁），航行针鲔单针（壬丙），航程四更到达。

第22条　自断节至双担驶巳亥二更收。

释义：在南沙，从断节（仁爱礁）开往双担（信义礁），航行针用单针（巳亥），航程二更到达。

第23条　自双担至海公驶乾巽辰戌三更收。

释义：在南沙，从双担（信义礁）开往海公（半月礁），航行针用缝针（乾巽和辰戌的中间线），航程三更到达。

第24条　自海公回双担驶壬丙三更直收。

释义：在南沙，从海公（半月礁）开往双担（信义礁），航行针用单针（壬丙），航程三更到达。

第25条　自双担下鸟串驶乙辛二更收。

释义：在南沙，从双担（信义礁）开往鸟串（仙娥礁），航行针用单针（乙辛），航程二更到达。

第26条　自鸟串回银饼驶壬丙兼二线巳亥五更收。

释义：在南沙，从鸟串（仙娥礁）开往银饼（安达礁），航行针用缝针（壬丙加二线巳亥），航程五更到达。

第27条　自铁岛至铜金驶辰戌二更收。

释义：在南沙，从铁岛（中业岛）开往铜金（杨信沙洲），航行针用单针（辰戌），航程二更到达。

第28条　自铜金至银饼驶乾巽二更收。

释义：在南沙，从铜金（杨信沙洲）开往银饼（安达礁），航行针用单针（乾巽），航程二更到达。

第29条　自银饼回黄山马驶卯酉三更收。

释义：在南沙，从银饼（安达礁）返回黄山马（太平岛），航行针用单针（卯酉），航程三更到达。

第30条　自黄山马至牛桅驶乾巽二更收。

释义：在南沙，从黄山马（太平岛）开往牛桅（牛轭礁），航行针用单针（乾巽），航程二更到达。

第31条　自黄山马落南蜜驶壬丙一更收。

释义：在南沙，从黄山马（太平岛）开往南蜜（鸿庥岛），航行真用单针

（壬丙），航程一更到达。

第32条 自牛杞至目镜驶壬丙巳亥平九更收。

释义：在南沙，从牛杞（牛轭礁）开往目镜（司令礁），航行针用缝针（正对着壬丙和巳亥的中间线），航程九更到达。

第33条 自目镜至无乜线驶乾巽兼辰戌三更收。

释义：在南沙，从目镜（司令礁）开往无乜线（无乜礁），航行针用缝针（乾巽和辰戌的中间线），航程三更到达。

第34条 自无乜沙至深圈驶壬丙三更收。

释义：在南沙，从无乜沙（无乜礁）到深圈（榆亚暗沙），航行针用单针（壬丙），航程三更到达。

第35条 自无乜沙落恶落门驶寅申三更收。

释义：在南沙，从无乜沙（无乜礁）开往恶落门（南华礁），航行针用单针（寅申），航程三更到达。

第36条 自深圈下半簸驶甲庚兼四线寅申二更收。

释义：在南沙，从深圈（榆亚暗沙）开往半簸（簸箕礁），航行针用缝针（甲庚加四线寅申），航程二更到达。

第37条 自半簸下铜章驶寅申兼二线甲庚一更收。

释义：在南沙，从半簸（簸箕礁）开往铜章（南海礁），航行针用缝针（寅申加二线甲庚），航程一更到达。

第38条 自铜章到光星仔驶壬丙二更收。

释义：在南沙，从铜章（南海礁）开往光星仔（光星仔礁），航行针用单针（壬丙），航程二更到达。

第39条 自光星仔到石公厘驶子午一更半收。

释义：在南沙，从光星仔（光星仔礁）开往石公厘（弹丸礁），航行针用单针（子午），航程一更半到达。

第40条 自石公厘到五百贰驶癸丁平三更收。

释义：在南沙，从石公厘（弹丸礁）开往五百贰（皇路礁），航行针用单针（正对着癸丁），航程三更到达。

第41条 自五百贰到单节驶癸丁丑未平三更收。

释义：在南沙，从五百贰（皇路礁）开往单节（南通礁），航行针用缝针（正对着癸丁和丑未的中间线），航程三更到达。

第42条 自铜章到海口线驶辰戌兼一线乾巽三更收。

释义：在南沙，从铜章（南海礁）开往海口线（柏礁），航行针用缝针（辰戌加一线乾巽），航程三更到达。

第 43 条　自海口线落大铜铳驶乾巽五更收。

释义：在南沙，从海口线（柏礁）开往大铜铳（东礁），航行针用单针（乾巽），航程五更到达。

第 44 条　自铜铳仔下大铜铳驶甲庚一更收。

释义：在南沙，从铜铳仔（华阳礁）开往大铜铳（东礁），航行针用单针（甲庚），航程一更到达。

第 45 条　自铜铳下弄鼻驶乙辛二更收。

释义：在南沙，从铜铳（东礁）开往弄鼻（西礁），航行针用单针（乙辛），航程二更到达。

第 46 条　自弄鼻下鸟仔驶艮坤申二更收。

释义：在南沙，从弄鼻（西礁）开往鸟仔峙（南威岛），航行针用缝针（寅申加二线艮坤），航程二更到达。

第 47 条　自黄山马到南乙峙驶壬丙一更收。

释义：在南沙，从黄山马（太平岛）开往南乙（鸿庥岛），航行针用单针（壬丙），航程一更到达。

第 48 条　自南乙到秤钩驶癸丁二更收。

释义：在南沙，从南乙（鸿庥岛）开往秤钩（景宏岛），航行针用单针（癸丁），航程二更到达。

第 49 条　自秤钩到荷乐门驶子午四更收。

释义：在南沙，从秤钩（景宏岛）开往荷乐门（南华礁），航行针用单针（子午），航程四更到达。

第 50 条　自荷乐门到六门驶乾巽兼辰戌一更收。

释义：在南沙，从荷乐门（南华礁）开往六门（六门礁），航行针用缝针（乾巽和辰戌的中间线），航程一更到达。

第 51 条　自六门到铜章驶壬丙四更收。

释义：在南沙，从六门（六门礁）开往铜章（南海礁），航行针用缝针（壬丙和子午的中间线），航程四更到达。

第 52 条　自六门到石盘驶乾巽兼辰戌平二更收。

释义：在南沙，从六门（六门礁）开往石盘（毕生礁），航行针用缝针（乾巽和辰戌的中间线），航程二更到达。

第 53 条　自石盘到上戊驶乾巽巳亥平四更收。

释义：在南沙，从石盘（毕生礁）开往上戊（永暑礁），航行针用缝针（乾巽和巳亥的中间线），航程四更到达。

第 54 条　自上戊到大铜铳驶癸丁四更收。

释义：在南沙，从上戊（永暑礁）开往大铜铳（东礁），航行针用单针

（癸丁），航程四更到达。

第 55 条　自石盘到大铜铳驶甲庚兼四线卯酉四更收。

释义：在南沙，从石盘（毕生礁）开往大铜铳（东礁），航行针用缝针（甲庚加四线卯酉），航程四更到达。

第 56 条　自黄山马到劳牛劳驶寅申三更收。

释义：在南沙，从黄山马（太平岛）开往劳牛劳（大现礁），航行针用单针（寅申），航程三更到达。

第 57 条　自劳牛劳到恶浪门驶壬丙五更收。

释义：在南沙，从劳牛劳（大现礁）开往恶浪门（南华礁），航行针用单针（壬丙），航程五更到达。

第 58 条　自秤钩到石盘驶丑未兼一线艮坤四更收。

释义：在南沙，从秤钩（景宏岛）开往石盘（毕生礁），航行针用缝针（丑未加一线艮坤），航程四更到达。

第 59 条　自劳牛劳下上戊驶寅申四更收。

释义：在南沙，从劳牛劳（大现礁）开往上戊（永暑礁），航行针用单针（寅申），航程四更到达。

第 60 条　自染青石到无乜线坐子午壬丙平四更收。

释义：在南沙，从染青石（染青东礁）开往无乜线（无乜礁），航行针用缝针（子午和壬丙的中间线），航程四更到达。

第 61 条　自铁峙下铁线驶丑未一更收。

释义：在南沙，从铁峙（中业岛）开往铁线（铁线礁），航行针用单针（丑未），航程一更到达。

第 62 条　自铁峙下丑未驶艮坤二更收。

释义：在南沙，从铁峙（中业岛）开往丑未（渚碧礁），航行针用单针（艮坤），航程二更到达。

第 63 条　自丑未下黄山马驶乾巽四更收。

释义：在南沙，从丑未（渚碧礁）开往黄山马（太平岛），航行针用单针（乾巽），航程四更到达。

第 64 条　自鱼鳞到乙辛亦是驶单辛三更收。

释义：在南沙，从鱼鳞（仙宾礁）开往（东头）乙辛（蓬勃暗沙），航行针用单针乙辛，航程三更到达。

第 65 条　自鸟仔峙到乙辛亦是驶乙辛二更收。

释义：在南沙，从鸟仔峙（南威岛）开往（西头）乙辛（日积礁），航行针用单针（乙辛），航程二更到达。

第 66 条　自铁峙往下三用巳亥二更收。

释义：在南沙，从铁峙（中业岛）开往下三（南钥岛），航行针用单针（巳亥），航程二更到达。

第 67 条　自下三往黄山马用子午二更收。

释义：在南沙，从下三（南钥岛）开往黄山马（太平岛），航行针用单针（子午），航程二更到达。

第 68 条　自红草下沙排驶辰戌一更收。

释义：在南沙，从红草（西月岛）开往沙排（长滩），航行针用单针（辰戌），航程一更到达。

第 69 条　自鱼鳞下断节驶卯酉二更收。

释义：在南沙，从鱼鳞（仙宾礁）开往断节（仁爱礁），航行针用单针（卯酉），航程二更到达。

第 70 条　自银饼往鸟串驶乾巽二更辰戌五更收。

释义：在南沙，从银饼（安达礁）开往鸟串（仙娥礁），航行针用缝针（乾巽加二线辰戌），航程五更到达。

第 71 条　自红草往第三峙驶艮坤三更收。

释义：在南沙，从红草（西月岛）开往第三峙（南钥岛），航行针用单针（艮坤），航程三更到达。

第 72 条　自丑未往双王驶辰戌二更收。

释义：在南沙，从丑未（渚碧礁）开往双王（双黄沙洲），航行针用单针（辰戌），航程二更到达。

第 73 条　自铁峙往双王驶壬丙二更收。

释义：在南沙，从铁峙（中业岛）开往双王（双黄沙洲），航行针用单针（壬丙），航程二更到达。

第 74 条　自双王往黄山马驶壬丙二更收（黄山马离半更开在东北有浅海硬浪）。

释义：在南沙，从双王（双黄沙洲）开往黄山马（太平岛），航行针用单针（壬丙），航程二更到达。

第 75 条　自第三往银饼驶辰戌三更收。

释义：在南沙，从第三（南钥岛）开往银饼（安达礁），航行针用单针（辰戌），航程三更到达。

第 76 条　自铜金往银饼驶巳亥二更收。

释义：在南沙，从铜金（杨信沙洲）开往银饼（安达礁），航行针用单针（巳亥），航程二更到达。

第 77 条　自银饼往牛杞驶癸丁二更收。

释义：在南沙，从银饼（安达礁）开往牛杞（牛杞礁），航行针用单针（癸丁），航程二更到达。

第 78 条　自目镜往深圈驶寅申二更收。

释义：在南沙，从目镜（司令礁）开往深圈（榆亚暗沙），航行针用单针（壬丙），航程二更到达。

第 79 条　自南蜜峙往浅沟峙驶壬丙二更收。

释义：在南沙，从南蜜峙（鸿庥岛）开往浅沟峙，即称钩岛（景宏岛），航行针用单针（壬丙），航程二更到达。

第 80 条　自浅沟往六门驶癸丁五更收。

释义：在南沙，从浅沟峙（景宏岛）开往六门（六门礁），航行针用单针（癸丁），航程五更到达。

第 81 条　自恶浪门往半簸驶壬丙四更收。

释义：在南沙，从恶浪门（南华礁）开往半簸（簸箕礁），航行针用单针（壬丙），航程四更到达。

第 82 条　自光星仔往大光星驶卯酉一更收。

释义：在南沙，从光星仔（光星仔礁）开往大光星（光星礁）；航行针用单针卯酉，航程一更到达。

第 83 条　自大光星往石公厘驶乾巽，二更收。

释义：在南沙，从大光星（光星礁）开往石公厘（弹丸礁），航行针用单针（乾巽），航程二更到达。

第 84 条　自大光星往海口沙驶子午四更收。

释义：在南沙，从大光星（光星礁）开往海口沙（柏礁），航行针用单针（子午），航程四更到达。

第 85 条　自红草下铁峙驶卯酉四更收。

释义：在南沙，从红草（西月岛）开往铁峙（中业岛），航行针用单针（卯酉），航程四更到达。

第 86 条　自鸟仔峙回老沙白峙仔驶癸丁丑未更收。

释义：在南沙，从鸟仔峙（南威岛）开往老沙白峙仔（盘石屿），航行针用缝针（癸丁和丑未的中间线）。

第 87 条　自女青石往无乜沙用丙兼巳五更收对东南。

释义：在南沙，从女青石（染青东礁）开往无乜沙（无乜礁），航行针用缝针（壬丙和巳亥的中间线），航程五更到达，航行方向对东南。

第 88 条　自丹节往海口沙北风用癸丁十更。

释义：在南沙，从丹节（南通礁）开往海口沙（柏礁），如果是北风，航行针用单针（癸丁），航程十更到达。

第 89 条 自五百贰往海口沙北风用午丁七更。

释义：在南沙，从五百贰（皇路礁）开往海口沙（柏礁），如果是北风，航行针用缝针（子午和癸丁的中间线），航程七更到达。

第 90 条 自红草沙排下裤归用丁未二更。

释义：在南沙，从红草沙排（长滩）开往裤归（库归礁），航行针用缝针（癸丁和丑未的中间线），航程二更到达。

第 91 条 自半路往北海用乾巽二十八更收贡士沙。

释义：在西沙，从半路（中建岛）开往北海（南沙群岛）的贡士沙（贡士礁）航行针用单针（乾巽），航程二十八更到达。

第 92 条 自三圈往北海向巳亥壬丙二十八更收奈罗。

释义：在西沙，从三圈（浪花礁）开往北海（南沙群岛），航行针用缝针（巳亥和壬丙的中间线），航程二十八更到达奈罗（北子岛）。

第 93 条 自奈罗北边角下贡士沙用甲庚，一更收。

释义：在南沙，从奈罗北边角（永登暗沙）开往贡士沙（贡士礁），航行针用单针（甲庚），航程一更到达。

第 94 条 自南边奈罗角用乙辛驶下收贡士沙。

释义：在南沙，从南边奈罗角（乐斯暗沙）开往贡士沙（贡士礁），航行针用单针（乙辛）。

第 95 条 自双峙沙仔下铁峙沙排壬丙二线巳亥二更又有犬殿沙一个。

释义：在南沙，从双峙沙仔（双子群礁）开往铁峙沙排（铁峙礁），航行针用缝针（壬丙加二线巳亥），航程二更到达，又遇到犬殿沙（梅九礁）。

第 96 条 自鱼鳞往鲎藤向子午四更收回向亥壬。

释义：在南沙，从鱼鳞（仙宾礁）开往鲎藤（鲎藤礁），航行针用单针（子午），航程四更到达。返回时航行针用缝针（巳亥与壬丙的中间线）。

第 97 条 自那孔往五风向壬丙一更收回向癸丁收

释义：在南沙，从那孔（马欢岛）开往五风（五方礁），航行针用单针（壬丙），航程一更到达。返回时航行针用单针（癸丁）。

第 98 条 自红草往火衰向子午一更收

释义：在南沙，从红草（西月岛）开往火衰（火艾礁），航行针用单针（子午），航程一更到达。

第 99 条 向火衰往三角用乾巽四更回用壬丙收。

释义：在南沙，从火衰（火艾礁）开往三角（三角礁），航行针用单针（乾巽），航程四更到达。返回时航行针用单针（壬丙）。

第 100 条　自断节往双担向丙已二更回子癸收。

释义：在南沙，从断节（仁爱礁）开往双担（信义礁），航行针用缝针（壬丙和巳亥的中间线），航程二更到达。返回时航行针用缝针（子午和癸丁的中间线）。

第 101 条　自双担往鸟串向辛酉二更半收。

释义：在南沙，从双担（信义礁）开往鸟串（仙娥礁），航行针用缝针（乙辛和卯酉的中间线），航程二更半到达。

第 102 条　自断节往鸟串向癸丁未二更收。

释义：在南沙，从断节（仁爱礁）开往鸟串（仙娥礁），航行针用缝针（癸丁和丑未的中间线），航程二更到达。

第 103 条　自断节往五风向癸丁四更收回向壬丙。

释义：在南沙，从断节（仁爱礁）开往五风（五方礁），航行针用单针（癸丁），航程四更到达。返回时航行针用单针（壬丙）。

第 104 条　自红草沙排上红草峙向乙卯一更收回用戌字。

释义：在南沙，从红草沙排（长滩）开往红草峙（西月岛），航行针用缝针（乙辛和卯酉的中间线），航程一更到达。返回时航行针用单针（辰戌）。

第 105 条　自那（罗）孔往鲎藤向乙卯一更半收回乾巽。

释义：在南沙，从那孔（马欢岛）开往鲎藤（鲎藤礁），航行针用缝针（乙辛和卯酉的中间线），航程一更半到达。返回时航行针用单针（乾巽）。

第 106 条　自鲎藤往鱼鳞向已亥四更收回用子午。

释义：在南沙，从鲎藤（鲎藤礁）开往鱼鳞（仙宾礁），航行针用单针（巳亥），航程四更到达。返回时航行针用单针（子午）。

第 107 条　自鱼鳞往东头乙辛沙向乙辛三更收回乾巽。

释义：在南沙，从鱼鳞（仙宾礁）开往东头乙辛沙（蓬勃暗沙），航行针用单针（乙辛），航程三更到达。返回时航行针用单针（乾巽）。

第 108 条　自鱼鳞往那孔向壬丙子午四更收回乾巽巳亥。

释义：在南沙，从鱼鳞（仙宾礁）开往那孔（马欢岛），航行针用缝针（壬丙和子午的中间线），航程四更到达。返回时航行针用缝针（乾巽和巳亥的中间线）。

第 109 条　自鱼鳞往石龙向壬丙四更收回用子午癸。

释义：在南沙，从鱼鳞（仙宾礁）开往石龙（舰长礁），航行针用单针（壬丙），航程四更到达。返回时用航行针缝针（子午和癸丁的中间线）。

第 110 条　自鱼鳞往断节向卯酉一更半收回用癸丁。

释义：在南沙，从鱼鳞（仙宾礁）开往断节（仁爱礁），航行针用单针（卯酉），航程一更半到达。返回时航行针用单针（癸丁）。

第111条　自五风往断节向壬丙四更收回向癸丁。

释义：在南沙，从五风（五方礁）开往断节（仁爱礁），航行针用单针（壬丙），航程四更到达。返回时航行针用单针（癸丁）。

第112条　自铁峙铜金峙仔向乾巽贰更收。

释义：在南沙，从铁峙（中业岛）开往铜金峙仔（杨信沙洲），航行针用单针（乾巽），航程二更到达。

第113条　自铜金去艮锅向乾巽二更收回向丙。

释义：在南沙，从铜金（杨信沙洲）开往银锅（安达礁），航行针用单针（乾巽），航程二更到达。返回时航行针用单针（壬丙）。

第114条　自艮锅去鸟向乾巽已亥六更收回上壬。

释义：在南沙，从银锅（安达礁）开往鸟串（仙娥礁），航行针用缝针（乾巽和已亥的中间线），航程六更到达。返回时航行针用单针（壬丙）。

第115条　自铁峙沙驶去丑未沙向丑未驶半更收。

释义：在南沙，从铁峙沙（中业岛）开往丑未沙（渚碧礁），航行针用单针（丑未），航程半更到达。

第116条　自丑未驶去第三向辰巽驶贰更收。

释义：在南沙，从丑未（渚碧礁）开往第三（南钥岛），航行针用缝针（辰戌和乾巽的中间线），航程二更到达。

第117条　自铁峙驶去双玨（王）沙仔向壬丙驶二更收。

释义：在南沙，从铁峙（中业岛）开往双玨沙仔（双黄沙洲），航行针用单针（壬丙），航程二更到达。

第118条　自双玨沙仔驶去黄山马向壬丙一更回用癸丁收。

释义：在南沙，从双玨沙仔（双黄沙洲）开往黄山马（太平岛），航行针用单针（壬丙），航程一更到达。返回时航行针用单针（癸丁）。

第119条　自女青石驶去无乜沙向子午驶四更收。

释义：在南沙，从女青石（染青东礁）开往无乜沙（无乜礁），航行针用单针（子午），航程四更到达。

第120条　自无乜沙驶往目镜用巽辰三更收回用癸丁驶。

释义：在南沙，从无乜沙（无乜礁）开往目镜（司令礁），航行针用缝针（乾巽和辰戌的中间线），航程三更到达。返回时航行针用单针（癸丁）。

第121条　自目镜驶往深圈用庚申驶二更收。

释义：在南沙，从目镜（司令礁）开往深圈（榆亚暗沙），航行针用缝针（甲庚和寅申的中间线），航程二更到达。

第122条　自光星仔驶往大光星向卯西一更收。

释义：在南沙，从光星仔（光星仔礁）开往大光星（光星礁），航行针用单针（卯酉），航程一更到达。

第 123 条 自大光星驶往石厘（石公厘）向巳巽二更收回用子午。

释义：在南沙，从大光星（光星礁）开往石公厘（弹丸礁），航行针用缝针（巳亥和乾巽的中间线），航程二更到达。返回时航行针用单针（子午）。

第 124 条 自钉积（丹节）驶往墨瓜线向丑未六更收。

释义：在南沙，从钉积（南通礁）开往墨瓜线（南屏礁），航行针用单针（丑未），航程六更到达。

第 125 条 自秤钩沙驶往六门用癸丁五更收。

释义：在南沙，从秤钩沙（华礁）开往六门（六门礁），航行针用单针（癸丁），航程五更到达。

第 126 条 自荷那门驶往援（簸）箕用壬丙四更收回用癸丁。

释义：在南沙，从荷那门（南华礁）开往援箕（簸箕礁），航行针用单针（壬丙），航程四更到达。返回时航行针用单针（癸丁）。

第 127 条 自六门驶往援箕向壬丙巳亥驶四更收。

释义：在南沙，从六门（六门礁）开往援箕（簸箕礁），航行针用缝针（壬丙和巳亥的中间线），航程四更到达。

第 128 条 自六门驶往石盘向辰戌二更收回乾巽。

释义：在南沙，从六门（六门礁）开往石盘（毕生礁），航行针用单针（辰戌），航程二更到达。返回时航行针用单针（乾巽）。

第 129 条 自六门驶往海口沙向甲庚寅申三更收。

释义：在南沙，从六门（六门礁）开往海口沙（柏礁），航行针用缝针（甲庚和寅申的中间线），航程三更到达。

第 130 条 自荷那门驶往铜钟向癸丁四更收。

释义：在南沙，从荷那门（南华礁）开往铜钟（南海礁），航行针用单针（癸丁），航程四更到达。

第 131 条 自铜钟驶往海口沙向辰戌贰线乾巽过头。

释义：在南沙，从铜钟（南海礁）开往海口沙（柏礁），航行针用缝针（辰戌加二线乾巽过一点）。

第 132 条 自海口沙驶往锅盖峙向寅申四更收。

释义：在南沙，从海口沙（柏礁）开往锅盖峙（安波沙洲），航行针用单针（寅申），航程四更到达。

第 133 条 自海口沙驶往铜铳仔向巳亥五更收。

释义：在南沙，从海口沙（柏礁）开往铜铳仔（华阳礁），航行针用单针（巳亥），航程五更到达。

第 134 条　自铜铳仔驶往大铜铳向庚酉一更收。

释义：在南沙，从铜铳仔（华阳礁）开往大铜铳（东礁），航行针用缝针（甲庚和卯酉的中间线），航程一更到达。

第 135 条　自大铜铳下弄鼻仔向辰戌驶二更收。

释义：在南沙，从大铜铳（东礁）开往弄鼻仔（中礁），航行针用单针（辰戌），航程二更到达。

第 136 条　自弄鼻仔下大（弄）鼻向卯酉一更①收。

释义：在南沙，从弄鼻仔（中礁）开往大鼻（西礁），航行针用单针（卯酉），航程一更到达。

第 137 条　自鸟仔峙驶去西头乙辛沙向辛二线酉二更。

释义：在南沙，从鸟仔峙（南威岛）开往西头乙辛沙（日积礁），航行针用缝针（乙辛加二线卯酉），航程二更到达。

第 138 条　自石盘驶往上戊向乾亥平四更收。

释义：在南沙，从石盘（毕生礁）开往上戊（永暑礁），航行针用缝针（正对着乾巽和巳亥的中间线），航程四更到达。

第 139 条　自上戊驶往铜铳仔向午四更收。

释义：在南沙，从上戊（永暑礁）开往铜铳仔（华阳礁），航行针用单针（子午），航程四更到达。

第 140 条　自上戊驶往大铜铳向丁午四更半收。

释义：在南沙，从上戊（永暑礁）开往大铜铳（东礁），航行针用缝针（丁癸和子午的中间线），航程四更半到达。

第 141 条　自铜铳仔回大秤钩向寅申九更半收。

释义：在南沙，从铜铳仔（华阳礁）开往大秤钩（赤瓜礁），航行针用单针（寅申），航程九更半到达。

第 142 条　自劳牛劳驶往大秤钩向巽辰三更收回壬子。

释义：在南沙，从劳牛劳（大现礁）开往大秤钩（赤瓜礁），航行针用缝针（乾巽和辰戌的中间线），航程三更到达。返回时，航行针用缝针（壬丙和子午的中间线）。

第 143 条　自南蜜沙仔下劳牛劳向甲庚二更收。

释义：在南沙，从南蜜沙（南熏礁）开往劳牛劳（大现礁），航行针用单针（甲庚），航程二更到达。

第 144 条　自铜钟驶往大光星向子午二更收回丑未。

释义：在南沙，从铜钟（南海礁）开往大光星（光星礁），航行针用单针

---

① 疑 "O 更" 其中漏字。据考证，是一更。

（子午），航程二更到达。返回时航行针用单针（丑未）。

第145条 自荷乐门驶往深圈向巽辰三更收回壬子。

释义：在南沙，从荷乐门（南华礁）开往深圈（榆亚暗沙），航行针用缝针（乾巽和辰戌的中间线），航程三更到达。返回时航行针用缝针（壬丙和子午的中间线）。

第146条 自第三峙驶往银锅向巽戌三更收回壬子。

释义：在南沙，从第三峙（南钥岛）开往银锅（安达礁），航行针用缝针（乾巽和辰戌的中间线），航程三更到达。返回时航行针用缝针（壬丙和子午的中间线）。

第147条 自三角回银锅向乙辛驶三更收。

释义：在南沙，从三角（三角礁）开往银锅（安达礁），航行针用单针（乙辛），航程三更到达。

第148条 自双门回银锅向戌驶四更收。

释义：在南沙，从双门（美济礁）开往银锅（安达礁），航行针用单针（辰戌），航程四更到达。

第149条 自红草沙排往铁峙向辛酉驶三更收。

释义：在南沙，从红草沙排（长滩）开往铁峙（中业岛），航行针用缝针（乙辛和卯酉的中间线），航程三更到达。

第150条 自银锅往高不向辰戌驶一更收。

释义：在南沙，从银锅（安达礁）开往高不（舶兰礁），航行针用单针（辰戌），航程一更到达。

第151条 自三角往断节向辰戌驶四更收。

释义：在南沙，从三角（三角礁）开往断节（仁爱礁），航行针用单针（辰戌），航程四更到达。

第152条 自劳牛劳往六门向丙午驶六更收。

释义：在南沙，从劳牛劳（大现礁）开往六门（六门礁），航行针用缝针（壬丙和子午的中间线），航程六更到达。

第153条 自劳牛劳往石盘向丁未驶五更半收。

释义：在南沙，从劳牛劳（大现礁）开往石盘（毕生礁），航行针用缝针（癸丁和丑未的中间线），航程五更半到达。

第154条 自劳牛劳下上戊向申驶四更收。

释义：在南沙，从劳牛劳（大现礁）开往上戊（永暑礁），航行针用单针（寅申），航程四更到达。

第155条 自荷乐门下六门向戌辛驶二更收。

释义：在南沙，从荷乐门（南华礁）开往六门（六门礁），航行针用缝针

（辰戌和乙辛的中间线），航程二更到达。

第156条　自双门往鸟串向午二线丁驶二更收。

释义：在南沙，从双门（美济礁）开往鸟串（仙娥礁），航行针用缝针（子午加二线癸丁），航程二更到达。

第157条　自库归往铜金峙仔向午驶一更收。

释义：在南沙，从库归（库归礁）开往铜金峙仔（杨信沙洲），航行针用单针（子午），航程一更到达。

第158条　自南蜜往女星石峙仔向巽驶二更收。

释义：在南沙，从南蜜（鸿庥岛）开往女星石峙仔（染青东礁），航行针用单针（乾巽），航程二更到达。

第159条　自南蜜峙下沙仔向辛戌驶半更有二个沙仔。

释义：在南沙，从南蜜峙（鸿庥岛）开往南蜜沙仔（南熏礁），航行针用缝针（乙辛和辰戌的中间线），航程半更可看到两个暗沙。

第160条　自南蜜峙到南蜜沙仔驶卯酉兼一线乙辛一更收。

释义：在南沙，从南蜜峙（鸿庥岛）开往南蜜沙仔（南熏礁），航行针用缝针（卯酉加一线乙辛），航程一更到达。

第161条　自南蜜有二只沙仔壬丙对沟内亦过船。

释义：在南沙，从南蜜（鸿庥岛）往返二只暗沙，航行针用单针（壬丙），水道内可通船。

第162条　自秤钩峙下大秤钩向丁午驶一更收。

释义：在南沙，从秤钩峙（景宏岛）开往大秤钩（赤瓜礁），航行针用单针（子午），航程一更到达。

第163条　自秤钩峙往南蜜沙仔向子壬驶一更半收。

释义：在南沙，从秤钩峙（景宏岛）开往南蜜沙仔（南熏礁），航行针用缝针（子午和壬丙的中间线），航程一更半到达。

第164条　自无乜沙下荷乐门向申驶三更收。

释义：在南沙，从无乜沙（无乜礁）开往荷乐门（南华礁），航行针用单针（寅申），航程三更到达。

第165条　自黄山马下南蜜沙仔向丁未驶一更收。

释义：在南沙，从黄山马（太平岛）开往南蜜沙仔（南熏礁），航行针用缝针（癸丁和丑未的中间线），航程一更到达。

第166条　自红草沙排下贡士沙向戌乾驶三更收。

释义：在南沙，从红草沙排（长滩）开往贡士沙（贡士礁），航行针用缝针（辰戌和乾巽的中间线），航程三更到达。

第 167 条 自双门往一沙驶巳亥兼一线壬丙二更收向西北。

释义：在南沙，从双门（美济礁）开往一沙（禄沙礁），航行针用缝针（巳亥加一线壬丙），航程二更到达。航行方向对西北。

第 168 条 自一沙往火哀驶巳亥兼一线壬丙四更收向西北。

释义：在南沙，从一沙（禄沙礁）开往火哀（火艾礁），航行针用缝针（巳亥加一线壬丙），航程四更到达。航行方向对西北。

第 169 条 自火哀回铁峙驶乙辛辰戌三更收向西北。

释义：在南沙，从火哀（火艾礁）开往铁峙（中业岛），航行针用缝针（乙辛和辰戌的中间线），航程三更到达。航行方向对西北。

第 170 条 自光星往石公里向午驶二更收回向癸丁。

释义：在南沙，从光星（光星礁）开往石公里（弹丸礁），航行针用单针（子午），航程二更到达。返回时航行针用单针（癸丁）。

第 171 条 自铜铳下鸟仔峙驶甲庚兼三线卯酉四更收。

释义：在南沙，从铜铳（东礁）开往鸟仔峙（南威岛），航行针用缝针（甲庚加三线卯酉），航程四更到达。

第 172 条 自丑未下第三峙驶辰戌兼二线乙辛二更收对西南。

释义：在南沙，从丑未（渚碧礁）开往第三峙（南钥岛），航行针用缝针（辰戌加二线乙辛），航程二更到达，航行方向对西南。

第 173 条 自第三峙往银锅驶辰戌兼二线乾巽二更半收对东南。

释义：在南沙，从第三峙（南钥岛）开往银锅（安达礁），航行针用缝针（辰戌加二线乾巽），航程二更半到达收帆泊船，航行方向对东南方向。

第 174 条 自劳牛劳往六门驶壬丙兼二线巳亥五更收对东南。

释义：在南沙，从劳牛劳（大现礁）开往六门（六门礁），航行针用缝针（壬丙加二线巳亥），航程五更到达，航行方向对东南。

第 175 条 自双门往鸟串驶子午癸丁平二更半收对西南收。

释义：在南沙，从双门（美济礁）开往鸟串（仙娥礁），航行针用缝针（子午和癸丁的中间线），航程二更半到达，航行方向对西南。

第 176 条 自劳牛劳往石盘驶子午兼一线癸丁四更收对南。

释义：在南沙，从劳牛劳（大现礁）开往石盘（毕生礁），航行针用缝针（子午加一线癸丁），航程四更到达，航行方向对南。

第 177 条 自六门中央硐到铜钟驶壬丙兼一线子午四更半对南。

释义：在南沙，从六门（六门礁）中央开往铜钟（南海礁），航行针用缝针（壬丙加一线子午），航程四更半到达，航行方向对南。

第 178 条 自火哀下库归驶乙卯二更收对西驶收。

释义：在南沙，从火哀（火艾礁）开往库归（库归礁），航行针用缝针

（乙辛和卯酉的中间线），航程二更到达，航行方向对西。

第 179 条 自红草沙排下铁峙用甲庚二更收对西南驶。

释义：在南沙，从红草沙排（长滩）开往铁峙（中业岛），航行针用单针（甲庚），航程二更到达，航行方向对西南。

第 180 条 自红草到五风用辰戌驶四更收对东南。

释义：在南沙，从红草（西月岛）开往五风（五方礁），航行针用单针（辰戌），航程四更到达，航行方向对东南。

第 181 条 自双门往双担用乾巽驶四更收对东南。

释义：在南沙，从双门（美济礁）开往双担（信义礁），航行针用单针（乾巽），航程四更到达，航行方向对东南。

第 182 条 自断节往五风用癸丁驶四更半收对东北。

释义：在南沙，从断节（仁爱礁）开往五风（五方礁），航行针用单针（癸丁），航程四更半到达，航行方向对东北。

第 183 条 自罗孔往五风用午丙驶一更半收对南驶。

释义：在南沙，从罗孔（马欢岛）开往五风（五方礁），航行针用缝针（子午和壬丙的中间线），航程一更半到达，航行方向对南。

第 184 条 自五风往断节用壬丙驶四更半收对东南。

释义：在南沙，从五风（五方礁）开往断节（仁爱礁），航行针用单针（壬丙），航程四更半到达，航行方向对东南。

第 185 条 自五风头上往半路沙驶乾巽二更收对东南。

释义：在南沙，从五风头（五方头）开往半路沙（半路礁），航行针用单针（乾巽），航程二更到达，航行方向对东南。

第 186 条 自五风往鱼鳞驶辰戌四更收对东南。

释义：在南沙，从五风（五方礁）开往鱼鳞（仙宾礁），航行针用单针（辰戌），航程四更到达，航行方向对东南。

第 187 条 自荷乐门往深圈驶辰戌四更收对东南。

释义：在南沙，从荷乐门（南华礁）开往深圈（榆亚暗沙），航行针用单针（辰戌），航程四更到达，航行方向对东南。

第 188 条 自铜金下第三驶甲庚一更收对西南。

释义：在南沙，从铜金（杨信沙洲）开往第三（南钥岛），航行针用单针（甲庚），航程一更到达，航行方向对西南。

第 189 条 自西头乙辛往六安驶乾巽相对二十二更收对西北驶收。

释义：在南沙，从西头乙辛（日积礁）开往六安，航行针用单针（乾巽），航程二十二更到达，航行方向对西北。

第 190 条　自火哀下第三驶甲庚二更半收对西南驶收。

释义：在南沙，从火哀（火艾礁）开往第三（南钥岛），航行针用单针（甲庚），航程二更半到达，航行方向对西南。

第 191 条　自若沙到火哀驶巳亥兼三线壬丙四更收。

释义：在南沙，从若沙（禄沙礁）开往火哀（火艾礁），航行针用缝针（巳亥加三线壬丙），航程四更到达。

第 192 条　自双门头上往若沙驶壬丙巳亥平二更收对西北。

释义：在南沙，从双门（美济礁）东北边开往若沙（禄沙礁），航行针用缝针（壬丙和巳亥的中间线），航程二更到达，航行方向对西北。

第 193 条　自双王下沙仔到黄山马东驶乾巽巳亥二更收对东南驶收。

释义：在南沙，从双王（双黄沙洲）经过沙仔，开往黄山马东（敦谦沙洲），航行针用缝针（乾巽和巳亥的中间线），航程二更到达，航行方向对东南。

3 苏德柳本和彭正楷本《更路簿》南海诸岛俗名起源与传说

3.1 立东海更路（西沙更路）[①]

1. 大潭是海南省琼海市潭门镇的渔港。

2. 东海，是个特称俗名，多见于《更路簿》各版本首篇篇目中，是历代渔民对西沙群岛的通称，有别于中国地理学上的东海。每年立冬过后，渔民们就乘借东北信风，扬帆远航西沙群岛。东海即东航首抵的西沙群岛海域。东，海南渔民常用特称方位词。

3. 三峙，其标准地名为南岛。我国渔民一直称南岛为三峙，因为它位于七连屿的中部，排行第三，故名。

4. 干豆是北礁的俗名。相传很久以前，曾经有人在北礁上捡到成袋干燥的豆子，因此，北礁俗称干豆。另外，远望北礁时，它的形状好似豆仁。据韩振华考证，葡萄牙人初来中国，经过南海进入广东省境的西沙群岛最北面的北礁时，便以 cantao（广东）相称，后译为中文"干豆"。

5. 海南渔民习惯上把永乐群岛称为石塘，石塘是永乐群岛的俗名。明朝永乐至宣德年间，郑和七次下西洋，命名石塘为永乐。明成祖朱棣（1360—1424），明代皇帝，年号永乐。在位期间（1402—1424），他派郑和七次出使西洋，促进了中国与亚非各国在经济文化上的交流。

6. 二圈标准名称为玉琢礁，是永乐群岛上分布着四个形似箩筐的环礁之一。四礁中华光礁最大，渔民俗称大圈，或大筐；羚羊礁最小，俗称圈仔，或筐仔；玉琢礁和浪花礁大小居中，俗称二圈（或二筐）、三圈（或三筐）。海南方言中，"筐"和"圈"两者同读（huan），同音同义不同形。

[①] 说明："苏德柳本和彭正楷本《更路簿》南海诸岛俗名起源与传说"的资料主要参考了韩振华等《我国南海诸岛史料汇编》，东方出版社1988年版；韩振华：《南海诸岛史地研究》，社会科学文献出版社1996年版；广东省地名委员会编：《南海诸岛地名资料汇编》，广东省地图出版社1987年版；郭振乾：《南沙群岛渔民地名综述》，载《南海诸岛地名资料汇编》1987年版，第515-527页；王彩：《海南渔民抄本〈更路簿〉所载南海诸岛俗名再研究》，载《海南热带海洋学院学报》，2015年第3期，第17-26页；张江齐、宋鸿运等：《〈更路簿〉及其南沙群岛古地名释义》，载《测绘科学》，2017年第12期，第69-76页。在此对所有作者致以衷心感谢。

7. 猫注，或猫峙、猫驻，是海南渔民给永兴岛起的俗名。永兴岛是西沙群岛中最方便抛锚泊船的地方，故得名锚岛。因渔民习称岛为峙，故锚岛又俗称锚峙。另外一个原因可能是，远眺永兴岛，其形状好像猫蹲着的样子。猫峙中的"猫"应是"锚"之讹读。猫注、猫驻和猫峙属于同音异字现象。

与永兴岛位于同一礁盘上的石岛也有三个俗名，分别是猫峙仔、猫注仔和猫驻仔，是渔民根据猫峙、猫注、猫驻给石岛起的俗名。在海南（潭门）方言中，"仔"是有意义的词尾，表示小。《更路簿》中，凡在岛礁地名后加"仔"的俗名，都与它们的主名称所指岛屿形成彼此相邻、一大一小的对应关系。例如，猫峙仔与猫峙呈对应关系。

8. 下峙渔民俗称下八岛或西八岛，位于西沙的西南。"下"是渔民的特指方位词，指西、南方位。下峙特称西沙的永乐群岛。在海南话里，"峙"有高耸、耸立的岛之意。

在位置上与"下峙"相对应的是"上峙"，海南渔民还俗称为"上七岛"或"东七岛"，指宣德群岛，由七个岛屿和沙洲组成，俗称"上峙"。"上"是方位词，是渔民使用的另一特称方位词，特指该岛在西沙群岛的东北方向。

9. 曲手应为晋卿岛与石屿之间的一条弯曲150°像手臂似的礁盘带。我国渔民称西沙的全富岛为全富峙或曲手。

10. 海南渔民把水道叫"门"或"江"。在永乐群岛西南方向的环礁上，从最大的全富峙数起，到晋卿岛旁正好有四条水道，晋卿岛因处在第四条水道旁而被取名为四江、世江门、四江门，或四江峙。海南方言中，"四"和"世"是同音字，"世"是"四"的讹写。

11. 银峙的标准名称为银屿，银峙是海南渔民根据传说而取的岛屿俗名。相传这个岛上早期遗落银子，故名。银屿是位于鸭公岛东北一海里多的一个小沙洲，礁盘上有一深坑，水呈蓝黑色，深不见底，水温较低，渔民称为龙坑。

12. 猫兴是东岛的俗名，即海南渔民称东岛为猫兴或巴兴。猫兴意为树木茂盛。巴兴是猫兴的近音讹记。因为东岛位于西沙群岛东侧，故名。猫兴是西沙群岛第二大岛。

13. 半路或半路峙是中建岛的俗名，位于西沙群岛通往南沙群岛的中途，海南渔民认为从西沙到南沙捕鱼到此已走一半路程，故称其为半路或半路峙，这是以航程距离取的名。中建岛是为纪念1946年中国政府派"中建号"军舰接收西沙群岛而命名的。

14. 海南渔民对南海海域的方位有一种习惯认同，他们称东或东北为"头"，西或西南为"尾"；另又以靠近家乡处为"头"，离家乡远处为"尾"。金银岛位于永乐群岛的最西边，渔民按习惯俗称其为尾峙、尾岛。金银岛得名有二说，一说是曾在岛上挖出不少钱币。另一说是此地产鲍鱼和其他名贵海产，到此捕捞常获厚利。

15. 白峙仔，它是盘石屿的俗称，在这一环状礁盘的北侧有一个低平的小沙洲，堆有白沙，因其面积不大，渔民称其为白峙仔或白树仔。

16. 红草门是指七连屿礁盘与永兴岛之间的水道。在七连屿南半部，由南往北依次排列着南沙洲、中沙洲、北沙洲，都生长着红色的马齿苋草，渔民俗称红草。渔民把南沙洲、中沙洲、北沙洲分别俗称为红草一、红草二、红草三。

17. 双帆，也叫尖石，是高尖石的俗名。高尖石为其标准名称，是西沙群岛中唯一由火山爆发形成的两块玄武岩石，呈塔形叠置状，它高突海面，远望似渔船扬着的双帆，因此得名。

18. 船岩尾，也叫船暗尾，或船坎尾，是西沙洲的俗名，西沙洲处于赵述岛所在礁盘的尾端，位于七连屿的最西面，渔民按方位称其为船岩尾。

19. 老粗门是中国西沙群岛的珊瑚岛和甘泉岛之间的通海水道，因珊瑚岛土名老粗岛而得名。该水道宽达2400米，水深有些地方在2米以内，深处可达45米。老粗门底部为珊瑚碎屑，少见活珊瑚生长。由海南岛来的船只都是先到这个岛，然后由老粗门进入永乐群岛的。

20. 三脚是琛航岛的俗名，位于中国西沙永乐群岛之永乐环礁里，在永乐主岛晋卿岛西边2800米处，与广金岛同居于琛航岛礁盘上。琛航岛中部平坦，四周沙堤包绕，呈弯曲三角形，面积约0.43平方公里（千米）。岛中部挖有水井，但不能饮用。该岛因纪念清末到此的"琛航舰"而得名。

3.2 立北海更路（南沙更路）

1. 北海指南沙群岛。海南渔民观念中，中国的中心在遥远的北方，因此，"北"具有遥远之义。据此，他们把远方俗称北方，把遥远的大陆俗叫北山。南沙群岛因处在遥远的南海海疆而被称为北海。

2. 永乐群岛上分布着四个形似箩筐的环礁，华光礁最大，渔民俗称大筐（圹），或大圈；羚羊礁最小，俗称筐仔，或圈仔；玉琢礁和浪花礁大小居中，俗称二筐（圹），或二圈和三筐（圹），或三圈。海南方言中"筐（圹）"和"圈"两者同读（huan），同音同义不同形。

3. 双子群礁至少有两个俗名：双峙、耐（奈）罗。双峙因岛礁为双数而得名；双子峙统称北子岛、南子岛；耐（奈）罗上峙则以传说故事取名。相传很久以前，有一位渔民带着自己的年少的儿子居住在北子岛以打鱼为生，因长期困在海岛，其子深感无聊寂寞，多次闹着要父亲带他返航回家，父亲每次都安慰儿子"耐罗"（潭门方言，有"忍耐着"之意），由此而得名。海南话"罗""着"同读 lɔ。

4. 红草线，或南奈罗角，是乐斯暗沙的俗名，后者是标准名称，由稳没水下的一群礁石组成。

5. 铁峙是中业岛的俗名，位于中业群礁的环形礁盘上，串接着三个珊瑚礁，它们看上去就像铁链一样，所以，渔民俗称其为"铁链"。因为中业岛基于铁链所在礁盘上，所以被称为铁峙。1946年抗日战争胜利后，中国政府派"中业号"军舰接收了该岛，并命名为中业岛。

6. 红草是西月岛的俗名，岛上不生树木，只长荒草，草近红色，因此渔民称该岛为红草，又称红草峙。此"红草"区别于西沙群岛的"红草"，前者为岛屿，后者为沙洲。

7. （红草）线排是长滩的俗名，位于西月岛西边，道明群礁东北部，是一包括蒙自礁在内的东北—西南走向的长条浅滩，故名长滩，它是个暗沉沙滩，渔民俗称红草线排。

8. 海南渔民远航南沙群岛，到达的第一站为双子群礁，第二站为中业群礁，第三站为道明群礁。道明群礁惟一的岛屿南钥岛俗称第三峙，简称第三。中国渔民自宋朝以来就一直以此岛为捕捞基地，在岛上种植树木，建造房屋和神庙，且挖有水井。

9. 锣孔，或罗孔，或大罗孔，三个俗名均指马欢岛，它是居于圆形环礁中的绿岛，远眺像大铜锣中间的"孔"，因得俗名锣孔。罗孔中"罗"为"锣"之讹写。马欢岛因毗邻一旁，且比俗称罗孔仔的费信岛大，另得俗名大罗孔。另外，马欢岛是以纪念明代跟随郑和下西洋的翻译官马欢而命名的。

10. 火艾或火哀，是火艾礁的俗名。海南（潭门）方言将火把称作火艾。火艾礁看上去很像火把，因此得名。"艾"与"哀"同音同义不同形。

11. 裤归为库归礁的俗名。它是指杨信沙洲东北 3 海里多的两个南北排列的珊瑚礁，涨潮淹没，退潮露出。该两礁明显同基于一礁盘上，形似裤裆，海南潭门渔民俗称裤归。

12. 三角礁东西长约为 5 公里（千米），退潮露出，环礁完整，无礁门，为三角形环礁，故海南渔民俗称三角或三角礁。

13. 双门是美济礁的俗名。美济礁南侧有两个礁门，均可进船，渔民因称双门或双门沙。这里盛产马蹄螺、砗磲等各种海参类，是海南渔民渔业生产的主要场所。

14. 五风是五方礁的俗名。五方礁礁盘有五个不同朝向的礁台，渔民分别俗称五风头或五方头，位于环礁的西南端；五风北或五方北，位于环礁的北部边缘；五风西或五方西，位于环礁的西部边缘；五风南或五方南位于环礁的南部边缘；五风尾或五方尾位于环礁的西南端，通称"五风"或"五方"，意为五个地方有礁石。海南方言"风"和"方"同音。

15. 断节，又名断节线，是仁爱礁的俗名。位于美济礁东南约 14 海里。其南北长约 15 公里（千米），东西宽约 5.6 公里（千米），北半环较完整，南环之礁盘带断开数段，彼此互不相接，渔民俗称之断节；断节地带因底下有暗沙，所以又名断节线。

16. 仙娥礁是标准名称，鸟串是它的俗名。仙娥礁位于信义礁西约 25 海里。仙娥礁是一个环礁，南北长约 7.4 公里（千米），东西宽约 4.6 公里（千米）。涨潮淹没，涨潮时也有若干点礁出露，退潮露出。环礁完整，无礁门。仙娥礁形状如一个巨大的鸟嘴，渔民因称鸟串。海南方言"串"和"嘴"读同音，鸟串即鸟嘴的同音讹写。

17. 双挑或双担是信义礁的俗名。信义礁上南北两边各有一条长长的礁带，远望如两条扁担横架海面，渔民因称双担或双挑。

18. 牛车轮礁俗名牛车英，位于仙宾礁的西南，在信义礁东北约 19 海里。涨潮淹没，退潮露出，形状似牛车轮子，这一礁盘外形浑圆，如木制的牛车轮。"英"，为车轮滚动的拟声词。

19. 脚坡，或脚钵，是海南渔民给海口礁取的俗名。海口礁为一完整的环礁，无礁门，长约 2.6 公里（千米），宽约 1.8 公里（千米）。礁湖水深，退潮时整个环礁露出，形状与洗脚盆相似，海南渔民将其称为脚钵。海南方言中，"坡"和"钵"为同音同义。"钵"被讹写为"坡"。

20. 石龙是标准名称舰长礁的俗名。舰长礁因有一个礁石洞，渔民于是称之为石洞。海南方言习惯称洞为笼，所以，石洞也叫石笼。笼、龙为同音字，石龙为石笼之讹写。

21. 鱼鳞是仙宾礁的俗名，仙宾礁是标准名称。仙宾礁的东南部和西北部均有突出的礁石，它们成片排列，形状像鱼鳞，因而得名鱼鳞。

22. （东头）乙辛海南渔民俗名，标准名称为蓬勃暗沙。实际上，它为一直径约2公里（千米）的环礁，退潮露出。礁湖水深在29～32米，为沙质底，无礁门。海南渔民俗称东头乙辛。

23. 鲎是甲壳类海洋动物，带藤状长尾。鲎藤礁在退潮时显露出一串串棱状礁岩，如同鲎所产的卵，故得俗名为鲎藤。号藤是鲎藤的同音讹记。

24. 海公为半月礁的俗名，后者是标准名称。渔民信奉海上高、大、强一类的自然物，俗称其为某公，如大鲸鱼因身躯庞大而被渔民称作海公。半月礁由于酷似鲸鱼，渔民们将其比喻为海公。另外，半月礁为不完整的环礁，呈半月形，故以其为标准名称。

25. 银饼，或银锅，是安达礁的俗名，安达礁是标准名称。该礁为一大锅形礁盘，像圆饼，又像圆锅。据说，渔民先辈曾从该礁盘中打捞到银锭，于是将之俗称为银饼或银锅。

26. 半路线是半路礁的俗名，半路礁是标准名称。它位于五方礁与仙宾礁的中间，分别相距25海里，即"半路"意思的来源。俗名中的"线"表明它是一滩暗沙，即中央有沙带。"半路"是半路线的省称。这个俗名有别于西沙群岛中的"半路"，前者为"线"，后者为"峙"。

27. 五方头是五方礁中一礁石，位于环礁的东北端，故名。

28. 铜锅为杨信沙洲的俗名，是一个直径仅100米的小沙洲，发育于长轴为1.4公里（千米）的椭圆形的礁盘中心，礁盘浑圆，似铜锅。相传，有渔民曾在该沙洲拾到黄金，因数量多而疑其为铜，故称此地为铜金、铜锅。另外，铜金的标准名称是以明成祖（1402—1424）时期的一位名叫杨信的重要官员命名的。

29. 丑未是渚碧礁的俗名。渚碧礁海区是个丰产的渔场，马蹄螺优丰。据说先发现的渔民从铁线礁启航，取丑未针向到达那里。渔民以罗盘针向"丑未"指代渚碧礁，以此记住该渔场。

30. 铁峙线排，是铁峙礁的俗名，铁峙礁为标准名称。它是接近铁峙的一座暗沙，且形体较小，故得名。"沙""线"和"线排"一样，都是渔民用以俗称暗沙的特称词。

31. 双黄是双黄沙洲的俗名，双黄沙洲为标准名称。双黄沙洲由两座大小不一的小沙洲构成，形状略似两个蛋黄，渔民因称双黄。海南方言中"黄"和"王"同读 wang，双王是双黄的同音异写。

32. 铁线是铁线礁的俗名，铁线礁为标准名称。位于中业群礁西部。为东北—西南一线排列的三个珊瑚礁的总称，我国渔民因此称为铁线。

33. 太平岛上的礁岩为黄色，其状如马，渔民因此将其取名为黄山马或黄山马峙。另外，太平岛是因纪念1946年抗日战争胜利后中国政府派往南沙群岛接收黄山马峙的军舰"太平号"而命名的。

34. 牛厄是牛轭礁的俗名，牛轭礁为标准名称。它位于九章群礁的东北端，是群礁中最大的环礁，退潮时露出，形态神似牛轭，故名。

35. 劳牛劳，也叫流不流或刘牛刘，为大现礁之俗名，大现礁为标准名称。大现礁是环礁，该礁盘海域暗流湍急，礁岩因受到洋流冲击经常发出呼呼声响，而表面海水处流不动，似流不流，故渔民俗称此礁为流不流。海南方言中，刘、劳、流同音，牛是不的谐音，所以，劳不劳又讹记为刘牛刘和流不流。

36. 南忆（乙）或南乙峙，也有讹写为南密或南蜜，是鸿庥岛的俗名，鸿庥岛为标准名称。海南渔民的先人初航至鸿庥岛时，误认为它是南海最南端的一个岛屿，为了便于记忆，特别取名为南忆。"忆"与"乙"为同音谐音，因此，南忆又讹记为南乙。此外，该岛的标准名称是为纪念1946年中国政府派往接收南沙群岛的中业舰副舰长杨鸿庥。

37. 秤钩是景宏岛的俗名，景宏岛是标准名称。它是九章群礁中的两座岛屿之一，尾端弯曲如秤钩状，故名。景宏岛的标准名称是为纪念随同郑和下西洋的副使王景宏。

38. 秤钩线，是华礁的俗名，位于九章群礁西部边缘，因暗沙形状像小秤钩而得名。

39. 目镜，或眼镜是司令礁的俗名，司令礁是标准名称。它是一个东西长约15公里（千米）的环礁，低潮时整个环礁露出，其上有两个潟湖，潟湖被一条突起的0.6米高沙滩分隔成东西两半，整个形态像一副眼镜，故渔民因形命名为眼镜。海南话"眼""目"同义。

40. 深匡（筐），或深圈，是榆亚暗沙的俗名，它所在礁盘中有潟湖，其水极深，难以触及底部，渔船进入潟湖时，不必找深水道进入，从礁盘上任何地方都可以进入，所以渔民称其为深匡（筐）。

41. 无乜线是无乜礁的俗名，这一海域海产稀少，海南渔民在此打鱼经常一无所获，于是给其取俗名"无乜"。由于无乜礁暗沙沉底，看似长线，因此就叫无乜线。

42. 女青石，或染青石，是染青东礁的俗名，位于染青沙洲的东面。染青沙洲附近海水颜色青绿，像是染上青绿色颜料一样，因有俗称染青峙。"女青石"和"汝青石"中的"女"和"汝"字可能是"染"的形讹。

43. 簸箕，或坡箕，为簸箕礁的俗名，簸箕礁为标准名称。该礁礁盘面积不大，形体略圆，中有礁石成片，整体形似簸箕，故名。

44. 铜章，或铜钟，是南海礁的俗名，南海礁为标准名称。它是一座完整环礁，无礁门。因其形似铜钟而得名铜钟。铜章是铜钟的同音讹记。

45. 海口线是柏礁的俗名，柏礁为标准名称，是南海中最大、最长的礁盘，底下有宽长的沙带，好像海岸边宽阔的入海口，因此得名海口线或海口排。

46. 海南潭门人俗称金星为光星。光星礁和光星仔礁都位于同一纬度上，夜晚行船时，渔民总能看到这两座岩礁和金星、针位在同一条直线上，成为极好的航标；再由于它们为一东一西、一大一小，渔民们就分别俗称大光星和光星仔。

47. 石公篱（离），或石公里，为弹丸礁的俗名。海南渔民敬称突出海面的礁岩为石公。弹丸礁这一环礁边上立着几块突出的礁岩，排列成篱笆状，渔民们形象地称其为石公篱。石公离、石公里是石公篱的同音讹记。篱、离、里，在海南潭门话中三字同音。

48. 五百二，或五百式，是皇路礁的俗名。此名有两种来源说法，一说是古代渔民曾在此捉到一只罕见的大玳瑁，它重达五百二十斤；另一说法为曾有渔民在此捡到五百二十个锡锭。"式"和"二"为同音同义不同形。

49. 丹积，或丹节，或单节，是南通礁的俗名，南通礁为标准名称。南通礁为一座完整环礁，无礁门，环礁成节不连续，只有一段礁石突出海面，因此得名单节。海南方言中，"单"与"丹"为同音字，"节"与"积"同音，因单节又异记，就记为了丹节、丹积。

50. 墨瓜线为南屏礁的俗名。这一海域盛产黑海参，海参外形像小长瓜，被渔民俗称为瓜，色黑如墨，因称墨瓜。南屏礁海底有暗沙，因而又得俗名墨瓜线。

51. 荷扐门，即恶落门，又称荷落门、阿落门等，是南华礁的俗名。南华礁有条水道，内宽外窄，口朝东南，不对风向，加上此水道口前面连接着弯曲的航道，渔船驶入该水道时非常艰难，因此得名恶落门。海南潭门话以"恶"训"难"，以"落"或"扐"训"入"。荷扐门、阿落门等都是恶落门的讹写。

52. 六门是六门礁的俗名。六门礁为一椭圆形环礁，因环礁西南部有六条大小不等的水道进出潟湖，故名。

53. 石盘为毕生礁的俗名，毕生礁是标准名称。毕生礁礁盘上的礁岩形状如磨盘，故海南渔民称其为石盘。

54. 上戊，或尚戊、上武等，都是永暑礁的俗名，永暑礁是标准名称。这

201

里的"戊"可能是指平地拱起土堆。永暑礁远望似海上拱起的土堆，故名。上戊、尚戊、上武均为同音异写。

55. 铜铳，也称大铜铳，为东礁的俗名。海南渔民把火药武器叫作"铳"。渔民曾在东礁所在礁盘发现铜制大炮，故称此地为铜铳。相对于东邻的华阳礁而言，东礁形体较大，所以渔民又称它为大铜铳。此外，铜铳的标准名称为东礁，因为它是位于尹庆群礁东部的一环礁，故名。

56. 龙鼻是西礁的俗名，西礁是标准名称。海南潭门话中"弄""窿""龙"同音。"窿"有"外露"之义，引申义为"大"。因此，"弄鼻"和"龙鼻"实为窿鼻的讹记。西礁形状像外露鼻孔的鼻子形状，因此得名弄鼻。相对其附近形体更小的中礁，弄鼻又称大弄鼻。

57. 鸟仔峙是南威岛的俗名，南威岛为标准名称。海南潭门方言称鸟为鸟仔，南威岛因为栖息着许多鸟类而被称为鸟仔峙。南威岛为纪念1946年接收该岛广东省政府主席罗卓英（号慈威）而得名，兼有接收舰队威震南疆之意。

58. （西头）乙辛是日积礁的俗名，日积礁为标准名称。该礁位于南沙群岛西部，而且从南威岛来日积礁罗盘上用乙辛方位，故名。（西头）乙辛是中国渔民在南沙捕捞作业时西部落脚点之一。

59. 南乙峙仔，也叫作南乙沙仔，是南薰礁的俗称，它坐落在鸿庥岛西边，是一座比后者形体还小的暗沙。"线仔"或"沙仔"，指小暗沙。

60. 禄沙，也叫一沙或一线，是禄沙礁的俗名，位于三角礁东北，为一个珊瑚礁，退潮露出，底有暗沙，海南渔民因此称一线/沙。

61. 黄山马东，也叫作马东，是敦谦沙洲的俗名，因其位置在太平岛东边而得名。太平岛上的礁岩为黄色，其状如马，渔民因此取名为黄山马或黄山马峙。其标准名称是纪念1946年中国政府派往接收南沙群岛的"中业号"军舰舰长李敦谦而命名的。

62. 九章是九章群礁的俗名。因此处有很多礁滩、暗礁遍布，给行船造成诸多障碍，因而得名九章。海南潭门方言"九"有"多"之义。这里"章"与"障"同音同义不同形。九章是九障的同音讹记。

63. 铜铳仔为华阳礁的俗名，华阳礁为标准名称。华阳礁位于东礁（其俗名为铜铳，或大铜铳）之东，形体较小，因此得名铜铳仔。

64. 贡士沙，或贡士线，为贡士礁的俗名，贡士礁为标准名，它位于中国南沙群岛的双子群礁东北端，与北子岛相距1海里，为三角形暗礁，无礁门，水下多暗沙堆积，并随着涨潮退潮或淹没或浮现。

65. 奈罗角（永登暗沙）位于双子群礁东北16海里。为沉没环礁，深海中型环礁，与乐斯暗沙组成连座复环礁，该礁形似纺锤，面积64平方公里（千米）。我国渔民俗称该礁为奈罗角、奈罗谷。

66. 犬殿沙，或梅九，其标准名称为梅九礁，梅九礁位于铁峙礁西南约 2 海里，是指发育在中业群礁中部的 V 形礁，开口向东。梅九礁是中国固有领土，行政上隶属于海南省三沙市。

67. 锅盖峙，是安波沙洲的俗名，长约 300 米，宽约 140 米，面积约 0.02 平方公里（千米），海拔约 2 米。洲上杂草丛生，但无树木，缺淡水。该洲形似锅盖，故我国渔民向称锅盖峙。

68. 弄鼻仔是中礁的俗名，位于西礁附近，因其形体小于被渔民俗称为弄鼻的西礁，故被称为弄鼻仔。

69. 赤瓜线是赤瓜礁的俗名。赤瓜礁是九章群礁中一座暗礁，位于环礁的西南端。此礁外环有棕色火山岩，内环为白色珊瑚礁。我国渔民向称赤瓜线，因此处产赤瓜参较多而得名。

70. 高佛，也称高不，是舶兰礁的俗称。位于郑和群礁的北端。礁形近椭圆，长约 1.8 公里（千米），宽约 1.3 公里（千米）。涨潮淹没，退潮露出。

参考文献

[1] BASSNETT, LEFEVERE. Translation, History and Culture [M]. 上海：上海外语教育出版社，1987.

[2] 巴斯奈特. 翻译研究（第三版）[M]. 上海：上海外语教育出版社，2010.

[3] 方梦之. 应用翻译研究：原理、策略与技巧 [M]. 上海：上海外语教育出版社，2013.

[4] 方梦之. 我国的应用翻译：理论建设与教学——第四届全国应用翻译研讨会侧记 [J]. 中国翻译，2011（3）.

[5] 格特. 翻译与关联：认知与语境 [M]. 上海：上海外语教育出版社，2004.

[6] 高帆. 浅析应用翻译理论体系的构建 [J]. 长江大学学报（社会科学版），2011（4）.

[7] 郭振乾. 南沙群岛渔民地名综述，南海诸岛地名资料汇编 [M]. 广州：广东省地图出版社，1987.

[8] 广东省地名委员会. 南海诸岛地名资料汇编 [M]. 广州：广东省地图出版社，1987.

[9] 韩振华. 南海诸岛史地研究 [M]. 北京. 社会科学文献出版社，1996.

[10] 韩振华，等. 我国南海诸岛史料汇编 [M]. 北京：东方出版社，1988.

[11] 黄忠廉，孙秋花，李亚舒. 方梦之应用翻译理论形成考 [J]. 上海翻译，2014（4）.

[12] 贾文波. 历届全国应用翻译研讨会综述 [J]. 上海翻译，2014（3）.

[13] 赖斯. 翻译批评：潜力与制约 [M]. 上海：上海外语教育出版社，2004.

[14] 李捷，何自然. "名从主人"？——名称翻译的语用学思考 [J]. 中国外语，2012（6）.

[15] 李永. 论"南海更路簿"国际法上的证据资格：以苏德柳抄本"水路簿"等12种"南海更路簿"为样本 [J]. 海南大学学报（人文社会科学版），2020（2）.

[16] 李彩霞. 苏承芬本《更路簿》外洋地名考证 [J]. 海南大学学报（人文社会科学版），2019（1）.

[17] 李金明. 《更路簿》与《东西洋考》针路之研究［J］. 南海学刊，2016（4）.

[18] 李文化，高之国，黄乐. 《癸亥年更流部》暹罗湾地名的数字人文考证［J］. 地理研究，2021（5）.

[19] 李文化，夏代云，吉家凡. 基于数字"更路"的"更"义诠释［J］. 南海学刊，2018（1）.

[20] 李文化. 南海《更路簿》数字化诠释［M］. 海口：海南出版社，2019.

[21] 林勰宇. 现存南海更路簿抄本系统考证［J］. 中国地方志，2019（3）.

[22] 刘国良，李钊瑾，曾超莲. 《更路簿》的历史价值研究［J］. 海南大学学报（人文社会科学版），2017（6）.

[23] 刘宓庆. 文体与翻译（增订版）［M］. 北京：中国对外翻译出版公司，1998.

[24] 奈达. 翻译科学探索［M］. 上海：上海外语教育出版社，2004.

[25] 奈达，泰伯. 翻译理论与实践［M］. 上海：上海外语教育出版社，2004.

[26] 诺德. 目的性行为：析功能翻译理论［M］. 上海：上海外语教育出版社，2001.

[27] 秦晓华. 南海诸岛礁名称的中国传统文化内涵及其意义［J］. 南海学刊，2016（1）.

[28] 孙冬虎. 南海诸岛外来地名的命名背景及其历史影响［J］. 地理研究，2000（2）.

[29] 斯珀波，威尔逊. 关联性：交际与认知［M］. 北京：外语教学与研究出版社，2001.

[30] 王利兵. 南海航道更路径研究：以苏德柳本《更路簿》为例［J］. 中国边疆史地研究，2016（2）.

[31] 王彩. 海南渔民抄本《更路簿》所载南海诸岛俗名再研究［J］. 海南热带海洋学院学报，2015（3）.

[32] 吴绍渊，曾丽洁. 南海更路簿中粤琼航路研究［J］. 中国海洋大学学报（社会科学版），2021（2）.

[33] 许盘清，安俊丽，曹树基. 航线与里程：文昌七洲洋与西沙七洲洋的地理位置［J］. 中国历史地理论丛，2022，37（1）.

[34] 夏代云. 卢业发、吴淑茂、黄家礼《更路簿》研究［M］. 北京：海洋出版社，2016.

[35] 许桂灵，司徒尚纪. 海南《更路簿》的海洋文化内涵和海洋文化风格［J］. 云南社会科学，2017（3）.

[36] 阎根齐. 论海南渔民《更路簿》的内容及习惯用语［J］. 南海学刊，

2017（1）.

[37] 阎根齐. 论海南渔民《更路簿》中地名命名的科学与合理性［J］. 南海学刊，2016（3）.

[38] 阎根齐，吴昊. 海南渔民《更路簿》地名命名考［J］. 社会科学战线，2021（6）.

[39] 阎根齐，李旷远. 郑和船队从广东至西沙群岛海域的航线和地名辨析［J］. 吉林大学社会科学学报，2020（1）.

[40] 周伟民，唐玲玲. 南海天书：海南渔民"更路簿"文化诠释［M］. 北京：昆仑出版社，2015.

[41] 张朔人，张若城. 南海维权的民间证据：《更路簿》内涵与面世抄本研究［J］. 云南师范大学学报，2018（4）.

[42] 张江齐，宋鸿运，欧阳宏斌，等.《更路簿》及其南沙群岛古地名释义［J］. 测绘科学，2017（12）.

后　　记

　　2014年，笔者在撰写一篇探讨如何翻译海南非物质文化遗产的文章时首次接触《更路簿》。次年秋天，笔者指导一名海南大学翻译硕士生撰写毕业翻译研究报告时，该生正苦于找不到合适的翻译材料，碰巧赶上了周为民、唐玲玲两位教授编著的《南海天书——海南渔民〈更路簿〉文化诠释》一书的首发出版。浏览全书后，笔者对《更路簿》有了比较全面的了解，就推荐给该学生，让她选用该书第四章和第五章作为其汉译英翻译研究论文撰写的源语文本，尽管翻译难度很大，但在师生共同努力下，最终还是完成了。该生论文答辩结束后，此研究报告得到了同行的充分肯定。这进一步激发了笔者对《更路簿》翻译研究的兴趣。于是，2020年，笔者申报了广东省哲学社会科学冷门绝学专项"南海更路簿翻译研究：以苏德柳和彭正楷抄本为例"，并获批立项。

　　直到目前，研究《更路簿》翻译的学者仍寥寥无几。因为《更路簿》与其他应用文本相比，有其独特的海南方言文化特征，其中翻译的疑难杂症的确不少，包括海南方言、南海岛礁的俗名、航海路线以及古指南针术语等文化负载词。因而需要认真研读、广泛查阅资料、反复琢磨其意义，还要请教专家和老渔民，除了《更路簿》中所涉及的南海诸岛的俗名（海南渔民起的乳名或土地名），还要彻底弄清楚它们的具体地理坐标位置、渔船上所使用的古罗盘针及航行路线、俗名的海南方言读音、岛礁的起源与传说等。特别要提及的是，"苏本"中涉及东南亚国家（越南、柬埔寨、泰国、印度尼西亚、马来西亚、新加坡）更路中提及的个别岛礁不止有一个俗名，同一个俗名又涉及不同的岛礁，导致部分岛礁的地理位置难以确定，个别岛礁所对应的中英文名也无法查到等。翻译中遇到的这些困难或许就是很少有译者愿意啃这块硬骨头的原因。然而，经过近两年的不懈努力，笔者及团队终于把这块硬骨头啃下来了。

　　根据课题立项时的任务安排，作为课题负责人，除了负责整个项目的统筹安排、统稿、译文校对、撰写译作的前言和后记，笔者还和团队成员共同翻译完成了苏德柳本《更路簿》的第一部分"立东海更路"（西沙更路），第二部分"立北海各线更路相对"（南沙更路），第三部分"驶船更路定例"和涉及海南岛至东南亚各国（南洋）的更路，即第四部分的1～4段以及第五、第六、第七部分，制作了"苏德柳本和彭正楷本《更路簿》南海诸岛信息一览表""苏德柳本《更路簿》中东南亚（外洋）地名中英文信息一览表"和"苏德柳本《更路簿》海南岛沿岸至广东省沿岸地名中英文信息一览表"3 个信息表，同时付出大量精力修改和校对项目组成员的译文初稿。吴素贞和翟秋兰两位老师完成了彭正楷本《更路簿》和苏德柳本《更路簿》第四部分的 5～12 段译文初稿，陈兆毓老师翻译了"前言"和"后记"。

本译作的立项和顺利完成，应归功于各方的协作与努力。

首先，要感谢广东省哲学社会科学规划项目的资助、匿名评审专家的辛勤劳动以及广州应用科技学院相关部门的大力支持。

其次，要衷心感谢海南大学周为民教授为本译作写序。周教授已 90 岁高龄，仍思维敏捷，在通读了本书稿后，他欣然同意为此写序。

再次，在项目实施过程中，得到了海南大学张朔人教授、秦晓华教授、李文化教授、李彩霞教授、陈虹馆员等《更路簿》研究领域专家学者的无私专业指导；陈虹老师在百忙中，花费了大量时间和精力为《苏德柳本更路簿》中南海岛礁俗名和东南亚国家相关岛屿俗名标注海南话读音；华南理工大学经济与管理学院在读博士胡晓丽女士在资料收集和文字处理方面给予了许多帮助；意大利籍美国英文教师 Aymie Michael George 在译文修改方面提出了具有建设性的建议；我爱人吕红老师默默承担了更多的家务劳动。在此对以上专家学者、同事和家人的辛勤付出表示衷心感谢！

最后，要特别感谢广州中山大学出版社有限公司和编辑张蕊女士为本译著的修改、编辑、出版所付出的辛勤工作。

本课题或许是国内学者首次尝试的《更路簿》翻译研究，英译文中可能存在一些不尽如人意之处，甚至存在不少错误，敬请读者、专家学者批评指正。

贾绍东

2024 年 3 月 26 日